THE
THREE
COUNT

THE THREE COUNT

MY LIFE IN STRIPES
AS A WWE REFEREE

Jimmy Korderas

Foreword by
Adam "Edge" Copeland

ECW Press

Published by ECW Press
2120 Queen Street East, Suite 200, Toronto, Ontario, Canada M4E 1E2
416-694-3348 / info@ecwpress.com

LIBRARY AND ARCHIVES CANADA CATALOGUING IN PUBLICATION

Korderas, Jimmy, 1962–
   The three count : my life in stripes as a WWE referee / Jimmy Korderas.

ISBN 978-1-77041-084-8
ALSO ISSUED AS: 978-1-77090-408-8 (PDF); 978-1-77090-409-5 (EPUB)

    1. Korderas, Jimmy, 1962–. 2. Wrestling—Officiating—United States.
3. Wrestlers—Anecdotes. 4. World Wresting Entertainment, Inc.—Biography.
I. Title.

GV1196.K67A3 2013   796.812092   C2012-907528-0

Editor for the press: Michael Holmes
Cover and text design: Tania Craan
Back cover photo: Charles Robinson
Typesetting and production: Carolyn McNeillie
Printing: Friesens   2   3   4   5

The publication of *The Three Count* has been generously supported by the Ontario Arts Council, an agency of the Government of Ontario. We also acknowledge the financial support of the Government of Canada through the Canada Book Fund for our publishing activities, and the contribution of the Government of Ontario through the Ontario Book Publishing Tax Credit. The marketing of this book was made possible with the support of the Ontario Media Development Corporation.

Canada | ONTARIO ARTS COUNCIL / CONSEIL DES ARTS DE L'ONTARIO | Ontario / Ontario Media Development Corporation

50 YEARS OF ONTARIO GOVERNMENT SUPPORT OF THE ARTS
50 ANS DE SOUTIEN DU GOUVERNEMENT DE L'ONTARIO AUX ARTS

PRINTED AND BOUND IN CANADA

This book is dedicated to those who dare to dream . . .
Dreams really do come true.

and

For my wife, Audra. Without her never-ending encouragement, I would not have been able to finish this book. She believed in my dream.

Table of Contents

So I'm sitting in my recliner with my teacup poodle (he's very tough) in my lap, and I'm reminiscing. Pleasant thoughts. The kind that are surrounded by fluffy clouds with breezy ukulele music as the soundtrack. Okay, got sidetracked, but I'm trying to set the mood here, folks. Let's just say these thoughts make me happy. Thoughts of my career. A career that has seen me main-event *WrestleMania*s. Win 31 championships in the WWE. TLC matches. Triple ladder matches. Money in the Bank matches. A Hall of Famer. A smile adorns my face. Until the record scratches. The lazy chords of the Hawaiian music slam to a halt in my brain, the clouds dissipate, and I crash back to Earth in a heap, suddenly realizing that a certain individual has been a part of all of these moments. A Canadian. No, not the Canadian who has annoyed me and audiences worldwide for years as Christian. But a Canadian nonetheless. A prematurely balding Canadian who admittedly used to rock a serious frullet (fro-mullet) that would make Billy Squier proud and the rest of us cringe. A certain Canadian who has parlayed his experience in the WWE into becoming a pretty successful analyst of the industry now on the ol' Canadian boob tube. I suddenly realize this man is the Forrest Gump of my career. He's been there, lurking, just barely out of focus. Oh, but he's there. You can't mistake that hollowed-out hair and mirror-like dome. Right over my shoulder or my prone body as the Undertaker plans to do his worst to me. That man is Jimmy Korderas. Now, as Lance Storm would say, *if I can be serious for a minute*, Jimmy and I go back. Way back. To 1996, when my WWE quest was being realized. I was a young up and comer, and Jimmy was already a road horse who had logged hundreds of thousands of miles as a WWE referee. One of the toughest jobs in the industry, and one that flies under the radar. Because if you are doing it the right way, your job is not to be noticed. Not to take away from the match and performance. Help tell the story, but not be the story. The narrator who furthers everything, but you never see his face. He's Daniel Stern in *The Wonder Years*. It can be a thankless job. Being a referee means you log all the same miles, but without the fame and glory. Put up and tear down the ring. Also the occasional bumps. Not an easy gig to say the least, but Jimmy always did it with a smile on his face and a horrible joke on the tip of his tongue.

What made a great guy even better was the fact that he was one of the best referees ever in the industry. And there've been some good ones. He really was there for so many of my pivotal moments. *WrestleMania 2000* triple ladder match. Check. TLC 1. Check. TLC 2. Check. TLC 3. Check. Money in the Bank. Check. I made sure he was there for the biggest match of my career. Yes, I personally requested Jimmy as the referee for my match in the main event of *WrestleMania XXIV* against the Undertaker. He got booted in the face by Taker and took it like a champ. Here's the thing: we knew he would, and that's why we wanted him.

Since those early days of my WWE career we've remained friends. He's one of the good guys. You hear that term tossed around a lot, and while it may be cliché and overused, with Jimmy, it couldn't be more fitting. To be honest, there are not many people I will stay in contact with in this business. I can count them on two hands. But Jimmy will be one of them.

Technically this little tidbit is usually named a "foreword." A few hopefully entertaining anecdotes that kick off an interesting journey you, dear wrestling fan, are about to embark on. I look at it as something different. This is more of a thank you note from one friend and colleague to another. Thank you, Jimmy, for being my Forrest Gump, but more importantly my friend.

Adam "Edge" Copeland
March 2, 2012
Asheville, North Carolina

Never in my wildest imagination as a young boy growing up in the heart of Toronto's GreekTown would I have thought I would be in the main event of a *WrestleMania*. March 30, 2008, the it's *WrestleMania XXIV* and there I am, lying on my side under the bottom rope, just staring out into a crowd of almost 75,000 screaming WWE fans. I have just been kicked in the head by a size 16 boot that sent me crashing to the canvas. The other end of that boot belonged to the WWE's most revered superstar of all time, the Undertaker. For me it was a badge of honour to have taken that kick from a legend. The other participant in the match was none other than fellow Canadian and good friend of mine, Edge. This was truly a dream match for any referee to officiate and I was fortunate to be chosen for this match. I was not originally scheduled to ref the main event, but I will get to that story in due time.

While I was lying there, so many things raced through my mind. The predominate thought was, "How did the kick to my head look?" After that, my thoughts turned to, "How do you top a moment like this?" I can't describe how much being a part of this match in WWE history means to me. It was so overwhelming; however, as I lay there I could see that the crowd was standing on their feet and apparently cheering — I just couldn't hear them. These are the moments guys like me dream about. These are the moments that make a guy like me proud and humbled to be a part of something that people will remember for a long time. This one moment in particular was the crowning achievement of a long career and a dream come true for a kid from Toronto, Canada. It was the culmination of a lot of sweat, tears, and yes, even some blood and broken bones. All the while my passion and love for this business never faded. It was a long and at times difficult journey to achieve this dream but I finally got there and this is my story.

CHAPTER 1

How It All Began

My journey began many years prior to that moment in Orlando, a long time before I began working for the premier wrestling/ sports entertainment company on the planet. Watching wrestling on TV was not high on my Greek immigrant parents' priority list. Excelling in school and going on to college or university was all that mattered to them. If that did not happen, plan B was to follow my father into the family business. My dad was a licensed auto mechanic who owned a gas station and repair shop in the heart of Toronto's GreekTown, affectionately called the Danforth after its main street. As much as I respected my father's wishes and as much as I liked tinkering with cars, the garage business was not what I wanted to get into. I did however work for him part-time while I attended school. When it became clear that a post-secondary education did not appeal to me, it was pretty much set in my parents' mind that I would work full-time for Dad. One thing was certain, I had not given up on a very different dream that I wanted to pursue. It was extremely difficult not to be a wrestling fan growing up in the epicentre of the Canadian wrestling scene,

Toronto. Let me explain by taking you back to where my passion for this unique form of entertainment originated.

Before the days when World Wrestling Entertainment ruled the sports entertainment landscape, before the Rock 'n' Wrestling Connection, and even before the Incredible Hulk Hogan, professional wrestling was a territorial business. Promoters divided North America into specific regions with the agreement that they would not run wrestling shows in the others' territory. Although they often worked together by trading talent and so forth, there was also a healthy competition between them.

Arguments arose among wrestling fans as to which area of North America had the best wrestling on television. After all, St. Louis had *Wrestling at the Chase*, Texas had *World Class Championship Wrestling*, there was the AWA in the midwest, plus the NWA and WWF, just to name a few. As a diehard wrestling fan growing up in Toronto, Ontario, I believe that I had access to the best wrestling on television you could possibly get anywhere. Each weekend provided me with countless hours of enjoyment watching my favourite sports heroes — outside of the Toronto Maple Leafs of course. I am a proud Canadian, after all!

Let me run down for you what a typical weekend of watching wrestling on television consisted of for me. On the weekends, we here in Toronto were able to watch the AWA on Global Television Network, Stampede Wrestling from Calgary on CKVR Channel 3 from Barrie, International Wrestling from Montreal on CityTV, All Star Wrestling from Vancouver airing on CKOC Kitchener, Mid-Atlantic Championship Wrestling on Buffalo's Channel 4, WWF on Channel 29 from Buffalo, and of course Maple Leaf Wrestling on CHCHTV Channel 11 out of Hamilton. I can't think of anywhere else on the continent where you could watch that many different promotions on TV in one city. There were a few others, but these were the major players for me.

Many a Saturday afternoon Mama Korderas would break out the floppy slipper (or as we call it in Greek, the *pandofla*) trying to drag me away from the television set to do my homework or maybe some chores, or even go outside and do something, anything other than watch wrestling on television. I was *hooked*, though. There was no chance I was going to give up watching guys like the Original Sheik, Tex Mckenzie, the Tolos Brothers, Hartford and Reginald (the Love Brothers), and the rest of those crazy characters that I loved to watch. For some reason, I really enjoyed Tex Mckenzie and Chief Jay Strongbow as a youngster. Tex was tall and lanky. I loved when he did this high knee lift, followed by this cowboy stomp around the ring, and finished off his opponent with the dreaded Bulldog. Chief Jay I liked because when he got angry, he did this little "war dance" while giving his opponent tomahawk chops. Maybe the dancing both guys did was what I found entertaining. I was always drawn towards the more colourful characters.

So I continued to defy my mother and entrench myself smack dab in front of that black and white set. There was colour television back then; we just could not convince my dad it was worth it to buy one. My mom also thought that we would go blind from colour TV. When I wasn't watching wrestling on TV, I was outside playing with my friends. The odd thing about that was although we would talk for hours on end about wrestling and who our favourites were and what happened this past week, we never "play-wrestled" with each other. We thought that if we performed the moves we saw on television on each other, someone would get hurt really badly. We believed everything in wrestling was real and didn't want to take any chances that would jeopardize our weekend ritual by getting hurt imitating our heroes. My, how times have changed.

Another sign of the times in those days was that wrestling action figures were nonexistent. That didn't stop me. Even at a young age, I showed some creativity. I made a makeshift wrestling ring out of an old box. Substituting for my favourite wrestlers was a bendable Gumby, his sidekick, Pokey, and a few G.I. Joes, including one with the kung fu grip. Not quite what the kids have access to today but hey, you make do with what you have.

After years of watching my favourite wrestlers on the tube and dreaming of the opportunity to see my heroes in person, on June 6, 1971 I finally got the chance to see these larger-than-life characters *live*! My neighbour and best friend was Billy Koufis. His father was taking him to a special Maple Leaf Wrestling event that was being held outdoors at Varsity Stadium in Toronto. They asked me if I wanted to join them. It took almost two full days of begging and pleading with my mom, but, reluctantly, she gave in. I was going to my first live wrestling show at the tender age of nine. It was an amazing night for me and my best friend. We rode the subway, which was so cool. Not only did we see our first live wrestling show, we actually snuck down onto the field and watched the matches up close. We found it strange that no one asked to see our tickets or even bothered to question us. *Awesome!* The main event this night was the NWA world champion Dory Funk Jr. defending his title against the Original Sheik. They fought to a double count out. It was a brutal and bloody match but I loved it. I had been hooked before, but now I was netted and landed in the boat.

The next time I got to attend a live wrestling event was in the company of my older brother Peter and his friends. Peter is nine years older than I am. The way he and his friends viewed pro wrestling was far different than the way I understood it. Let me explain. My brother Peter not so willingly allowed me to accompany him and his buddies to see a show at Maple Leaf Gardens. I was so happy and excited until the unthinkable happened. My brother and his cohorts began cheering for all the bad guys. As the lawyer Jackie Childs in an episode of *Seinfeld* said, "I was shocked, chagrined, and stupefied." How could my older brother, who I looked up to, cheer for these dastardly villains? The people around us were screaming obscenities at my brother and his friends while I attempted to hide under my seat, dodging popcorn and soda. At six feet two inches tall and 265 lbs — of muscle not fat — Peter was not intimidated by the little old ladies, scrawny men, and little kids in attendance. It wasn't until after we had gotten home that

Peter explained his reasoning for his behaviour. He got a kick out of inciting the crowd. For him and his friends, pro wrestling was strictly entertainment. They did not take it seriously, whereas I believed it to be very real. I guess you could say Peter Korderas understood the term "sports entertainment" long before Vincent Kennedy McMahon made the phrase famous. Too bad my brother did not trademark that phrase. He might be a rich man today.

It would be many years before I got to attend another wrestling event at Maple Leaf Gardens. We moved to the suburbs in 1972 when I was ten years old and my brother stopped going to shows with his friends. I guess he outgrew wrestling, but of course I just couldn't let it go. For years I continued to watch it on television religiously. More years passed; I was now 16 years old with a driver's license and my own beater of a car. I didn't need anyone to take me to see wrestling any longer. I was more than capable of getting to Maple Leaf Gardens on my own. To help pay for my obsession, I had two part-time jobs. One was working as a pin chaser at a bowling alley and the other was helping my dad out at his gas station after school and on most weekends. It didn't matter to me if I had company or if I went alone. I was a regular at all "the Gardens" shows.

After I became a regular at the Gardens, I noticed that many of the other regular patrons were sitting in the same seats week after week. There were the female twins who sat front row ringside for every show. You could not miss them as they always dressed and had their hair styled as if they were trapped in the '50s or '60s. There were other fans but one I remain friends with to this day is Steve Argintaru. Steve also enjoyed taking photos at events and we often compared pictures. That and we both hung out on Wood Street, behind the Gardens, trying to get autographs from the wrestlers as they arrived or when they were leaving. It was hit or miss as there were many others trying to do the same. Steve now works in Toronto at TSN, Canada's first all-sports TV station. We still attend events these days, but now Steve brings his boys with him. We are influencing another generation of wrestling fans.

Seeing as I was going to every show at MLG, I had to find out whether there was such a thing as season tickets for wrestling. So, one day I decided I was going to visit the Tunney Sports Inc. wrestling office, located directly across the street from Maple Leaf Gardens to find out if I could get season tickets. When I got there I knocked on the door and a familiar voice boomed, "Come in." I opened the door and walked in, and there standing behind a counter was none other than the legendary ring announcer for Maple Leaf Wrestling, Mr. Norm Kimber. He asked me how he could help me. I shyly asked him how to go about getting the equivalent of season tickets to the wrestling shows. Mr. Kimber pulled out a seating chart and showed me what was available. I chose two floor seats, second row ringside, right beside the ramp that stretched from the entrance all the way to the ring. Mr. Kimber noted my seat selection in his ledger and told me my tickets would be at the box office before every show. I thanked him and left the office extremely excited. I couldn't wait for the next wrestling event. Finally, that day arrived. I went to the box office, picked up my tickets and rushed to my seat. The seats were amazing. I couldn't have asked for two better seats. If I couldn't get a friend to go with me, I would sell the ticket at the show, usually for a small profit. This led me to my next brilliant idea.

I began bringing a camera with me to all the shows and taking pictures of all the wrestlers. Sitting right beside the entrance ramp made taking pictures that much easier. I was able to get some terrific shots of the guys. Here's where the brilliance comes in. I would get the film developed and get a second set of prints for a dollar; that way I could keep one set of the photos and sell the other ones. That is exactly what I did. I would show up early to the next event with pictures in hand ready to sell to the wrestling fans waiting outside. Believe it or not, I was getting two dollars a picture. I more often than not sold all of my pictures, which paid for the developing of the photos, my ticket for the show, and parking, and still left me with more than few bucks for refreshments. As a matter of fact, I was turning a small profit. That was until I got busted by one of Jack Tunney's employees.

Elio Zarlenga was responsible for making all the programs for the events, which included taking photographs during the matches that would be used for the programs. What I did not know was that he was also the person licensed by Tunney Sports Inc. to sell pictures of the wrestlers. Another thing that I didn't realize was that by selling pictures without a license, I was breaking the law. Elio approached me one day outside Maple Leaf Gardens and asked to see my pictures. Not knowing at the time who he was, I handed him my photos. As he looked through them, he complimented me on them, saying that I did good work. After I thanked him, he told me that I could be arrested for selling copyrighted material. I asked him what the hell he was talking about — these were my pictures. He replied, "You don't have permission from Tunney Sports and don't lie because I work for Jack Tunney." I began to panic. Here I was, almost 20 years old, thinking I'm going to go to jail. I guess Elio saw the panic on my face and went easy on me. He told me I could sell my pictures, just not in front of Maple Leaf Gardens. He suggested I could sell the pictures a little farther down the street and he wouldn't say anything to anyone. From that day forward, Elio and I began to become friends.

A few months passed and Elio finally decided it was time for him to introduce me to none other than WWF president Jack Tunney. I felt somewhat intimidated meeting him. Jack was a large man who had this aura surrounding him. He appeared stern and serious, but in actuality, he was a kind-hearted man with a good sense of humour. I guess he took a liking to me as he told Elio that they would "find something for me to do." Jack told me that he had only a few simple rules for me to follow. First, he said that I needed to be on time and never be late. Second, he said he expected an honest day's work of me. The third and final request he made of me was that as long as the boys showed up on time and in condition to work, he did not want to know about any of the goings-on away from the ring. He said that I was going to see a lot of things that would go on in this business, whether in the locker room, on the bus, in the hotel, or anywhere else. In a nutshell, he basically told me not to be a stooge. I had no problem with that.

To say that I was ecstatic about landing a job with the World Wrestling Federation would be a gross understatement. But not everyone shared my excitement. When I informed my parents that evening about my big job score, the look of disappointment on their faces caught me completely off guard. I asked them what the problem was. My mother said to me, in Greek mind you, "What kind of future could you possibly have working with all those crazy guys from the TV?" My dad did not say a word, but you could tell he was not happy at all. Again, I could not understand for the life of me what the problem was. It was several weeks later when I realized that both my parents, particularly my father, had expected me to follow in his footsteps and take over the family business one day. I consider myself a car guy and don't mind working on them. But it was not the career I envisioned for me. I must say, they did eventually come around.

As it turned out, my very first job for Jack Tunney and the WWF was to transport talent from Toronto to Brantford, southwest of the city, for television tapings. It was November 1985 and at that time the WWF ran shows at Maple Leaf Gardens every three weeks on Sunday nights. On the following Monday, they would tape three weeks' worth of their syndicated TV show *Wrestling Challenge*, which aired all over the world. Jack Tunney rented two minibuses for Elio and me to drive. One of us would drive the babyfaces while the other was assigned to take the heels. We alternated each week between faces and heels. We got to hang out all day at the Brantford Civic Centre watching pre-taped interviews, talking to the boys, watching the matches; basically I was having the time of my life and I was getting paid for it. My life in wrestling was just beginning.

CHAPTER 2

Not Quite a Ref Yet

So there I was, working for then–WWF president Jack Tunney. I say president but that was only his onscreen persona. Jack was in charge of the Canadian office for the WWF; he was only the figurehead president on television. As I stated earlier, my duties were for the most part transporting the wrestlers. Usually he would rent those two minibuses for Elio and me to drive. Sometimes, Jack would hand me the keys to his Cadillac Fleetwood, a cruise ship on wheels if ever there was one, and have me pick up main event talent from their hotels and bring them to Maple Leaf Gardens for the shows. I was given the great honour of chauffeuring everyone from Andre the Giant, Rowdy Roddy Piper, and Hulk Hogan, among other greats. I was even given the responsibility on occasion to drive none other than the boss himself, Vincent Kennedy McMahon. The one good thing about having huge superstars in the car with you is that it can help get you out of trouble.

I remember one instance when Jack asked me to take his car and go to the Carlton Place Hotel by the airport in Toronto to pick up "Macho Man" Randy Savage and Miss Elizabeth. On my way

there, the traffic was horrible. I was running a little late. I absolutely
hate being late for anything, so I began driving aggressively — a
little too aggressively as it turns out. Eventually, I got pulled over by
one of Metro Toronto's finest, who was about to issue me several
tickets. At first I thought, *Great, this guy's going to make me even
later than I already am to pick up Savage and Liz.* Among the tickets
he was threatening me with were speeding, unsafe lane changing,
and reckless driving. This officer was ready to throw the book at
me. I was now in complete panic mode. All I kept thinking was
that Jack was going to *kill* me, then fire my ass, and in that order.
At one point, the officer began questioning me on the ownership
of the car. Uh-oh, here we go, now he thinks I've stolen the car.
Sure, here's a guy in his early 20s driving a Cadillac with *YENNUT*
(*Tunney* spelled backwards) on the plates, not suspicious at all.
Almost shaking, I told him it belonged to my boss Jack Tunney
and that I was late to pick up "Macho Man" Randy Savage and Miss
Elizabeth. All of a sudden, the policeman changed his tune. Now he
was Mr. Nice Guy. He started telling me that his son was a huge fan
of the wwf and how the kid had all the action figures, the toy ring,
and so on. He was talking to me as if this traffic stop was really cool,
stopping Jack Tunney's car on the way to pick up a pair of wwf
superstars.

We were only stopped about a mile from the hotel when I had a
brainstorm. I looked this cop in the eyes and said, "Would you like
me to ask the Macho Man and Miss Elizabeth if they would give
your son an autograph?" His eyes lit up and he said, "I'll follow you
to the hotel. If you can get me the autographs, I will let you off on
all the tickets." That's all I needed to hear. I told him to follow me to
the hotel and I would see what I can do. On the way there, I thought,
*What if Randy doesn't want to help me out? What if he's in a crappy
mood and won't sign?* Still, I had to try it or risk losing my job.

When we got to the hotel I called up to Randy's room and Liz
answered the phone. After exchanging pleasantries, I explained my
situation to her. She said it would not be a problem at all and that

she would make sure Randy and she would autograph an eight-by-ten for the officer's son. She was truly a wonderful lady, a real sweetheart. Five minutes later, the first couple of the WWF came into the lobby. In his gruff voice, Randy said hello to the policeman. He then pulled out an eight-by-ten of himself and Liz and they proceeded to autograph it for the cop's kid. The policeman thanked us all and left without even mentioning the plethora of fines he had wanted to bestow upon me. I was off the hook thanks to Macho Madness. I thanked Randy and Liz for doing this for me. They were so cool about the whole thing. We all had a good laugh about it. When I think back on that incident, boy did I get away with one. Thanks again, Randy and Liz. You both saved my job!

Having superstars in the vehicle did not always get me out of trouble with the law, though. After a set of television tapings for *Wrestling Challenge* in Brantford, I loaded up the minibus and prepared for the trip back to Toronto. The drive generally took about an hour and 20 minutes to an hour and a half. It was now 11:30 p.m. In the bus were the likes of Terry Funk and Hercules Hernandez, among many others. One passenger was the great Harley Race, who asked me what time last call was at the hotel bar. I told him that in Toronto, they stop serving at one a.m. He as well as the others told me to put the pedal to the metal to make it to the hotel for last call. One brief look at all those wrestlers and I knew what I was going to do: everyone buckle up, because here we go. I was never afraid to drive fast; as a matter of fact, back in the day I did it quite often. We were making great time when — you guessed it — I got pulled over by the Ontario Provincial Police, the equivalent of a State Trooper. The strange thing about this was that I was more concerned about getting back to the hotel before last call than I was about the ticket. That wrestling business mentality had already infiltrated my mind. Despite the valiant attempts of Harley Race and Terry Funk to talk the officer out of writing the ticket, I ended up getting one anyway.

Once we got back on the road, Harley and Terry took up a

collection from everyone to pay for the ticket. We arrived at the Howard Johnson's hotel by the Toronto airport about 12:40 a.m., a good 20 minutes before last call. Everyone got out quickly and went straight to the bar. Harley handed me some money. He said, "Here kid, this is to pay for your speeding ticket." I counted it and told him it was $110 too much. He replied, "Keep it, kid, you earned it. By the way, you're one hell of a driver. Thanks." *Wow!* What a compliment coming from the legendary Harley Race. I must've been grinning from ear to ear. I thanked him, parked the bus, and joined the boys for a drink.

Not everyone had words of encouragement on those trips to the TV tapings in Brantford. One day, I had a veritable who's who of wrestling on a particular trip to the TV station. Sitting shotgun was "Classy" Freddie Blassie, an old-school wrestler who was now a manager. Sitting behind us was the Manager of Champions, Captain Lou Albano; Mr. Fuji, a former wrestler also turned manager; and former world heavyweight champion, now colour commentator, Bruno Sammartino. I didn't really say much to them other than hello. I guess I was just a little intimidated. All the managers knew who I was but this was the first time I had had the honour of meeting Bruno. About half an hour into the drive, Bruno decided to strike up a conversation with yours truly. He asked me where I was from, how old I was, how long I had been working in the business, and so forth. It almost felt like an interrogation at times but I understood that he was old school and very protective of his profession. After I had told him that I was only six months into my wrestling career, he did have one more question for me. He asked if I wanted a bit of advice. I thought, *Are you kidding me? Bruno Sammartino wants to offer me advice — damn right I do.* He said, "My advice is to get out of the business before it gets into your blood. Once it is in your blood, you will never get it out."

What did I just hear? The former champ just told me to get out of the business before I get hooked? Not knowing how to answer, I just thanked him for the advice. That's when Blassie, Albano, and

Fuji piped in and told Bruno to "leave the kid alone." "If this is what he wants to do, no need to scare the shit out of him." Hearing those guys stick up for me was awesome, but it was too late anyway; it was already in my blood, I'd been bit by the bug and there was no turning back. I was not going to let Sammartino's words of wisdom get me down. I felt the wwf was where I wanted to be and I was prepared to do whatever it took to live my dream.

I could go on and on with stories about being the chauffer to some of the biggest superstars of the wwf, but I'll save those for another time or maybe even another book.

As much as I really enjoyed transporting some of the most famous and recognizable people in the world around the Canadian countryside, Jack Tunney had other plans for me. My next assignment was to become a member of the ring crew. The person in charge of hauling around and setting up the ring was former wrestler and now referee John Bonello. That name may sound familiar to some of you for less than pleasant reasons but Bonello did treat me very well and I considered him a friend. He took me under his wing and showed me how to set up the ring that he had actually built himself. This particular ring was 18 feet by 18 feet. The wwf rings were generally 20 feet by 20 feet. This may not sound like a huge problem to most people; however, there are very noticeable adjustments one must make when you are working in a different-sized ring. Running the ropes, ring positioning, and timing all have to be taken into consideration when working in rings of various sizes.

Speaking of working inside the ring, after having the ring setup routine pretty much down pat, I began learning something new. After John and I had the ring set up, well before any fans would enter the arena, we would have our own little wrestling match. That's right; he was teaching me how to wrestle and take bumps. It was nothing too spectacular, just basic fundamentals. We actually had a pretty good little match worked out. The only people who ever got to see this match were a handful of arena workers and on one occasion the late, great Billy Red Lyons. One day, he showed up to the arena much earlier than usual and, unbeknownst to Bonello and me, watched our little match. He didn't bother interrupting us but rather sat back and watched as we went through our simple match. When we were finished, of course Bonello goes over, we heard a single person applaud. Red came over and told us we had a good little match worked out and that if the wwf needed a filler match one night, maybe fans would be interested in a ring-crew-member-versus-ring-crew-member match. We got a good chuckle out of his statement but deep down inside, I couldn't help wishing that one day it would happen for real. It never did, but that didn't stop me from dreaming about it.

Those were not the only duties I had. Sometimes, something unexpected came up and I might be asked to help out in other ways. One such time happened in December 1986 after a wwf card in Hamilton, Ontario, at the Victor Copps Coliseum. On this evening, my job was helping Elio manage the merchandise stands on the concourse level. Not a bad gig at all. We got a percentage of the sales as our pay. Commission paydays definitely make you hustle your butt off and this night was a very good night for us. Little did I know that I would be called into action shortly for a completely different assignment.

One of the matches that night featured the British Bulldogs, Dynamite Kid and Davey Boy Smith, versus the team of Don Muraco and Cowboy Bob Orton — four veterans of the ring who could put on a great performance. I wanted to watch this match but I couldn't see from my vantage point at the merch stand. Suddenly there was a strange sound coming from the crowd in attendance. It's hard to describe, but it sounded like a mixture of disbelief and confusion. After several minutes of wondering what was going on, I managed to get someone to watch the stand and went to take a peek to see what all the commotion was about. Paramedics were placing the Dynamite Kid, a.k.a. Tommy Billington, on a stretcher and wheeling him away. I never really found out what exactly had happened; all I knew was that he had been injured in the match and could not walk, let alone wrestle.

After spending the night in a Hamilton hospital on a gurney in an emergency room hallway, Dynamite was going to be transported via ambulance to Toronto International Airport and put on a flight back to a hospital in Calgary, Alberta, where he lived. One little problem though: because he was flying while on a stretcher, he was not permitted to fly alone. Someone had to accompany him on the flight. Tunney had asked me to accompany him on the plane ride. I would fly with him to Calgary, make sure he was put in an ambulance to take him to the hospital, and wait five hours for my return flight. Yes, for me it was a quick trip. When I found out I was going to be in Calgary for only a few hours, a slight measure of disappointment set in. This was my first trip to Alberta and there would be no time to see anything. I guess I should not complain. The trip was work related, plus I was being paid to do it. What the heck was I thinking? This poor guy was in severe pain, on medication with his career possibly in danger, and here I was thinking about sightseeing. I felt like an ass.

Despite the fact that I was a novice air traveller, when I got to the airport to check in, I wanted to look like a pro. It didn't quite work out that way. As I was checking in, the lady behind the counter asked how many bags I would be checking. I told her, "No bags to check."

She looked up at me and said in a smarmy manner, "Do you have any bags?"

As I began to explain the reason I had no bags at all, her smarmy expression slowly turned into a look of resentment. She then said, "Oh, you're travelling with the *wrestling guy*. All right, here is your boarding pass. Try to be at the gate at least 30 minutes before departure. Thank you and have a good flight." It was not what she said but rather how she said it. Her tone was aggravating.

She was the most condescending bitch I had ever encountered. I thanked her anyway and went to meet the ambulance. When

Dynamite arrived at the airport, the paramedics wheeled him straight to the gate. Since Dynamite was unable to walk, he was being boarded first and because I was his travelling partner, I was allowed to priority board with him. The aircraft we were flying on was a Boeing 767. On those planes, there are only two seats next to the window as opposed to three like on many other planes. In order to accommodate the stretcher, they folded forward the seat backs of two window seats immediately next to the emergency exit, making enough room for Dynamite to lay flat. I, on the other hand, had it pretty good. I was in the aisle seat next to him but the airline could not place a passenger in the seat directly in front of me. If they did, they would be sitting next to Dynamite's legs and feet. Picture someone sitting in the back seat of a car on the passenger side. Then imagine that this person was able to fold forward the passenger seat in front of them and stretch their legs straight out. The driver would have this person's feet beside them while driving. Not the most appealing proposition. That meant more room for me as I was able to lay the seat in front of me flat, put my feet up, and really get comfortable. The flight from Toronto to Calgary is usually between four and four and a half hours long. Not a problem for someone who can get up and move about the cabin, but for Dynamite it was a struggle. He just could not get comfortable and was in excruciating pain throughout the flight.

We arrived in Calgary at about seven p.m. local time. We were met at the airport by Dynamite's wife, Michelle, and Julie, Bret Hart's wife — they just happened to be sisters. I introduced myself to both of them. They both thanked me very much for accompanying him to Calgary. They then asked me what time my flight back to Toronto was. My flight was the red-eye, not leaving until 12:25 a.m. When they heard that, they asked if I would go with them to the hospital and said that they would make sure someone got me back to the airport for my flight home. I figured, *Why not*, so I hopped in the car with Julie. Michelle rode in the ambulance with her husband.

When we all arrived at the hospital, a few family members were there as well. The one individual I was most excited to meet was none other than Stu Hart. Julie walked me over to Stu and introduced me as the fellow who flew on the plane with Dynamite. I extended my hand to shake his and said that it was an absolute pleasure to meet him. He shook my hand firmly, looked me in the eyes while still holding on to my hand, and said, "So, you work for Jack, eh?"

"Yes, sir," I replied respectfully.

"Are you a worker?" was his next question. For those not sure, he was asking if I was a wrestler.

"No, sir," was my timid response.

Next, he would make me an offer that I didn't expect. In the way that only Stu can say it, he continued, "Well, if you, ahhhh, decide that you ever want to train to become a worker, ahhhh, let me know. I'd be happy to train you, tiger."

I could not believe my ears. The legendary Stu Hart offered to train me. How freaking cool was that? I thanked him and said that if I were to train to become a professional wrestler, he would be the first person I would want to train with.

Just to show you how much pull the Hart family has in Calgary, we were only there for maybe 20 minutes before Dynamite was admitted to a private room. That's when his wife, Michelle, came out and said that Dynamite wanted to see me. On my way to the room, I kept wondering why he wanted to see me. I entered the room. After asking him how he was doing, he said as good as can be expected, considering the pain. He thanked me for travelling with him and asked Michelle to bring him his leather jacket. He reached in the pocket, pulled something out, and called me over to the bed. He told me to stick out my hand. He extended his and placed some money in mine. I really felt uncomfortable taking it and told him so. He said that I better take it or he'd kick my ass — maybe not that day but one day. He then said, "Please take it and buy your girl something nice for Christmas."

When I said I didn't have a girlfriend at that time his reply was then to buy my mom something nice. So I just put it in my pocket without looking to see how much it was and thanked him. There was no need for him to do that; I was being paid for the trip. When I told him, he said that it didn't matter and to consider it a bonus. Just then Julie came in, said she was leaving, and that she could give me a ride back to the airport. I accepted the offer for the lift. I thanked Dynamite and Michelle for their generous gift, said goodbye to Stu, who reiterated his offer to train me, and left the hospital. Julie Hart was extremely nice to me and asked if I was hungry. She said she could stop if I wanted food. I lied and told her that I was not hungry — she was already going out of her way for me. She dropped me off at the airport and thanked me for helping them out. I said it was no problem and thanked her for the ride. She smiled and said it was no trouble at all. She drove off and I went inside to kill some time before my flight.

When I reached in my pocket, I remembered that Dynamite had given me some money. I pulled it out to see how much it was. He gave me $200! To me that was a large sum of money. I'll never forget his generosity. This trip also opened my eyes to the real dangers that pro wrestlers face every time they step into a ring. They put their bodies on the line for our entertainment. I always respected the wrestlers for that; however, on this day I gained a much deeper respect for their sacrifices.

Everything was going very well for me and I was extremely happy with my involvement in the WWF thus far. The year was coming to an end and I had no idea what 1987 had in store for me. That was until legendary WWE Hall of Famer Pat Patterson had a suggestion for Jack Tunney. Pat mentioned to Jack that the company was not happy with the referees the various athletic commissions assigned to the WWF events. They were looking to have their own full-time referees who worked specifically for the WWF. Pat thought that I would be a good candidate to fill one of those slots as I was already at the events setting up the ring. He figured, why not have me referee some matches as well? Jack contemplated the idea before replying to Pat that he didn't think the time was right to "smarten the kid up." Pat looked at Jack in disbelief, then said, "The kid has been working here for a year. All the boys know him. He's been in the locker room. What do you mean smarten the kid up? I think the kid knows by now the business is a work."

The funny thing about that conversation was that I was within earshot of the entire exchange. Pat even looked over at me, shrugged his shoulders, and laughed. I wasn't laughing. I was really upset. This was the opportunity of a lifetime and in my mind it had been taken away before it was even offered. Pat came over to me and said, "Don't worry, Jimmy, he'll come around. Leave it to me."

A few weeks later, Jack approached me and asked me if I would be interested in becoming a referee. I quickly answered him with an enthusiastic yes. At the same time, I thought, *How could he not know that I heard his whole conversation with Pat Patterson about my becoming a referee?* I was only a few feet away from them when they were discussing it. No way was I going to question it; this was the chance I had been waiting for.

At that time, the referees in the World Wrestling Federation wore a uniform similar to that of professional boxing officials. The standard garb was black pants, black wrestling boots or sneakers, a light blue dress shirt, and a black bow tie. Jack told me to go out and purchase the necessary attire and to carry it with me at all times because you never knew when I would be pressed into action. I guess the first question I should have asked him was who was going to train me and show me the ropes as far as learning to become a pro wrestling referee. I suppose I was just so excited to start that I didn't think at that time to find out. Nevertheless, I went out the next day and bought everything I needed to be a wwf referee. Maybe I should have thought ahead and bought more than one pair of black pants and one powder blue shirt but I will get to that in just a little bit. I had my uniform, carried it to every event where I was setting up the ring, and waited to be trained for my reffing debut. This is when things got interesting.

CHAPTER 3

Finally

It has been said many times that when you are anticipating something, no matter what it may be, the waiting is the hardest part. Let me tell you, whoever came up with that cliché was dead right. Here I was, travelling from show to show, continuing with my duties on the ring crew and carrying my newly acquired referee gear in my bag while I waited to begin my referee training. When was I going to be taught how to referee a wrestling match? Who was going to be the one to train me? This was not happening fast enough as far as I was concerned. To this day I think back to that moment and wonder why I didn't approach any of the other officials or even Pat Patterson himself and ask them for some advice or help. I wanted to start yesterday but I couldn't bring myself to "bother" anyone. Still very anxious to get this thing going, I decided that I would exercise patience and my chance would come. Not soon enough of course.

I do not remember the exact day, but it was in February 1987 and the wwf had an event in Newmarket, Ontario, less than an hour's drive north of Toronto. As usual, I brought my officiating gear with me to the show, not expecting to put it to use. John Bonello and I set up the ring early that afternoon. Like we had many times before, once we were done with the setup, we had our little match that we had worked out. It was just another day at the office for us. We got a quick bite to eat and returned to the venue waiting for the rest of the guys to show up. Every WWF/E event has what was referred to in those days as a road agent. The job of a road agent is to act as a liaison between the wrestlers and higher-level management. They gave instructions and guidance to the talent about what management wanted to happen in the matches on each and every live event. They were in charge of all aspects of the show. On this night, former wrestler Tony Garea was acting as road agent and the lead or head agent was WWF Hall of Famer Chief Jay Strongbow.

Chief, as we all called him, was a unique individual to say the least. He had a good sense of humour and was well known by those in the industry as being, shall we say, very thrifty. Chief didn't like to waste money. Not only his own; he didn't like spending the company's money very much either. Another thing that Chief was famous for was giving nicknames to everyone. Wrestlers and crew alike found themselves being given one of his original monikers. For example, Tony Chimel was given the nickname Chimmy Cham; John D'Amico was John Brown and I became Jimmy Jam. We all kind of felt that if Chief christened you with one of his tags, you were "over" with him.

When Chief had settled in and dropped off his Halliburton briefcase in the locker room, I bumped into him in the hallway. After we exchanged greetings and pleasantries, he asked me a question I was not prepared for: "So, Mr. Jimmy Jam, I understand that you are going to be refereeing for us."

"Yes, Chief. That's what I was told," I replied.

"Do you have your ref gear with you here today?" he continued.

I answered, "Yes, Chief. I always bring my ref gear with me. I was told to never forget it and to bring it with me to every show whether I am reffing or not."

Chief smiled, looked me in the eyes, and said, "Well, go get your stuff because you're working tonight."

I was in shock. I thought, *How am I going to ref tonight when I haven't had any training to become a referee?* I mentioned that to him and his response was classic Chief. He again looked me right in the eyes, leaned closer, and said, "Does that mean you don't want to ref?"

"No! No! No!" was my quick answer. "Of course I want to referee tonight. I was just saying . . ." Before I could finish my sentence, he told me to go get my stuff and that I would be working one match on the show. The match I was assigned to ref involved S.D. "Special Delivery" Jones versus the Red Demon, who was Jose Luis Rivera wearing a red mask. Before informing them that I was officiating their match, I sought out some help. That help came from Billy "Red" Lyons and referee Terry Yorkston. They both took the time to give me a crash course in pro wrestling refereeing 101. They gave me the rundown on the basics, told me not to worry too much, and re-enforced that everything would be just fine. I know I heard everything they told me but because I was so nervous about my first match, I couldn't remember much of what they explained to me. I thanked them both and proceeded down the hall.

Next order of business was to tell S.D. that I was reffing his match. I wasn't too sure how he would react to the news but it was now my job to find out what was happening in the match. That much I did know. S.D. was really a good guy and we had become pretty good friends, which helped calm me down for a little while at least. He gave me a brief summary of what he had planned but the most important thing he told me was to listen to him during the match and it would all work out just fine. Rivera was there in the locker room while I was talking to S.D. and just reiterated what S.D. had said. I thanked them both and went to put my referee gear on for my first match.

There were two matches on before mine so I figured the best course of action would be to watch the refs in those matches and keep mental notes. Red stood with me while I watched the matches and pointed out a few things that would be helpful to me. That's the kind of guy Red was: one of the nicest men you could ever meet. At the end of the second match, it was time for me to make my way to the ring. I was later told that from the way I was walking to the ring, you would have thought I was heading to the electric chair. Finally, I got to the ring and climbed the steps to enter. The only thing going through my mind was, *Please don't trip going through the ropes!* I didn't trip but I was already beginning to sweat. The thing about those powder blue shirts we all used to wear was that they absolutely showed when one is perspiring and I was pitting bad.

As the two combatants made their way to the ring, another thought entered my already frazzled mind. *What the hell was the finish of the match?* I completely drew a blank on all the stuff S.D. had told me. Thinking fast, as I performed the pre-match check of the wrestlers for any foreign objects, I whispered to S.D. that I had forgotten the finish and pretty much everything else. He calmly told me not to worry and to stay close to him and listen to what he told me to do. Sounded simple enough — only one little problem, though: how was I supposed to stay close to him without making it look like I'm staying close to him? This might sound confusing but I didn't want it to appear obvious that I was being instructed on what to do during the entire match. There was no time to dwell on it, so I signalled for the bell and the match was underway.

Even though I knew I was moving around the ring as if I were auditioning for the role of zombie in *Night of the Living Dead*, I followed S.D.'s instructions to the letter. Everything he told me to do, I did. Then they added a little wrinkle I was not expecting at all. Since Rivera was wrestling under a mask and working as a heel, they decided to introduce the dreaded foreign object. Here's how it played out. S.D. was selling and told me to stay with him and not look at Rivera for a few seconds. I did just that and as I backed off and gave him some space, Rivera gave him a head butt. S.D. sold it like he had been hit with a club. As green as I was, I had seen this scenario many times in the past. My instincts told me to go to S.D. and check on him, all the while keeping my back to Rivera. S.D. told me to go check Rivera's mask for an object. I did, found nothing, and returned to S.D. to inform him that all was well and that there was no object. Of course, while my back was turned, Rivera slipped the object back into his mask and gave S.D. another head butt, which he sold big time once again. We repeated this two or three more times, all the while never finding out what the dastardly Red Demon had done. In the end S.D. overcame the odds and won the match. I felt relieved — I had gotten through my first match. The feedback from the other referees and the guys in the match was encouraging but I knew I had so much more to learn and work on.

With my first match out of the way, I couldn't wait to get back in the ring. Not only that, I couldn't wait to make my Maple Leaf Gardens debut. After all, the Gardens was the Mecca of Canadian wrestling, not to mention hockey. How much better does it get than to referee for the World Wrestling Federation in the same arena that your favourite NHL team plays in? Not to mention that Toronto is where I was born and raised, which would make it that much more of a special event for me. A few months had passed and still my anticipation was building. During those months, I had the opportunity to continue to learn my craft at spot shows, shows the WWF held in smaller towns and venues. I wasn't complaining, mind you, but I was still waiting impatiently to get to ref a big show. Then, I got the call.

It was May 17, 1987. The moment had arrived. I was assigned two matches on a WWF card at a Maple Leaf Gardens event. The first was Johnny K-9 versus Sam Houston. K-9 was a local wrestler from Hamilton while Houston was the younger half-brother of Jake "The Snake" Roberts. The second match I was to work was

Outback Jack taking on Frenchy Martin. All the matches at Maple Leaf Gardens were taped for television at that time. So not only was this my MLG debut, it was my first time refereeing a match for TV. At ringside doing commentary for the matches were legends and Hall of Famers Gorilla Monsoon and Bobby "The Brain" Heenan. I can't say enough about those two gentlemen. Gorilla had a big heart and truly loved the business while Bobby was legitimately one of the funniest men I have ever met. Heenan was a really nice guy as well and he and Gorilla working together was pure magic.

What a feeling it was climbing the steps and walking to the ring along the entrance ramp that I had sat next to as a fan for so many years. At that time, I believe that Maple Leaf Gardens was the only arena in North America to have this unique setup. For years I had followed my idols as they made their way to the ring on the very same platform that I was now using. Johnny K-9 was next to enter the ring. He was not well received by the fans as they booed him loudly. The jeers turned to cheers as Sam Houston made his entrance, doing a little Texas Two Step as his music played. The introductions were made and the match was on, but little did I know that my long-anticipated MLG debut would be met with embarrassment.

As nervous as I was, I had a few months' worth of matches under my belt so I was gaining a bit of confidence — but not over-confidence. I just wanted to look like I belonged in the ring and not to seem out of place. The match itself was going smoothly until something happened that caught me by surprise. There was a pin attempt and, as any good referee would do, I dove to the canvas to make a count. That's when the unthinkable occurred: I experienced a wardrobe malfunction. The back of my pants split. Not just a small split, but a rather large gaping one. It began from the middle of my crotch, down near the taint, and ran all the way up the back of my pants to the belt loops. There is one little thing you learn once something like this happens: you learn to wear *black* undergarments or tights under your referee pants just in case of such an emergency. That day, I was wearing blue underwear, and not dark blue unfortunately, and it probably looked like a blue light flashing from the back of my pants. I could hear people laughing, but I chose just to ignore it and continue with my in-ring duties. I glanced over to the announcers' table at ringside where I saw Heenan in stitches while Gorilla just shook his head in disbelief.

Mercifully, the match ended soon after but the damage to my ego had been done. The other lesson I learned that evening was to carry a back-up pair of pants. Unfortunately, I had only one pair of ref pants with me. Who would have thought that I would need another pair? Obviously, you live and learn. But I had one more match to referee that evening. Where was I going to get another pair of black or even dark pants on a Sunday night in downtown Toronto? Thankfully, veteran referees Terry Yorkston and John Bonello offered me their spare pants. At that time, my waist size was 29 inches. Terry's pants were most likely closer to a size 38 and John's were too short. I ended up wearing Terry's pants. They were extremely big on me, but what choice did I have? The show must go on. Looking like a child in his father's pants, I made my way out for my second match. Other than the fact that I looked a little like a clown, the match went off without a hitch.

At the end of the show Bobby Heenan came up to me, still laughing, shook my hand, and patted me on the back. He said, "It's not that you split your pants open in the middle of a match that I find funny, it was the expression on your face and fact that you no-sold it that was hilarious." He then told me I did the right thing by continuing as if nothing happened. "You couldn't very well take a time-out to go change your pants. By the way, whose giant pants were you wearing for the other match?" he said, giggling.

I told him that I had borrowed them from Terry Yorkston and that from now on, I would have another pair in my gear bag.

He smiled and said, "See, kid, you're learning. Never stop learning in this business. The day you think you know it all, it's time for you to leave. Good job tonight."

Wow! What great advice from the one and only Bobby "The Brain" Heenan. To this day, I have not forgotten those words. I always prided myself on being a sponge, trying to absorb and learn as much as I could, and have done so throughout my career. Thanks, Brain — to this day, he is still one of my favourite people that I have had the pleasure of knowing. Not just in the wrestling business, but in life.

Gorilla, on the other hand, was a little more father-like with his assessment of my reffing work. He said I did fine with not letting my mishap distract me from my job but that in the future, I should be better prepared in the event of a repeat occurrence. He also said that to avoid something like that happening again, I should buy pants that were not so tight. I agreed and thanked him for his help. He patted me on the back as well and told me that I would be just fine and to keep working hard. I told him I would and thanked him again.

My very first Maple Leaf Gardens match didn't quite go the way I had hoped but it was a true learning experience. Of course, lesson number one: buy loose-fitting pants and wear black under them. I always did from that day forward. This was really only the beginning. The best was yet to come and, brother, did I have a blast. I know somewhere in the video archives of the WWF/E television studios, my blue butt lives forever.

CHAPTER 4

Making a Splash?

Things were beginning to look up with regards to my further involvement with the WWF, partly due to some unforeseen circumstances. The first occurrence that expanded my duties was Jack Tunney's eye surgery. It required him to wear dark glasses and also precluded him from driving his car for a few weeks. When the WWF held their TV tapings within a ten-hour drive of his home base in Toronto, Jack preferred driving there instead of flying. As I mentioned earlier, Jack was the figurehead president of the WWF at that time so he was needed at every taping. Usually he was accompanied by his longtime friend and confidant Billy "Red" Lyons. He and Red would split the driving to and from TV.

Before I get further into this story, let me tell you a little about the man who hired me. Jack Tunney is the nephew of one of the most respected promoters in all of wrestling, Frank Tunney. Jack's father, John, was a partner in the promotion with Frank. The brothers began promoting wrestling events out of their office directly across the street from the famed Maple Leaf Gardens. John passed away at the young age of 32. Frank continued to promote wrestling until his passing in 1983. Jack and Frank's son Ed Tunney took over the reins together, with Jack as the front man while Ed kept a lower profile. My eventual good friend Elio Zarlenga worked closely with the Tunneys as kind of their right-hand man.

For years, the Tunneys' main source of talent was a mixture of well-known local wrestlers as well as top stars from Jim Crockett Promotions, based in North Carolina. As the promotional battle between the WWF and the NWA heated up, Crockett felt the need to keep his top talent closer to home to combat the juggernaut that was the WWF. Without the bigger names from the NWA appearing on MLG cards, crowds dwindled. Jack saw the writing on the wall. He made the decision to join forces with Vince McMahon Jr. and become the WWF's head promoter for Canadian tours. This alliance seemed logical not only from a business standpoint but from a personal one as well. Frank Tunney and Vincent McMahon Sr. were not only business associates, they were good friends. So it only made sense their families would continue their relationship.

Jack was then named figurehead president of the WWF, a role that was primarily a television persona. Jack was likely chosen because he was a large man who looked very authoritative and in command at all times. Always well dressed and businesslike, he definitely looked the part and fit the role very well. That's where his backstage power ended. Of course he had some say on whom he could request to appear on his shows; his actual role was that of a regional promoter. Unfortunately for Jack, his run with the WWF ended in 1995 when Vince chose to run shows in Canada without any involvement from the Tunneys. Although I do not know the reason why, I do know Jack was forced out of the WWF and retired from promoting wrestling. There were rumours of Jack aligning himself with WCW to run against the WWF but as far as I know, they were just that, rumours. Jack disappeared from the wrestling scene. I hadn't heard anything about his whereabouts until Dave Hebner informed me in early 2004 that Jack had passed away. He told me a week after it had happened. I was not only sad to hear that the man who had given me my first job in wrestling had died, I was disappointed that I had been unable to attend his funeral.

I never got to say it, but thank you, Jack, for taking a chance on a young kid with big dreams and no clue what he was getting into.

Okay, back to the story. Jack called me one day and asked if I would meet him at his office. I told him of course and made my way downtown. When I got there, he explained to me that because of his eye surgery, he wasn't able to drive to upcoming TV events. He then asked me if I was available to join him and Red on their next trip to help with the driving. Jack also thought it would be a good idea for me to bring my referee gear because you never knew when you might be needed. Not only that, it would be good for me to be seen and to meet people who worked for the WWF that I would not generally get to meet at house shows. I jumped at the chance and told Jack that I would be more than happy to help them out. It didn't hurt that I was getting paid for it as well, but even if I hadn't been, it was a great opportunity to get noticed, and I was not going to pass that up.

Just as I was about to leave Jack's office he added one more reason why he wanted me to accompany him and Red on their road trips. Jack told me that Red was notorious for driving not one mile per hour above the posted speed limit. Not only that, Red made frequent coffee stops, which according to Jack added to their travel time. He hoped that with me taking over much of the driving and with Red sitting in the back seat, maybe there would be less frequent coffee stops. When I laughed at what Jack said about his buddy, he looked at me seriously and said, "I'm not kidding. Red is the safest driver I know — sometimes a little too safe." Then he smiled and said, "Thank you, James, talk to you soon." Jack often called me James. He was the only one to call me James and it never sounded odd or out of place to me. It was actually cool in a way.

My first road trip with Jack and Red was to the television tapings first in South Bend, Indiana, for *WWF Superstars*. The next day took us to Rockford, Illinois, for a taping of *Wrestling Challenge*.

It was actually in Rockford that I made my syndicated television debut. It was not as a referee but rather as an attendant. It was after the match where the Ugandan Giant Kamala had soundly defeated Moondog Spot. Moondog was left lying in the ring and I was one of the ringside attendants helping to stretcher him out. For me, that was an awesome moment. I called everyone I knew to tell them that I would be on television. I don't think they quite understood my excitement over being a stretcher bearer. Nevertheless, in my mind I was on my way to becoming a regular on TV. Just not quite the way I had envisioned.

I made several more road trips with those two and ended up doing the majority of the driving. Even back then, I was a terrible passenger. I preferred being the guy behind the wheel and to this day, that still applies. We journeyed to many places that I had never been to before, some interesting and some not so much. On one trip through Pennsylvania on our way to Hershey, the Chocolate Capital of America, we passed a sign that read *Intercourse 11 miles*, with an arrow pointing to the left. We were near Lancaster, Pennsylvania, and when I saw the sign, I turned to my two passengers and said, "So, am I making a left or is that place just a tourist trap?"

Red laughed, while Jack had this look of someone who was not amused by the comment. He might have found my attempt at humour funnier had we not been terribly lost. Yes, I had made a wrong turn somewhere an hour or so prior which added almost three hours to the trip. Red didn't mind as long as we stopped for a six-pack. As it turned out, as well as coffee Red also liked to indulge in a brewski or two. Jack just wanted to get to our destination and check into the hotel so he could get some rest. You may think that being a passenger even in your own car is relaxing, but that is not true, especially for larger individuals, and Jack definitely fit into that category. Anyway, in my mind, it was probably one of the funniest road signs I have ever seen. We finally made it to our destination, Hershey, P.A., checked into our hotel, and crashed for the night. I will say this about Jack's choice of hotels; everywhere we travelled we stayed at only good and clean hotels. Maybe not always a high-end brand-name establishment but for sure the quality was there.

Unfortunately for me, on this particular trip I did not make it onto TV. No stretcher bearing, no cleanup in the aisle, not a darn thing. I was really only mildly disappointed because at the same time I realized that I was making contacts with WWF personnel and the crew, as well as getting to know the talent better. I was truly enjoying myself. Now it may sound to some like my only objective was to be on television but that was not the case at all. I just thought it was cool to make the occasional cameo that I could brag to my friends and family about. Who wouldn't want to be on TV? Plus, it beats working a "real" job. My father said to me once that if you like your job and you enjoy going to work every day, you are one lucky person and I knew how fortunate I was to be associated with this group.

Things were going very well for me as I continued to be a part of the Canadian ring crew as well as referee matches on those shows. The thing I found kind of odd was that Jack had told me that I would accompany him and Red because of Jack's eye surgery; several months had passed and Jack's eyesight was just fine but he still had me driving with them to the TV tapings that they did not fly to. There had to be a reason why I was still performing this duty. I never found out why it continued but I wasn't going to complain. Then it happened. The day I had been waiting for finally arrived.

It was June 1987 and on this trip, the three of us were driving to the television tapings in Glens Falls and Lake Placid, New York. As usual, I brought my referee gear, thinking it would not get used as was the norm at TV. On this day, though, things changed that impacted me for the rest of my career. Let me explain the situation that led to my TV reffing debut. John Bonello was a Canadian referee and appeared on *WWF Superstars* and *Wrestling Challenge* every week. It was never made clear to me why but the WWF wanted a Canadian presence on the TV shows, particularly the ones that aired in Canada. I always assumed it was because of the Canadian content rules that apply to stations in this country. In a nutshell, this means Canadian TV and radio stations have to air a certain percentage of what they deem "Canadian content." That could mean shows shot and produced in Canada or having Canadian performers. I may be mistaken but I was under the assumption that was the reason for having a referee from Canada on the show. He would be considered a performer and thus labelled as "Canadian content."

John had been refereeing at every TV taping for a while now. The WWF flew him in for the tapings when it was too far for him to drive. They also paid for his rental car and hotel rooms. All travel expenses were taken care of and the only thing he had to pay for was food and booze. Of course on TV days there was catering so if got your fill there, it would limit your food cost away from the arenas. Anyway, at the previous tapings in New Jersey, John ran into some flight trouble and no-showed the scheduled TVs. Flight delays and cancellations are very much a part of the wrestling business. It is inevitable that it will happen sooner or later. From what I was told, John made one small error in judgement; he didn't call anyone to let them know of his dilemma. This did not sit very well with the bosses. They were surprised that someone with so many years of experience as a wrestler and a referee would not inform anyone of the situation. One rule you learn almost immediately when you begin in the business is if you run into any kind of trouble and you know you will be late or even not make it to the venue for the show, you need to notify the proper people or person. The "office" was not satisfied with John's explanation of what happened and they decided not to bring him to a few television tapings as a sort of punishment. After all, what would happen to anyone if they just didn't show up for work without calling or giving a valid reason for being absent? I think we all know the answer to that.

Not to sound like Captain Cliché, but one person's loss is another person's gain, and being in Glens Falls, New York, that day was my gain. I was approached by the man responsible for starting me on my refereeing career, Pat Patterson. He asked me if I had brought my gear with me. I did but I had left my bag at the hotel a few blocks away. I wasn't going to tell Pat that, so I just nodded and said that I did indeed have my gear. He told me to put it on because I would be working. I was ecstatic. I was finally going to get my chance to referee on TV and be seen back home. I found the nearest exit and took off running towards the hotel where my bag was. I must have broken some land speed records because I was back at the arena changing into my ref clothes in no time. After getting dressed, it was time to get my ref assignments for the three weeks' worth of programming.

I set out to find the other referees to find out which matches I'd be reffing. I don't remember how many other refs were also working that night. I do recall Joey Marella being the one who informed me which matches I had. Joey was the son of Gorilla Monsoon. Even though he had that New Jersey swagger about him, he was very helpful in getting me to relax. As you may have guessed, I was very nervous to say the least. Dave Hebner was also there, which made me more at ease because I had known Dave for over a year by this point and we had become good friends. As a matter of fact, Dave pretty much took me under his wing and mentored me throughout my career. I couldn't have asked for a better teacher. There was one more referee there that evening that I remember. Jack Lotz was assigned to the event by the New York State Athletic Commission. Jack was not your ordinary ref from the Commission. He was very cooperative, unlike others who were known by those in the WWF as "Commission Refs," which wasn't a flattering label to have. Jack was different; he was a very nice man who was more than willing to help a young greenhorn like myself. He was also a licensed professional boxing referee, which I found interesting. Then I found out that he had been in the boxing movie *Raging Bull*, starring Robert DeNiro and Joe Pesci. How cool was that! He downplayed it when I asked him about it. He was a real humble guy who I got to know pretty well over the years, a real class act. There may have been other referees working that night but those three are the only ones I can recall.

Later on, Hebner asked me if I was okay with the matches I had been given to work and I said that everything was fine. His final instructions were on how to get the time cues from the timekeeper at ringside. It was not a complicated process and I assumed that I would pick it up in no time at all. I just had to remember to look in the direction of the timekeeper every so often during the match and to let the wrestlers know how much time was remaining. It didn't always work out that way. My very first WWF television match involved George "The Animal" Steele versus an enhancement talent — in other words, a guy who makes the superstar look like a superstar. During this match, I totally blanked on giving the Animal time cues. George kept staring at me and I just stared back, thinking it was part of his character. He did portray a wild and unpredictable wrestler, so I just chalked it up to him doing his thing. After tearing open one of the corner pads and pretending to eat the stuffing, which was one of his trademarks along with having a green tongue, he turned to his opponent and placed him in his finishing move, the Flying Chicken Wing. It goes without saying, that maneuver was very painful, or at least appeared to be. The no-name wrestler submitted; I called for the bell and went over to raise the Animal's hand in victory. As I did just that, George had other plans. Suddenly he dropped to the ground, locked his legs around my ankles, and sent me falling backwards to the canvas. Shocked, I scurried out of the ring and George proceeded to chase me to the backstage area. Once we got there he came over to me and said, "Did I scare you?"

I said, "Yeah, a little."

"Well, maybe next time you won't forget to give me the time cues!" he snapped.

I apologized for not giving him the cues and assured him it wouldn't happen again. Just as he was about to walk away, he turned to me, smiled, and said, "I'm just messing with you. I really do need you to give me those cues but I'm not mad. Just ribbing the new kid."

What a relief! The last thing I wanted to do was to piss off one of the boys, especially one of the veterans. Just as I was getting over that fiasco, Pat Patterson came up to me and informed me that there was a change and that I would be refereeing the One Man Gang's match in the final hour of the taping. He said to find out what the Gang wanted to do. Now the One Man Gang, whose real name was George Gray, was six foot eight inches tall and close to 400 pounds, with a mohawk and tattoos on the shaved portion of his scalp. He was one scary-looking dude but in reality, he was super nice. I always thought how amazing it was that so many of the boys were so unlike their wrestling personas.

So off I went to find the Gang to see what he wanted me to do. I found him sitting quietly in the locker room. I walked over and softly said to him, "Pat told me that I am reffing your match now and to get with you to find out what you want me to do."

George nodded approvingly and gave me the run-down of what was going to happen. "Okay, first I'll beat up on the guy for about a minute or two. Then I'll hit my finish on him. After the one-two-three, raise my hand. Then I'll shove you out of the way, grab the guy, and hit my finish on him again. After the second time, you get in my face and start giving me shit. I'll stick my finger in your face then you stick your finger in mine."

As soon as he said that, I knew right then and there that it was not going to end well for me. He continued with the plan, saying, "At the right moment, I will get mad, grab you, and give *you* my finish."

Trying hard not to look stunned, I told him, "I've never taken that finish before; what do you need me to do?" I had never taken anyone's finish before but I wasn't going to tell him that. I was trying to sound like a grizzled old veteran but somehow, I don't think he bought it.

"Nothing!" he replied. "Just keep your face turned to one side so you don't land on your nose. I'll take care of the rest. Don't worry, you'll be just fine."

I thanked him and left the locker room thinking, *I hope I don't screw this up.* This was a huge opportunity for me to show them I was capable of doing whatever they needed me to do. Just then Pat walked over and asked if I had talked to the Gang. I told him I did. He then asked me if I was okay with doing it. Again I told him not to worry and that it would be fine. He smiled, gave me an encouraging pat on the back, and said, "Good luck, Jimbo."

It was now the moment of truth. Everything went exactly as the Gang had explained to me. After he hit his finishing move on his opponent for the second time, it was time for me to jump in his face and begin to read him the riot act. His rather large finger was now mere inches from my face and I continued to let him have it verbally. Out of nowhere, he reached out, pulled my head down, hooked his left arm around the back of my head, grabbed the waistband of my pants with his right hand, lifted me vertically in the air, and fell forward, dropping both of us belly first on the mat. He had just given me his finish, the 747. It is basically a vertical suplex, only instead of falling back with both men landing on their backs, he falls forward landing flat.

The impact was jarring. Even more than I was anticipating. Despite that, I thought I had better not budge after such a devastating move and just lay there until someone came to get me. That's exactly what I did. As I lay there motionless, there seemed to be a lot of commotion going on in the ring. Eventually Joey Marella and Jack Lotz pulled me out of harm's way and helped me to the back. Once I was through the curtains, the first person to check on me was Pat. He wanted to know how I was. I told him I was fine but he asked again just to make sure. There was so much adrenaline rushing through my veins, I was not feeling a damn thing. After I assured Pat that everything was okay, he said nice job and smiled as he walked away. I was then approached by Rick

Martel and Haku, two veteran wrestlers who I had become friends with. They were both genuinely concerned about my well-being. I reiterated to them both that I was fine. I reassured them that I was feeling good and they both said that the bump looked really good.

For me, that was like earning my stripes the hard way. There goes Captain Cliché again. After the tapings were done, Jack, Red, and I headed back to the hotel. They both complimented me on the bump, which again made my night. We were spending the night in Glens Falls and driving the two hours to Lake Placid in the morning. The only problem for me was that I was still so amped up from my first ever ref bump, there was no way I could sleep. I'm not sure what time it was when I finally fell asleep for a few hours. The wake-up call came way too early. I showered, got dressed, and met my riding partners in the lobby. There was no way I was going to let anyone know that I was now feeling the after-effects from the night before. I've never said this to anyone before, but I landed almost flat with my knees hitting the canvas slightly ahead of the rest of my body. My knees hurt, not too much but enough to feel it. We all piled into Jack's Cadillac Fleetwood and made our way to day two of TV.

The drive to Lake Placid seemed to take no time at all. When we got there, everything was business as usual. The only thing they said to me was that I would ref matches for the first two hours of *Wrestling Challenge*. I would not be on the third hour of the show because it was to air the same week as the One Man Gang 747 incident taped the night before. That made complete sense considering the magnitude of the bump. This night I was much better at relaying time cues to the talent and began to feel just a little more comfortable. Maybe that first bump helped settle me down. Whatever the reason, on day two I was a bit more composed.

After the tapings were over, I was met by Pat, who informed me that after talking to Terry Garvin, a former wrestler who was in charge of booking the refs for the WWF, I would be booked at all the TV tapings from now on. Basically, I was replacing John

Bonello as the "Canadian" referee on the weekly broadcasts. As bad as I felt for John, there was absolutely no way I would pass up this great opportunity. Thanking Pat, I immediately set out to find Terry Garvin. I thanked Terry for giving me this chance and we shook hands to seal the deal.

On a side note, John Bonello didn't do himself any favours with the company after he was charged with and convicted of counselling first-degree murder. According to the *Toronto Star* newspaper, he was sentenced to 18 months and ordered to perform 360 hours of community service during his three years' probation. The article states that Bonello paid an undercover officer a cash advance and gave him a house key with directions to shoot his wife while he was out of town reffing. A psychiatrist testified at the trial that Bonello was using steroids, marijuana, cocaine, and Benzedrine, which together contributed to a psychosis that could have given him delusions of grandeur.

I thought that this was very unusual as I never suspected any kind of strange behaviour from Bonello. He was always very confident, even a little cocky at times, but that was not uncommon to see in this business. I guess you just don't know what some people are thinking or are capable of. After this scenario, I was pretty sure nothing would shock me about this business but I would later find out that would not be the case.

Obviously this was considered a black mark on the company as the front-page photo in the *Star* was Bonello refereeing a match with the WWF champion Hulk Hogan. It was the kind of publicity the company didn't want or need. They were going through some legal battles of their own and this was just more ammo for those who disliked pro wrestling in general and in particular the WWF. Needless to say, this was the end of Bonello's wrestling career with the WWF. I understand he and his wife have reunited and are still together to this day.

I personally never had an issue with John Bonello. On occasions, we travelled together and he took it upon himself to be the "leader" of the Canadian referees, who included Terry Yorkston and me. Neither Terry nor I minded too much as that was just his character and we were both easygoing. All that being said, not to sound mean-spirited about it, the only influence John Bonello had over my career was that his misfortunes benefitted me.

Now back to the story. Jack, Red, and I piled into Jack's Caddy and we began our drive back home that very night from Lake Placid. Once we got on the road, Jack asked me what Pat and Terry wanted. I was taken aback, thinking that both he and Red would have heard the good news. After I gave them the skinny on what went down, they were both genuinely happy for me. I did feel a slight measure of trepidation from Jack though. Maybe he thought everything was happening too fast for me or maybe he was concerned that all this new responsibility would be too much for me to handle so soon. He may have even thought that all this new-found success would go to my head. Whatever the reason was, I could sense something in Jack's tone that suggested caution. After all, not everyone is cut out for the wrestling business and this was definitely going to answer any questions as to whether or not I was capable of handling the increased schedule.

CHAPTER 5

A Whole New World

In the summer of 1987 things really took off for me. All of a sudden, a whole new world opened up to this young kid from Toronto. I was travelling all over North America, all on the WWF's dime. Airfare, rental cars, hotels were all being paid for by the company. It was pretty much the same deal John Bonello had. Every few weeks, an itinerary would arrive at my house with my schedule for the upcoming tours. I wasn't working very many house shows in the United States, but mainly TV tapings. Of course I was still booked on all the Canadian shows. At that time, the WWF ran monthly tours in the Great White North. I was only working limited live events in the U.S., which I was perfectly fine with. I knew in my heart that sooner or later, I would be a full-time referee working a full schedule.

Along with getting to travel all over the USA and seeing just about every state in the union, I began to experience some lasting memories that would remain with me forever. I will admit that there were some days that were less than memorable. However, being a person who tends to focus on the positives in my life, or at the very least tries to, the good times are the ones most embedded in my mind. One such moment occurred on my very first trip to San Francisco. As a matter of fact, it was one of the first TV trips I made. I had flown into the City by the Bay the day before the tapings. After picking up my rental car, I was off to find the hotel that the office had me booked in. Did I mention this was my very first trip to San Fran? It did take awhile for me to find the hotel but then figuring out how to get into the parking garage was another issue. After eventually solving that problem, I checked myself into the Adam's Mark hotel. A king bed smoking room — yes, I was a smoker in those days. The reason I tell you this is because I discovered some new (to me anyways) information about the boss, Vince McMahon. Apparently, Vince was not fond of smoking. Pat Patterson smoked, Terry Garvin smoked, and they were top people in the company. In my mind it could not have been that big a deal; however, I was not willing to find out and was determined not to light up in front of the boss.

The remainder of that day I spent just walking around the town, getting a bite to eat, then going to bed somewhat early to be ready for the next day's television. Waking up early the next morning, I took my time getting ready to head to the Cow Palace, the arena in San Francisco. Before exiting my room, I lit up one last cigarette. Back in those days smoking was nowhere near as prohibited as it is today. You could smoke just about anywhere, even in California. Anyhow, I grabbed my gear bag and my smoke and made my way to the elevator. Waiting for it to arrive, I took one last drag and the doors opened. Standing right there in the elevator were Brian Blair, Brutus "The Barber" Beefcake, Hulk Hogan, and, as luck would have it, Vincent Kennedy McMahon. Now in full panic mode, I pull the butt out of my mouth, hiding it behind my back. I casually dropped the evidence in the ashtray by the door. I still had two lungs full of smoke in me when Vince said to me, "Well, what are you waiting for, come on in."

Hulk then piped in and said, "Yeah, brother, come on in."

Expelling as much smoke as possible away from the doors, I entered the elevator, not knowing what to expect. As soon as the doors closed, Vince began to lecture me on the evils of smoking. I nodded in agreement after every point he made, with the occasional "yes sir" thrown in for good measure. As that was going on, the other passengers in the elevator were enjoying the 22-floor ride down to the lobby. Hulk was not helping me out but giving me the odd poke in the ribs as Vince was speaking. I tried my best not to flinch but needless to say, it wasn't working.

Vince then asked me, "Are you all right?"

I answered the boss, "Yes sir, everything is fine and I appreciate your advice." The problem was, being as nervous as I was and with Hulk poking me in the ribs the entire time, I really have no idea what Vince was talking about other than smoking was bad for me.

"Just trying to look out for my guys" were Vince's last words to me before exiting the elevator.

My guys? Vince McMahon just called me one of his guys. How freaking cool was that? The rest of the guys got a good chuckle out of the whole thing and each wished me luck. I wasn't sure if they were joking but that's how I took it. The rest of the day at the arena, every time Hulk, Brutus, or Brian would walk by, they would ask me if I had a cigarette. Funny guys. All the friendly kidding gave me a sense of belonging and made me feel like part of the team.

Something else happened on this TV day in San Fran. The WWF had produced their second vinyl LP with original music entitled *Piledriver: The Wrestling Album 2*. The first album was mainly superstars' entrance music with one track being the company's own version of "Land of a Thousand Dances." A music video was made of this song featuring Rick Derringer, Meat Loaf, and Cyndi Lauper (wearing a brunette wig and sunglasses) playing instruments while the WWF superstars sang along with the song. It was very cheesy but looked like they were having a lot of fun.

The title song on this new album was sung by Koko B. Ware and that day, they planned to film footage from one of his matches to insert into the music video that was to accompany the release of the album. Little did I know the dark match assigned to me on this night would be the match filmed for the video. Koko was facing Barry Horowitz and I didn't clue in as to why earlier in the day they had been recording Koko giving Barry his finishing maneuver several times. There was one catch: they were shooting the sequence from under the ring. They didn't put the canvas on the ring; they slightly separated the plywood planks so that the camera could see up from under the ring. Koko would then administer the "Ghost Buster" on Barry and it would appear as if they were landing on the camera. It looked great. Now it was time for their actual match. Of course the WWF filmed the match but only used a very short clip from it in the music video. As short as the clip was, my face can be seen in the background. It's extremely brief but I am there. I had made it into a music video that was shown on MTV as well as on weekly syndicated TV. A small claim to fame, but I'll take it.

San Francisco turned out to be so much fun. I couldn't wait to see what else was in store. It didn't take long me to find out what life on the road was really all about.

The boys like to amuse themselves in so many different ways. Two gentlemen who really enjoyed creating a bit of a ruckus were Marty Jannetty and Shawn Michaels, collectively known as the Rockers. These two had a reputation of being partiers and getting a little overly rowdy. One night, I had the pleasure of falling victim to one of their pranks. It wasn't too bad, but it had me worried about the consequences. Let me elaborate.

We were in Indianapolis, Indiana, and after once again filming the WWF's television shows for the upcoming weeks, I hopped into my rented Ford Taurus and made my way back to the airport hotel I was staying at. What I didn't know was that most of the boys were staying there as well. It also became apparent that many wrestling fans were well aware of the location of the hotel the majority of the roster was staying in. As I pulled into the hotel parking lot, there were literally no spots available. After driving around for about 15 minutes, I stopped in the middle of one of the aisles to map out my next plan of attack. With the car still in drive and my foot firmly on the brake pedal, I felt a small nudge to the rear bumper. When I looked up in the rearview mirror, all I saw was Marty Jannetty in the driver's seat and Shawn in the passenger side waving hello. They were also in a rented Taurus and had their front bumper pressed up against my rear bumper. Thinking that was the end of it, I was just about to start moving forward when all of a sudden Marty floored his car and began pushing my car across the parking lot. I didn't think to take my foot off the brake. The sound of screeching tires echoed through the parking lot.

Panic mode set in. What the hell was he doing and why? In the mirror I could see them both laughing. They were getting a big kick out this and I was thinking about how much damage was being done to the car and how one might explain it to the rental car company. Just as suddenly as he hit the gas, he stopped. Not knowing what to expect from him next, the only thing I thought to do was hit the gas pedal myself and get away. Now the chase was on. It was almost as if he was offended that I would run or, in this case, drive away from them. It resembled a scene straight out of a movie: two identical Fords playing car tag in the parking lot. As luck would have it, there was a car backing out of a spot that forced me to stop. *Wham!* Marty rammed the back of my car pretty hard. The car that was backing out of his spot stopped. The driver looked over in our direction with fear in his eyes and sped away. I pulled into the vacant spot, shut off the engine, and got out. I then went to the back of the car, popped open the trunk, got my bag out, waved to the Rockers, and walked into the hotel. There didn't seem to be very much damage to the car so I chose to ignore it.

A little while later, I figured I'd go down to the bar for a nightcap. Most of the boys were there having a good time. Some were having too good a time. I didn't want to seem presumptuous by joining the party uninvited. Just then Shawn and Marty entered the bar. Uh-oh! What were they going to do when they spotted me? Thinking they hadn't seen me, I relaxed with a drink at the bar. That thought was a little premature. While sipping on my cocktail, I received an unexpected surprise; two hard and simultaneous slaps on my back. The Rockers had indeed spotted me and came over to discuss our brief encounter in the parking lot. I was caught off guard when they said they were not angry in the slightest. On the contrary, they were actually entertained by my handling of the matter. They thought it was funny how I no-sold the entire thing after parking my car. I confessed to them how terrified I had been during the whole fiasco and that my no-selling was more an act of fear and not an attempt at defiance. They laughed and they each bought me a drink. I thanked them for the drinks and for not hurting me. They laughed again and went off to do their thing.

The fun that evening didn't quite end there. Fun may not be the correct word in this instance. Let's just say that what happened next opened my eyes to whole new world of drunkenness. It wasn't pleasant. As I continued sipping my drinks while standing at the bar, three or four of the boys cozied up to the bar right beside me to order drinks. One in particular was very drunk and standing immediately to my right. Then the strangest and most unbelievable thing happened. This well-known WWF superstar began to urinate at the bar. He was hiding it very well with his blazer and his cohorts were covering for him. I probably would not have even noticed had this man not peed on my right foot. That's right; he was peeing on my right foot! I pulled my foot away the very second I noticed what was going on, but the damage was done.

Not knowing what to do next, I did the only thing I could do. I casually walked out of the bar and went into the nearest restroom. Then, I took off my shoes without using my hands. Next was getting my wet right sock off again without touching it. Grabbing a bunch of paper towels, I slipped off my soggy sock, left it and my shoe in the restroom, and proceeded to my hotel room. Once there, I took my pants off because they too had been infected with the urine of champions. I was not keeping any of the infected clothing so I was travelling home minus one pair of pants, one pair of shoes, and of course a single sock. It was a good thing my referee shoes were just black sneakers because I just wore them home.

I know what you all are thinking: who was the superstar responsible for this unusual moment and my loss of clothing? I don't like to name names but I will say this. He was a former Intercontinental champion and he was as solid as a "Rock." No, it wasn't Dwayne Johnson. I may have given it away to some of you but hey, the guy pissed on my foot so he had it coming.

Throughout my 20-plus years with the wwe, I have been privileged, honoured, and maybe just a tad bit lucky to have been a part of some firsts. I thought it would be appropriate to tell you a little story about my first Survivor Series experience. It just so happens that it was also the first ever Survivor Series.

The date, Wednesday November 25, 1987, the day before the inaugural Survivor Series pay-per-view, I was absolutely thrilled that I was booked to be a part of this historic event, which took place at the Richfield Coliseum in Richfield, Ohio. Because Richfield was not that far from Toronto, where I lived, I decided it would make more sense to drive to the event than to fly. After all, it was a one-shot deal, meaning it was the only show we had that weekend. One small problem: my car was acting up so I ended up borrowing my mom's K-Car to make the trip. For those of you who remember this classic vehicle, stop snickering! It had less than 20,000 kilometres on it, so it was still relatively new.

The drive to Ohio was uneventful. Of course I did have to make my obligatory Micky Ds pit stop along the way. It took less than five hours for me to make it from my driveway to the Holiday Inn located next to the Richfield Coliseum. After checking in to the hotel, I got a quick bite to eat in the hotel restaurant, had a few pops with the boys, then called it a night.

The day of the Survivor Series, Thanksgiving Day, I arrived at the building around noon to take advantage of the wwe's catering.

Hey, free food is free food and their catering was usually very good. After I made a total pig of myself, it was time to get to work. I didn't have to help set the ring up that day so I concentrated on my referee duties. That was when I found out that each match would have two referees assigned to officiate it. I was paired with Joey Marella. We were assigned two matches that night. The Women's Survivor Series match featured Team Sherri Martel versus Team Fabulous Moolah. For this match I would be the inside referee and Joey was the outside referee. The other match we were assigned was the main event, headlined by Team Hogan versus Team Andre. Joey was the inside referee and I was assigned the outside.

I thought the women's match went fairly well except for two small hiccups. The first faux-pas occurred when timekeeper Mel Phillips prematurely rang the bell during a pin attempt. I stood up and waved it off and the match continued on without an elimination. The second mishap occurred when one of the ladies, Velvet McIntyre, accidently hit her head on the canvas. She was in obvious pain. She did continue on until she was eliminated from the match. The highlight of the match was the Jumping Bomb Angels. They absolutely stole the show. For those who have never had the pleasure of watching them perform, do yourselves a favour and look them up; you won't be disappointed. Speaking of not being disappointed, being a part of the main event was definitely the biggest moment in my career at that time. Getting to read the riot act to Hulk Hogan and getting tossed into the ringside barricade by Andre the Giant further added to making my Survivor Series experience unforgettable.

Unfortunately, being a part of the main event was not the only unforgettable part of my journey. As I mentioned earlier, I had to borrow Mom's K-Car to make the trip. The drive home the next morning should have only taken about five hours or so. Mom's car had other plans for me. Everything started out fine as I made my way north on Interstate 271 and merged onto I-90 eastbound. This is where things went south, figuratively. After about half an hour of driving on I-90, the car started to sputter and backfire. A strange light lit up the dashboard. I thought, *Great, now what!* I managed to make it to the shoulder, where I sat for about 30 minutes contemplating my next move. Remember that in 1987, cell phones were not the norm as they are today. I was nowhere near an exit and it was a cold day so I really didn't feel like walking for miles. For some reason I tried turning the key and the car started. Now was the time to act fast. I put the car in drive and I was off again.

Just when I thought everything was all right, another setback. Same exact thing happened. After 45 minutes of driving, more sputtering and backfiring and coasting the vehicle onto the shoulder once more. What the heck was going on? The same dashboard light was on again. Once again, after about 40 minutes, I turned the key and the car was running like nothing happened. Okay! I put that sucker in drive and off I went. After one more similar occurrence, I managed to make it to Erie, P.A., where I pulled into a Chrysler dealership. I explained the situation to the service tech and he knew right away what the problem was. He explained to me that it was the pick-up coil located under the distributor cap. When the engine heated up to a certain temperature, the two copper wires in the coil would expand, touch each other, and short out the motor. When the engine cooled off, the wires would contract and separate, allowing the engine to run normally. I asked if he could fix it; after all, the car was under warranty. He told me that he could, but couldn't do it that day because the day after American Thanksgiving, or Black Friday as it is known, is their busiest day. I asked how easy it was to change it myself, figuring I have some mechanical knowledge and could repair it. He said it was very easy to replace but if I did it myself, it might void the warranty. I didn't want to do that. So I thanked him and left the dealership.

I went to a KFC a block away and sat down to a *big* meal. After making Colonel Sanders a healthy profit, my journey continued. The entire trip home was more of the same deal. Drive for about 30 to 45 minutes, engine cuts out, sit for approximately half an hour, then continue driving. Thank goodness it was a cold November day, which helped the motor cool down a little quicker. This was the pattern I followed all the way back to Toronto. Of course, there were a few more food stops along the way but that was a no-brainer as far as I was concerned. Whatever makes one happy, right? I arrived home at nine-thirty that night. I had left Richfield at nine that morning. There it is, what was normally a five-hour drive took me 12 and a half hours. I would have been even more upset about the whole car thing if it wasn't for all the food that kept me going.

Would I do it again? Absolutely! Being a part of the first ever Survivor Series, getting involved in the main event match, and being a small part of history was more than worth the "minor" inconvenience of car trouble. What can I say, when you have a passion for your work, these little problems don't seem so bad. There were plenty of bigger travel-related mishaps throughout my career and I will get to some of them a little later on.

CHAPTER 6

Ups and Downs

By now I felt like I was on top of the world, getting to share the ring with some of the most recognizable personalities in the world. They were awesome too. They made me feel welcomed almost from the very beginning and for that I was extremely grateful. By this time, my confidence had grown and I was feeling more relaxed in the ring and in front of the cameras. All was going well, or at least I thought it was. That was until I had another not so pleasant run-in with the Chairman himself, Vince McMahon, during a TV taping.

To be honest, I'm not sure what city we were in. One of the matches scheduled for this night was an eight-man tag-team match. The participants were "good guys" the Killer Bees, B. Brian Blair and Jim Brunzell, teaming with the Young Stallions, Paul Roma and Jim Powers, to take on the "bad guys" Nikolai Volkoff, The Iron Sheik, Sika the Wild Samoan, and the Ugandan Giant Kamala. Now that was a recipe for disaster, especially for a referee who had yet to have had the opportunity to officiate what would in all likelihood turn into, as we say, a clusterf#@k. I was about to get a crash course in what not to do ever again in a match.

Going into the match, as always, I asked the guys involved what they were planning to do. I got my instruction and waited for the moment of truth. The match began about as expected with the babyfaces gaining early control. Eventually the heels took over using underhanded tactics. Here is when the match took a turn for the worse. I wish I could describe the events more clearly but for lack of a better term, suffice it to say they buried the shit out of the referee — *me*! None of the wrestlers listened to me while I tried to enforce the rules. Guys kept entering the ring illegally and didn't adhere to the five count. It was a mess. It made me look very incompetent, even for a pro-wrestling referee. I'm not saying that none of it was my fault. On the contrary, I was just as much to blame for letting things get so out of hand and I was happier than Tony Chimel at an all you can eat buffet restaurant when the bell rang to end the match. With a sigh of relief, I made my way backstage to an awaiting boss.

The second I stepped through the curtain, it hit the fan. Vince took off his headset, stood up, and power-walked over to me. Right there in front of everyone, I got an earful about how terrible the match was, how I let them bury me out there, and how there was no possible way they could use that footage on TV. He told me several times that the match was a waste of film and money. After what seemed like forever, Vince ended his criticism, walked back to the monitor, and put his headset back on.

I was in complete shock. I know this will be hard for some to understand, but depression set in almost the second he was done. I couldn't help but think that my days with the company were numbered and my dream job with the WWF was quickly becoming a nightmare. Jack Lanza, a former wrestler and now road agent who witnessed the whole ordeal, came over to me immediately after Vince left. He put his arm around my shoulder and said, "Come with me."

Walking with Jack, I was trying not to show how upset I really was, but he knew. He led me around the corner out of view from the gorilla position and gave me a pep talk of sorts. The gorilla position is the staging area right behind the entrance curtain; one of the producers sits there, usually along with Vince McMahon, and cues the talent while monitoring the show. The first thing he said was "I know how intimidating Vince is, but don't feel too bad. At some point, everyone gets yelled at by Vince. The good thing is, in about 30 minutes or so, he'll come up and talk to you about what happened. He won't be yelling. It's kind of his way of saying he feels bad for what happened. You'll see, it'll all be just fine. Consider this a learning experience."

I thanked Jack for his kind words and told him that I had learned from this night. Sure enough, not 15 minutes later, Vince McMahon walked over to where I was standing. *Oh no, here we go again!* That's what was going through my mind. He must have sensed my panic because as he approached he smiled. Now panic turned to confusion. Why the heck was he smiling? Now remember, not only was Vince the boss, he is a large man, which in itself can be very intimidating. I was shaking in my referee boots.

Placing a hand on my shoulder, Vince said to me in a calm comforting tone, "Listen, I didn't mean to be so hard on you but I just want everything to be just so, in other words, perfect. At the same time I would like you to learn from mistakes and improve, get better and better. I really want you here with this company. If I didn't, you wouldn't be here, but you are and will be for a long time; or at least until you screw up again." After that last comment he laughed and gave me a good old pat, or should I say slap, on the back, and finished his short speech with, "We all make mistakes; we learn from them and we move on. Don't let tonight bother you too long. See you tomorrow, pal."

I was both relieved and confused at the same time. Then, the more I thought about it, the more I understood the boss. He wants his vision of the product to be the best it can be and also wants those working for him at their best at all times. He never dogs it or phones it in, ever. All he wants is an honest effort each and every day and that's what he got from me always. I smelled what the boss was cooking that night.

I was determined not to mess up a match ever again. No one is perfect, though, and my next mishap was soon to happen. Two short weeks after the lecture from Vince, the man who was the original calming force that evening, Jack Lanza, became the angry boss giving me the speech. This was 100% my fault. We were back at Maple Leaf Gardens in Toronto. It seems like that location was a hotspot for me. The match I was refereeing was another tag-team match. This time it was a conventional two versus two tag match. The Young Stallions faced the team of Sika and Kamala. They were having a good match and the crowd was very much into it. Now it was time for the finish. Of course I was aware of the planned ending to the match; unfortunately I jumped the gun, so to speak.

Here is how it was supposed to go down. Jim Powers was now in the ring and as Gorilla Monsoon would say, "He's a house of fire!" meaning he's dominating his opponents. At one point, all four men would be in the ring battling and at the right moment, I was to turn my attention to Paul Roma to try to get him out of the ring and back to his corner. With my focus on Roma and my back to the ring, the heels would cheat behind my back. Roma would give me the okay and I would then turn at the appropriate time to see Powers being pinned. For some reason that escapes me to this day, I turned around before Roma gave me the "Iggy" or signal just in time to see the illegal man, Sika, diving off the top rope and splashing Powers. Sika then rolled out of the ring while Kamala covered Powers for the pin. I should have just counted the pin but for some reason my brain told me to do something completely different. Roma kept shouting at me in carnie, "Just cizcount, cizount!" After a few seconds of frozen uncertainty, I called for the bell disqualifying the heels. Everyone in the ring looked confused, including me.

"The winners of this match, as a result of a disqualification, the Young Stallions!" the ring announcer informed the MLG faithful.

As I raised the winners' hands in victory, Roma leaned over, smiled, and quietly said to me, "Thanks for the win, Jimmy."

I looked him straight in the eyes and replied, "Think nothing of it." He laughed but I wasn't in a laughing mood. How pissed are Sika and Kamala going to be? How upset will the agents be? What happens when you screw up a finish? These were all questions racing through my mind. The incident at TV was different. The finish of that match wasn't ruined, just the body of the match.

After walking the "Green Mile" back to the locker room, the first thing I needed to do was to apologize to all the guys in the match for my error. To my surprise, none of the boys were upset in the least about the unplanned outcome. Each one of them told me not to sweat it. Everyone except Kamala that is, who just nodded while not saying a word, more or less staying in character. They reiterated that it happens to everyone and that it will most likely not be the last mistake I make. Thanking them for their understanding, I was about to leave the room when Jack Lanza stormed in. He tore into me almost as harshly as Vince had that night at TV two weeks prior. One small difference, Jack's verbal tirade was laced with F-bombs. Before he was done he removed me from the other match I was scheduled to referee that night as a punishment for my misdeed. He then stormed out of the room leaving me speechless in front of the guys who had just told me not to worry about it. Again, the boys tried to make me feel better, but my confidence was not quite at a high point.

Later that night at the hotel where all the boys stayed near the Toronto airport, Jack came over to me, apologized for the outburst, and told me to chalk it up as another learning experience and that it would not be the last time I made a mistake. What mattered was how one handled themselves afterwards and showing you have learned from it. I thanked him for the talk and the advice and went to have a few pops with the boys.

It's hard to describe how unnerving it is when you believe you have a grasp of things, only to find out that there is so much more that you really don't know. Thank goodness I found out early on in my career that you should not take any aspect of this business lightly. I kept thinking of the advice Bobby Heenan gave me that one day when he said that in wrestling you never stop learning. Boy was he right! I would never doubt "The Brain" but brother, was he ever right. After that night, never again did I take anything regarding the wrestling business for granted. "Always learning" was now my motto.

Learning experiences were not only reserved for the ring and refereeing, they also very much applied to out of the ring activities such as transporting and setting up the ring. By now I had taken over as the person in charge of the ring crew in Canada. There were several crews spread out across North America. There were rings in California, Colorado, Texas, Illinois, Florida, Pennsylvania, New Jersey, Connecticut, New Brunswick, and of course Toronto. I was in charge of the Moncton and Toronto rings as well as assisting at times with other crews on their rings. At that time, each crew was a two-man crew and occasionally a three-man crew, depending on the tour, the venues, and how difficult the setup might be. Not everyone is cut out for this kind of lifestyle. Among the tiresome duties were long drives between towns, the vast majority of which I handled. As I stated earlier, I am a terrible passenger and prefer to drive. Just ask my old ring crew partner Derek Casselman. He will tell you that the only thing I needed for any long trip was a pack of du Maurier cigarettes, a six-pack of Pepsi, and a radio. I could drive all night as long as I had my essentials for the drive.

Derek was added as my assistant on the ring crew after several failed attempts by the Canadian office to find me some help. Two of the potential candidates were the husbands or boyfriends of ladies who worked in the office for Jack Tunney. One was an older gentleman whose name I don't recall. A nice guy but the work was too difficult for him. There were two others who didn't pan out either for completely different reasons. One was not really any help at all and only had the job because Elio Zarlenga felt bad for him and wanted to help the guy out. Needless to say he didn't last long either as I finally had enough of his antics and needed someone who was an actual help and not a detriment to the job.

There was one fellow they tried out and he was Jack's secretary's boyfriend. At first he was a good worker; that is until he got a taste of being in the ring. Jack thought it would be a good idea to teach this guy to referee just in case I was not available for whatever reason. You never know what could happen — I could get hurt or get sick and that would leave them in a spot if I was the only one capable of doing the job. Smart thinking on his part. Unfortunately for all of us involved, once he got a taste of refereeing, it went straight to his head and he thought his worth was more than it really was. He developed an attitude that began to rub me the wrong way. It all came to a head on a trip that saw us travel to the east coast.

On this trip, we had to rent a 24-foot Ryder truck because the main events for the shows on the east coast tour were cage matches and we needed a bigger truck to carry both the ring and cage. After great shows in Fredericton and Moncton, New Brunswick, the final day had us in Halifax, Nova Scotia. Not wanting to start the long drive back to Toronto that night, we spent the night just outside of Halifax and got an early start in the morning. Now the drive from Halifax to Toronto in a Ryder truck takes between 22 and 24 hours of driving time, so I figured two days max to get home. We were on the road at about eight-thirty a.m. and, as always, I drove. Rivière du Loup, Quebec, was where I had planned to spend the night. It was about the halfway point of the trip but I wasn't too terribly tired just yet. I decided, much to the chagrin of my passenger, to drive the 200 or so kilometres to Quebec City.

After stopping to refuel just outside Quebec City, I felt like I could continue to drive for at least a few more hours so I just kept going. By now my assistant was passed out in the passenger seat unaware of the circumstances. I thought Trois Rivières and Montreal were not too far away so I could at least make it to one of those cities and crash. Wrong again! I found myself motoring right through Montreal and into Ontario. I was really in a zone and determined to go as far as my body would allow me to. As we were passing Kingston, Ontario, my colleague awoke from his slumber amazed by how far we had travelled. He didn't seem as upset as before because now we were so close to home.

We were in the home stretch and zipping through Oshawa, Ontario, when disaster almost struck. Out of nowhere my passenger yelled out, "Holy shit, look at that!"

Thinking that something was on the highway in front of us that I was not seeing, I hit the brakes as hard as I could, locking up all four wheels. Thank god it was five-thirty a.m. and there was practically no one on the road. With smoke billowing from all the tires and the sound of everything in the back of the truck shifting, I frantically asked what I had missed. He pointed to the sky and remarked, "There was a shooting star in the sky. Did you see it?"

The tires were not the only things smoking right about now. You could probably see the smoke coming out of my ears. I was absolutely furious. If you were to ask anyone who knows me, they will tell you that they could not picture me getting angry. I was always known as the calm, level-headed guy of the group. I uncharacteristically reared back and open-hand slapped him right in the side of the head and said, "Do you realize we could have had an accident or even worse rolled the truck, all because of your stupid little shooting star? We're almost home; just sit there and don't say a word until after we unload the truck into the storage unit." He was shocked, at the slap more than anything, I believe. He agreed to keep quiet for the rest of the trip, which was fine with me. We arrived at the storage unit and unloaded the ring and cage, before I drove the star-gazer home and then dropped the rental truck off and headed home myself.

Not too long after that incident, the young man was not a part of my ring crew anymore. His dismissal had nothing to do with this incident but rather a string of bad decisions made by him.

Derek was then given the opportunity to be my assistant and it turned out well for both of us. He accompanied me on so many trips, and we became good friends. We did have our own run-ins as well but usually with others and not each other. Nothing too intense, more fun encounters than anything. On one of our countless trips to Winnipeg, Manitoba, we had one of those run-ins. To be more accurate, the incident I'm referring to happened on the ride home from the "Peg."

The one thing Derek discovered about me very quickly was that I liked to get to my destination as soon as possible with minimal stopping, especially coming home on a long drive. What I discovered about Derek is that he has a self-professed small bladder which meant frequent rest room stops. So when he told me he had to go, I assumed that it was his usual pee stop. Like I had done many times before, I ignored his request for a pit stop so he could relieve himself. He repeated his request and I answered him by handing him an empty Gatorade bottle and said, "Here, use this." It's an old wrestlers' trick. Not really, but it has been done in the past in emergency situations. The thing here was that the Gatorade bottle would not solve this particular problem. It was not a number one that Derek was talking about.

Once I found out what he really meant, we looked for a good spot to pull the ring truck over so he could take care of business. We were much too far from anything that remotely resembled a town — we were smack dab in the middle of farm country. There were no gas stations, restaurants, or convenience stores for miles and Derek had no time to wait. I pulled over by a nice stretch of trees on the shoulder of the Trans Canada Highway. Derek grabbed the roll of toilet paper we kept in the truck and ran for the woods. Sitting in the truck, I lit up a smoke and chuckled to myself while waiting for him to finish. It didn't seem to take very long but all of a sudden, Derek emerged from behind the trees, running while trying to pull his pants up at the same time. Finally getting his pants on, he hopped into the passenger seat and screamed for me to drive. Just as he said drive, I noticed what I believe was a farmer also running towards the ring truck with what looked like a shotgun in his hands.

I put it in drive and floored the gas pedal getting us out of there as quick as possible. I looked over at Derek and asked him, "Did you at least get to do what you set out to do?"

Breathing heavily, he replied, "Pretty much. I think I'll be good for a while but I left the toilet paper in the woods."

We looked at each other and laughed our asses off. That is a story you tell your kids about, we agreed. Whenever I tell anyone that story, the first question they almost always ask is how can anyone stop and relieve themselves on the side of the road. I always answer them that it is infinitely more favourable than doing your business inside the truck. Anyway, I'm not sure why I chose this tale about my friend to share considering we've had some fun times. It's all good, though, because Derek went on to become a senior manager of venue merchandise. Not bad for a guy who craps in the woods.

CHAPTER 7

A Bump in the Road

For the next few years, I was living a dream. Nothing could bring me down from the high I was on, doing what only a privileged few were able to do. In my mind, I could do no wrong. Not that I would ever tempt fate, it just wasn't in my nature to push the envelope or rock the boat. Being a model employee (or independent contractor) was how my multiple duties were always approached. As with any job, you hope that your hard work doesn't go unnoticed and I felt that my hard work was beginning to pay off. My bookings increased and Dave and Earl Hebner had taken me under their wing. The twins and I became travelling companions and they passed on their referee knowledge to me as we drove from town to town.

I just remembered the very first time I met Earl Hebner. Dave had been a referee working for the WWF for several years while Earl was a referee for the National Wrestling Alliance, which was a rival promotion to the WWF. However, on February 5, 1988, both Dave and Earl would become the most famous referees in all of wrestling.

The WWF was presenting, for the first time since the 1950s, a live wrestling event on network television. Up until this point, they produced a monthly special for NBC called *Saturday Night's Main Event*. It was a replacement for *Saturday Night Live* once a month. This time, the WWF would be *live* in prime time and the main event for the broadcast was WWF champion Hulk Hogan defending his title against Andre the Giant. Andre was a villain and under the employ of the Million Dollar Man, Ted DiBiase. Dave was assigned to officiate this historic match.

I was there that night glued to a monitor just like the entire roster. As we like to say, "The monitor was sold out! It was standing room only." Now that I think about it, no one recalled seeing Dave Hebner all day. On the line-up sheet that listed the order of matches and who would referee each one, Dave's name was listed next to the main event. Remembering that it was odd we had not seen him all day, I asked Pat Patterson if Dave was there. He told me that he was in fact there but was not feeling well and was resting so that he would be fine for his match later that night. I didn't question Pat and just proceeded with my regularly scheduled work day.

Now, back to the infamous match. Watching it unfold on the monitor, I couldn't help but think to myself that Dave was looking a little slimmer and I remember remarking to someone that he looked like he had lost some weight and was looking good. As the match was coming to its conclusion, I turned around to get a drink at the beverage stand and lo and behold, who should I see leaning against the wall in the shadows watching the match, but Dave Hebner. I stared at him in astonishment. He smiled, put a finger to his mouth, and motioned *shhhh!* I nodded and turned back to watch the monitor to see what they were doing for the finish.

Confusion set in as my mind worked hard to figure out what the heck was going on. Then it hit me like a Triple H sledge hammer shot. Dave had a twin brother who worked for the NWA — that had to be the ref in the ring. Different scenarios were now going through my mind as to how this would all unfold on television.

Where were they going with this and was this a one-time deal for Earl? Not a single fan in the arena had any clue that the referee in the ring was in fact Earl. Most likely, many if not the majority of the boys didn't realize who was actually the referee in the ring.

Suddenly, the story became very clear. Andre attempted to pin Hogan and when the referee began to count, Hogan clearly lifted his shoulder well before the three count. After Hebner hit the mat for the three count, he called for the bell and awarded the title to Andre the Giant. At first, many thought that the finish was a mistake. They believed, and part of me did as well, that the ending to the match had not gone as planned. We all couldn't have been more wrong. It had gone exactly the way it was supposed to. In all the commotion, I didn't notice the real Dave Hebner slip out to the ring to confront his evil imposter. A brawl ensued, with Earl getting the better of his brother. Hogan then grabbed Earl, pressed him high over his head, and tossed him to the outside where he was to be caught by Andre, DiBiase, and Virgil. One problem though: the Hulkster threw Earl too far and the trio outside the ring could not catch the flying official. Earl landed on and damaged his shoulder, which required surgery. Of course, as far as I know, the WWF took care of all of his medical expenses. It was later revealed to fans that Ted DiBiase had paid someone to have plastic surgery to resemble Dave Hebner. They ran with that story for a while before finally letting the cat out of the bag and acknowledged that Earl and Dave were in fact identical twins.

When Earl was healed from the injury, he was brought back as a full-time referee. That was when I got to know Earl and we quickly became friends. I can't thank both Dave and Earl Hebner enough for all they have taught me not only about how to be a good referee but also how to conduct oneself in all areas of the wrestling business. Their mentoring proved to be invaluable to me and for that I am forever grateful. Thank you, Dave and Earl Hebner, for everything you did for me.

So far, I had nothing to complain about regarding my wrestling career. I was having a pretty good run, until a problem developed with one of my bosses. Terry Garvin was the man in charge of assigning which referees and ring crews would work each event. He was the one who would send me the monthly schedule that listed all my bookings. We had a good rapport and I never sensed that there was any trouble brewing. Now I wish I could go into detail as to why this tension developed between him and me but sometimes there are matters that are best kept private. In my mind, this is one of those instances where I believe it is best not to go into specifics. One of the reasons why I choose not to give details is because Terry passed away years ago and therefore it would do no good to make an accusation that no one can defend. Also, I am trying to keep a positive tone. Okay, maybe not the entire book, but for the most part I'm trying to stay encouraging.

This time in my wwf career was definitely the most difficult I had encountered up to this point. I found myself being booked far less than before. No longer was I booked for every tv taping. No longer was I booked for any house shows that were not drivable. In a nutshell, if there were any events that would require me to fly to the event, I was not booked. Although I was still in charge of the Toronto ring, the one that was stored in New Brunswick was a different matter. I found myself being phased out of my responsibilities for that ring and feared that my job was in jeopardy.

The man who had originally hired me noticed that something was changing, and not for the better. Jack Tunney called me into his office in downtown Toronto one day to question me about why my duties had diminished so drastically. He closed the door and sat down behind his rather large desk. He then leaned forward and straight out asked what had happened, telling me not to lie to him. It was a very intimidating sight to see him lean forward and look me in the eyes while he spoke. I didn't want to lie to Jack but at the same time I also didn't want to divulge what had transpired between Terry and me. Again Jack asked what had happened, this time sounding sterner. I explained to Jack that with all due respect, it was a matter that I didn't want to discuss and that hopefully it would all work itself out.

When I looked at Jack's face and his reaction to what I had just told him, there was this sense that he had an idea of what I was referring to. It was almost as if he already knew the circumstances surrounding my fall from grace. He told me he understood why I was reluctant to talk about it and that he would not press the issue any further. He also reassured me that as long as he was in command of the Canadian office, I had nothing to worry about as far as working any Canadian dates. I thanked Jack for his understanding and his vote of confidence in me. I got up and shook his hand, and as I was walking out of his office, his parting words were to let him know if there was ever anything I needed to talk about, not to hesitate and to make sure I talk to him about it first. He also said not to trust anyone in this business. I thanked him again and left his office feeling a little better than when I had walked in, but still not too good about my future with the company going forward.

With my drastically limited WWF schedule, there was now no choice; I had to find a second job. I was just not working enough for the WWF to make a decent living. It is a good thing I am of Greek heritage because to the Greeks, living with your parents is totally acceptable, at least until you are well into your 30s, so I had a long way to go before I needed to look for alternate living arrangements. I did have to look for a job that would not affect the times I would be working for the WWF. I did not want to give up the part-time ref/ring crew gig. Essentially, I needed a second part-time job to complement my existing part-time job. It might not have been the ideal situation I was looking for but I continued to dream.

As luck would have it, my closest friend Tom Kellesis was working at our local beer store. In Ontario, you can only buy beer from a government-run liquor distributor. The LCBO is where you can buy wine, spirits, and select beer products. Brewer's Retail, or the Beer Store, was where one would go specifically to buy beer. One

Friday evening, my friend Tom was working the late shift. We were planning to go out to a nightclub after he was done. I would often go early to meet him at work. Tom would let me sit in the lunch room and hang out watching TV. On this Friday, the store was short-handed as two people had called in sick, and they were very busy.

At most beer stores in Ontario you order at the counter and someone in the back cooler gets your beer for you and rolls it out on a conveyer where the customer picks up his order after paying. Tom was not only taking the orders at the cash register; he was also running to the back to get everyone's orders as well, while one of his co-workers was handling all the empty bottle returns, which also had a long line. Frustrated and desperate, my friend asked me if I would give him a hand. I told him of course I would and went into the back cooler to get the orders he called out over the intercom. I was not familiar with the setup but caught on quickly. At first, Tom would not only shout out the orders, he would give me quick directions to where all the different brands of beer were stacked. It took us an hour and a half to get the line cleared but we got it done. It was closing time and the store was empty of patrons. Tom locked the doors and we sat down to take a breather. Running around the huge cooler full of beer, slinging cases out to the buying public, was quite frankly a pretty good workout.

My friend, the other employee, and I sat in the lunch room and had a pop. Tom then asked me if I was interested in a part-time job with him at the Beer Store. Thinking about it for a few minutes, I told him that I was definitely interested. He told me he would run it by his manager the following Monday and let me know what he said. How cool was that? Not only potentially landing a job, but getting to work with my best friend. I couldn't wait to hear back. I hadn't given up on my wrestling dream, but I needed to do something in between wrestling bookings. This seemed like a good fit.

After talking to his boss, Tom called me and told me to go in to meet the manager of that store. I did, and found he was a good guy; we got along very well right from the start. I explained to him about my other job with the WWF and he said he had no trouble at all scheduling me around my wrestling schedule. I was hopeful the situation with the WWF would be rectified. For the time being, I was content with how things were progressing. Thanks to my friend Tom, I had a second job that worked for me on all fronts.

There was no shortage of memorable wrestling moments, even with my reduced schedule. Virtually every show I had the privilege to work provided moments that to this day remain special to me. One of the first cage matches I officiated involved "the Giant," the one and only Andre the Giant. This match became particularly special because Andre showed how much he trusted me.

The date was November 19, 1989, the place the venerable Maple Leaf Gardens in Toronto. The main event that evening: Intercontinental champion the Ultimate Warrior was putting his title on the line against WWE Hall of Famer Andre the Giant and yes, yours truly was assigned to man the cage door. This match had no referee inside the cage as the only way to win the match at that time was either exiting through the door or climbing over the top and having both feet hit the arena floor.

Things didn't get off to a good start for me. I walked out to the big blue cage — remember the one with the steel blue squares? — did a quick walk around to check the structure, and positioned myself at the door. Andre was the first to make his entrance. He came out, walked around the cage as well, and then began stalling, not wanting to enter the cage. I tried my best to convince him to climb the steps and get in the ring. At first he just laughed and then he started to get agitated. He yelled something to me, in French mind you, so I did not understand what it was he bellowed. Just then, he grabbed the cage door with his left hand and flung it wide open, hitting me in the noggin. As I lay there holding my aching head, the Giant laughed out loud and entered the ring.

The Ultimate Warrior entered the arena next. After a few laps around the ring, stopping occasionally to shake the cage, he helped me to my feet. He jumped into the cage, I closed the door, and the match was under way. It was what you'd expect from these two legends. Andre dominated most of the time with the Warrior getting in limited offence. Andre even gave the Warrior one of the earliest versions of the "Stinkface." He had the Ultimate One seated in the corner by the door and placed his rather large posterior directly into his face. That's when things got ugly. I heard the Warrior screaming for Andre to stop. A few seconds later, I realized why. The Giant thought it would be funny to just let it rip right then and there, if you get my drift. I got the drift and it was one of the nastiest things I had ever smelled. Andre as usual laughed his butt off. Andre was notorious for dropping "bombs" in the ring, and I don't mean punches or elbows. I don't know what Giants eat and really didn't want to find out.

Now back to the match. The battle continued. As Andre once again gained the upper hand, he began crawling on all fours to make his way to the door. As I opened the door for him to exit, I couldn't help but remember what happened before the match had begun, how this giant of a man got a thrill from knocking little Jimmy on his ass. As he stuck his head and shoulder out of the cage on his way out, I reared back and *slammed* the cage door on him. Yes! I slammed a cage door on Andre the Giant and the crowd went *banana*! (Yes, no S. That is how Pat Patterson would say it.) Just as that occurred, the Ultimate Warrior recovered from his beating and scaled the cage, climbing over the top and jumping down to the arena floor. I called for the bell, raised Warrior's hand, and ran to the dressing room.

When I got to the back, the only thing going through my mind was whether or not I had slammed the door too hard on the Giant. Everyone was back from ringside and relaxing in the locker rooms. I approached Andre and shook his hand, as is the custom, and asked if everything was okay with the match. I kept thinking that maybe I had swung the door too hard or maybe not hard enough. I just hoped that it looked fine. He looked at me, smiled, and said, "Perfect, Boss. Thank you." I was both relieved and ecstatic. Not only was one of the greatest WWF superstars of all time pleased with the match, he called me Boss. That was a sign. If Andre liked someone, he would call him Boss. I thanked him again; after all, having Andre's approval meant the world to me. I then went to thank the Warrior as well. All was good in my world that night. I was grinning from ear to ear. I had just helped the Intercontinental champion defeat a giant and had had my first brush with the 15 minutes of fame we all hope to get at least once in our lives. Not to mention, getting called Boss by *the Boss*! This match was taped but never televised, so somewhere in the archives of the WWE vault, this classic encounter still lives. Maybe one day, it will see the light of day.

After the show ended, Tim White, a longtime referee and a very good friend of Andre's, pulled me aside to have a chat. He said that Andre was very happy with how the match had turned out. He also said that if I wasn't doing anything after the show, Andre would like to buy me a drink back at the hotel. I was overwhelmed. I accepted the invite. After all, who would not want to have a drink with a true legend of the squared circle? I didn't know what I was getting myself into. I had heard some stories about how much beer or wine Andre could consume in one sitting. I had seen him in a bar or two before, but had never sat to drink with him and witness how much he drank. I was about to find out.

I met Andre and Tim at the hotel bar where they invited me to have a seat with them. Andre didn't like sitting at a table unless he was playing cards, so he usually sat at one end of the bar on a stool. He asked me what I was drinking. I told him a beer would be fine and he ordered me three. Before I could finish the third beer, two more found their way in front of me. Next thing I knew, I was more than a little tipsy. There was no way I could drive the 20 minutes home that night in my condition but I also didn't want to spring for the cost of a hotel room. Thanking Andre and Tim for their hospitality I told them I had to go and went to the lobby to collect myself.

As luck would have it, I didn't have to drive home or pay for a hotel room. Jack Tunney always had a complimentary suite in the hotel where the boys stayed because he booked 10 to 15 rooms for them at a group rate and the hotel threw in the suite at no extra charge. Jack would have a few cases of beer and some cold cuts for sandwiches and invited the crew up to drink and shoot the bull there. His logic was if the boys drank in a private setting, they would not get in any trouble in the bar. The party broke up early and Jack, noticing my inebriated condition, offered me the suite to sleep it off. At first I felt guilty accepting, but he insisted so I agreed. It was a very nice thing Jack did for me that night.

It wasn't the only time Jack bailed me out of an Andre drinkfest. On another occasion, before another Maple Leaf Gardens event, Jack once again handed me the keys to his Cadillac Fleetwood. He told me to pick up Andre and Danny Davis at the airport Marriott. Danny was filling in for Tim White on this trip. Gladly, I took the keys and was off to pick them up. I arrived at the Marriott and called up to Andre's room to let him know I was there. There was no answer in his room so I tried Danny's room. He said he would be down in a bit and to check the bar for the big man. Just as Danny suggested, there was Andre, sitting on a couch with two "friends" and his gear bag. I walked over to where they were sitting, and when Andre spotted me he bellowed, "Hey, Boss. Come on, sit down, have a drink."

I really wasn't sure how to answer him. When "the Boss" offered you a drink, he considered it an insult if you did not accept. I wanted to say no thank you but instead I replied, "Okay, I'll have one, a Jack Daniel's and Coke please." Now that was a huge error on my part. Andre called the waitress over and ordered me a *double* Jack and Coke. Not saying anything, I took the drink, thinking just one shouldn't be too bad. Danny finally came down to the bar to meet us, but not before I had two more double Jack and Cokes. Once again, the big man had succeeded in getting me drunk. One major problem, though: it was prior to the event and I still had to get them to the venue.

Danny looked at me and said, "Jimmy, are you okay to drive?"

DISCLAIMER: I do *not* endorse what I did next nor do I think in any way, shape, or form that what I did was acceptable.

I explained to Danny that if we were to arrive at the venue with him driving and anyone were to see that I was not driving, my job would be in jeopardy. He cautiously agreed to let me drive and sat shotgun to keep an eye on me. I could tell he wasn't happy about it but went along for my sake. I was not stumbling drunk but over the legal limit for sure.

We made it down to MLG without incident and I parked the car. We made our way to the locker rooms; all the while I was nervous that someone would find out I had been drinking before the show. Walking past Jack, I handed him his keys. He paused for a moment and called me back to speak with him. He looked me in the eyes and asked, "Have you been drinking?"

There was no denying it, so I confessed to having a few drinks. I wasn't going to put the blame on anyone else, so I just said yes. Waiting for his reply, the fear of losing my job took over. It seemed to take forever for him to say something and when he finally did, it shocked the hell out of me. He said, "The Boss cornered you in the bar, didn't he?" I nodded and he continued, "Go get some coffee in you and don't let any of the agents see you for a little while. You'll be okay." He half-smiled in an almost hope-you-learned-a-lesson-here kind of way and went to work. I on the other hand drank several cups of coffee, avoided everyone for about an hour, and got through the night's festivities. After that day, I never ever had a drink before a show again. They say you don't know what you have until it's gone; well sometimes all it takes is to almost lose something to really appreciate what you have. From that point on, I never took my job for granted. Lesson definitely learned.

CHAPTER 8

Back on Track

I had dodged a bullet and it was once again time to focus on where my career was heading. I was still working two part-time jobs. I liked working at the Beer Store but that wasn't my first choice as a career path. The WWF was where I wanted to be, but the scandal that revolved around Garvin and the WWF was taking its toll on the company. Terry had to go. Now don't get me wrong, I hate it when anybody gets let go from their job, but when I heard that Terry Garvin had been relieved of his duties, I began to think that this was my opportunity to go back to a full-time schedule at my dream job. Steve Taylor assumed Terry's position in the Event Operations department. Steve and I got along very well, going back to when Steve was the principal photographer for the WWF and their magazine. I kind of felt guilty for thinking this, but in my mind it was only a matter of time before Steve brought me back on the road the way it used to be. It didn't exactly turn out that way.

For the next few years it was pretty much the status quo. The only difference was that I was getting to work the occasional TV or pay-per-view event, but it was still nowhere near the amount I was hoping for. As usual, I didn't complain about it and just went along with the program. My work ethic had not changed. I continued to give 110% all of the time and never let on that I was unhappy that they had not offered me a full-time slot. My thinking was good things come to those who work hard and don't rock the boat. I knew nothing about the squeaky wheel getting the grease theory. So for the next few years I toiled at both jobs, hoping the WWF would see how valuable I was to them. Sometimes, though, they might not have seen it that way.

An error in scheduling caused me to miss an event in Fredericton, New Brunswick. It would not have been such a big deal had it not been for the fact that for this show, I was the scheduled ring crew. Let me explain. When the booking sheet came out for the month of the Fredericton show, I saw that I was the ring crew/referee for a Halifax event that took place the day after the Fredericton show. Jack Tunney insisted on getting the booking sheet sent to him directly for any Canadian events and then he would inform me of my bookings. Jack told me about the Halifax show. I mentioned to him that Fredericton was running the night before and asked if I would be doing that show as well. He said not to worry about that and that I was only booked for Halifax.

I booked my flight to Moncton to pick up the ring the day before the Halifax event. That was the same day as the other show I was told not to worry about. Flying into Moncton, I took a cab to where the ring truck was stored, started her up, and headed to Halifax. I pulled the truck into a weigh station at about eight p.m. The officer inside called out to me on the loudspeaker and asked if I was Jim Korderas. How did this guy know my name? I said, "Yes, I am Jim Korderas," and he said, "Can you park the truck and come inside please?"

Of course I did just as he asked. I entered the booth with no idea what was going on. My first thought was that something had happened at home, an emergency of some sort. The first words out of the officer's mouth were, "You need to call Steve Taylor ASAP!"

Piecing two and two together I had an inkling of what had happened. Using the pay phone outside, I called Steve at his home. He answered and right away asked me where I was. I told him where I was and he then said, "Why aren't you in Fredericton?"

A bit flustered, I explained the whole situation to him about not being told to be in Fredericton and not to worry about who would be the ring crew there. I could tell he was not a happy camper but he did understand my position and told me to proceed to Halifax. The Fredericton show was cancelled due to the miscommunication. From now on, though, he would send out booking sheets for the Canadian shows to Jack as usual but would also send one to me so that I would be aware of the dates. We both had great respect for Jack and didn't want to put the blame on him. Steve took the heat for the mishap. In the meantime, we had come to the conclusion that we would be on the same page from now on. It was the one and only time I failed to provide a ring for a show. It would never happen again on my watch.

With that miscommunication behind me, it was now time for me to decide which profession was going be the one for me. Sling beer or go forward and do what I believed I was born to do. Even as a youngster, I knew I belonged in the wrestling business. Not necessarily as a wrestler or a referee, but I just knew this business was for me. I waited for the chance to talk to Steve in person, not wanting to tell him of my intentions over the phone. The next set of TV tapings we were both at, I pulled him aside and asked him if he had a minute or two to chat. He said he did and we went out and sat in the stands of the empty arena. I explained to him that I wanted to be a full-time member of the Event Operations team, meaning ring crew/referee. I also explained that working two part-time jobs wasn't cutting it for me so it was time for me to choose one or the other. The job I wanted with all my heart was with the WWF. It was no contest. The WWF was where I wanted to be and where I felt I belonged.

Steve was somewhat taken aback. Telling him my intentions

and how I felt really surprised him because, as he put it, "I didn't know you felt that way. I thought your other job was your primary one and wrestling was secondary." Before I could rebut that statement he went on, "Now that I know what you want, I would love to have you with us full-time."

There was no hiding my elation. I gave Steve a big hug and told him I was in. I was back, even though I never really left, but I think you know what I mean. Even though I was back working a full-time schedule for the WWF, I was hired as an independent contractor and not an employee of the company, which suited me just fine. They were not very happy to hear it, but goodbye Beer Store! It was now game on for me. What followed were many years of great times and awesome memories. There were a few sad moments along the way but the good far outweighed the not so good.

By this time, the production values of WWF's flagship program, *Monday Night Raw*, had expanded from its beginnings when it was filmed at the Manhattan Center in New York City. Every two weeks we would be live on the USA Network and tape the following week's episode of *Raw* the Tuesday after the live show. On the weeks when the taped show aired, we ran non-televised live events so the travel schedule was hectic. Again I'm not complaining; it is the nature of the business and I took great pleasure in being a member of the WWF family. A family is what we were, especially those of us on the road crew.

Notice that I referred to us as the road crew. That is because we were not only responsible for setting up the ring, we were also entrusted to set up the protective barricades, help with erecting the stage and whatever else needed to be done to get the show ready. The crew and I were always friends but when I joined them on a permanent basis, we all became very tight. We all had each other's backs and really looked out for one another. Jack Doan, Mark Yeaton, John D'Amico, Mike Chioda, and Tony Chimel were all fixtures as part of Steve's Event Operations team. I was now a part of that team and they accepted me as such.

Being on the road so much again took a lot of getting used to. Flying to and from work every week, driving from town to town, and living out of a suitcase is not an easy lifestyle. It takes a certain kind of person to be able to survive life on the road. I had no problem with that while living the dream. It felt like the road and I were meant for one another. It didn't hurt one bit that being on the setup crew came with added perks. Those of us on the crew were paid for travel days to and from every tour. For example, we would be paid for the day we left home as well as the day we travelled back home. We were also paid a daily rate for setting up for the show. We were provided with rentals to get from town to town and our hotels were paid for as well. Add to this, for those of us who also refereed, getting paid for that as well and there was absolutely no reason for anyone to gripe. It was a great gig if you could get it, and we were the fortunate few that did get it. We were the select few and you just knew that with this motley crew, stories and lifelong memories were just around the corner.

CHAPTER 9

Road Worriers

When you are on the road as much as we were, and especially with the cast of characters I was involved with, there were bound to be too many funny occurrences to keep to oneself. Here are some amusing stories I would like to share with all of you. They will not be in chronological order as I will tell them as they pop up in my head. Where do I begin?

Probably the one person I spent the majority of my time with on the road was ring announcer/road crew member Tony Chimel. Chimel and I would eventually become constant and almost permanent riding partners. We were dubbed Waldorf and Statler by the others in the crew. I guess we reminded them of those grumpy old men who sat in the balcony trading barbs and heckling everybody on *The Muppet Show*. We both had similar likes and dislikes — the one thing we both genuinely loved was the wrestling business, but that didn't stop us from jokingly making our comments about everything. Most of our comments were reserved for the car rides. When discussing the day's activities on our ride to the next town, we would ultimately end each sentence with the phrase

"Stays in the car!" No one was immune from the friendly jabs we took at just about everyone. It was all in fun, but you never know how some might take it, so we just waited for our car ride to comment.

Many times we would have a third and even a fourth in the car but that didn't stop us from our usual routine. Here's how a normal trip would go. First we, or more accurately I, would pack our bags in the car. I had a knack for utilizing every square inch of truck space to avoid having bags in the seating area of the car. As Chimel would often say, "Korderas, you are one hell of a packer!"

Of course I would be behind the wheel almost 100% of the time because I preferred it that way. Chimel didn't mind that one bit and neither did any other passenger who happened to ride with us. Once on the road, our first order of business was a convenience store stop. We would stock up on healthy (yeah, right) snacks. For me it was normally a pack of smokes, a Pepsi or two, and some kind of munchies. As I stated previously, as long as I have those goodies with me, I can drive all night long.

From there, the conversation turned to a critique of the show that evening. We started from the opening match and went over what we liked and what we didn't like. Naturally there were some comedic undertones to our analysis. Well, it was funny to us anyway. Depending on who was in the car with us, we were very careful what we said and about who. When it was just us two, no one was off limits. A select few passengers were privy to our banter. Not just anyone could ride with us. You had to earn that spot. That or we were ordered by the higher-ups to let another crew member ride along. Either way, if you were in our car, you had to abide by the prime directive of the car: "Everything said in the car stays in the car!"

On one long drive between towns, Chuck Palumbo asked if he could ride with us. We told him absolutely. He said the guys he was travelling with had very little room in their car. We never refused anyone if we had the room, so he rode with us. I know this sounds contradictory but an unwritten rule of the road is "you never leave anyone behind!" It was a rare circumstance to allow a "non-regular" in the car, but we occasionally did. Chimel gave him the rules of the car and ended his instructions with "The last thing you should know is Korderas sings along with the radio and he knows the words to every song ever recorded."

Another reason I liked driving the majority of the time was because the one driving the car had control of what radio station we listened to. Chimel was pretty much a classic rock guy. I like classic rock as well, but I also enjoy a wide range of other music, from old school hip hop to some country music and everything in between. I was not really into heavy metal but there were some songs I liked. Now I never professed to have a good singing voice or be able to memorize song lyrics but when I hear a song I know, the words all come to me and I sing along as I'm driving. Chimel used to joke that I knew the words to every song ever made. I only knew them as the song was playing, not by memory. That may not make much sense to some people but that's the way it is for me.

Chuck found that very funny and said that it was fine with him. Chuck actually played guitar in a band so for me the pressure was on to not suck. At the end of the trip, Chuck thanked us for letting him ride with us. He said he was thoroughly entertained listening to the two of us and would like to do it again one day. It was a nice compliment and we told him no problem.

After a complete rundown of each match on the show, the conversation turned into open mic night. We debated everything from music to religion to politics, whatever came up. People who know Chimel will tell you that his view of the world is unique. Whenever he discussed any serious topic, we all referred to his point of view as "The World According to Chimel." Many believed that he was purposely being antagonistic to entertain all who listened to his diatribes. His arguments with the likes of Kane and Val Venus were some of the most comical exchanges I have ever heard. Both Kane and Val have very libertarian ideologies and Chimel — well let's just say his take on various matters do not fall into any political category known to mankind. Hot button topics such as abortion, gun control, the role of government, among others left all of those who were fortunate enough to be within earshot of Chimel's perspectives shaking their heads. That is why we all thought that he was "working" everyone. We were never sure if he was or not.

One of the daily rituals, for lack of a better term, that Tony and I did was a five- to six-minute routine where we would just start cracking on each other. We would trade barbs and insults, again in a comedic fashion, mainly in the presence of some unsuspecting bystanders to see if we could amuse them. Sometimes I think it was done more to amuse ourselves. Whether it was in the production office, at ringside during set-up, or loading the truck at the end of the night, it was game on for us. We would go through every type of insult imaginable. From you're so old to you're so fat to even yo' momma jokes. Here is a little example of how our interactions went:

Chimel: You're so old, your first driver's license was written in hieroglyphics!

Korderas: You're so fat, you're not just a [beep] on the radar, you are a [*beeeeeeeeeeeeeeeeeeeeeeeeeeeeeeeeeeeeeeeeeeeeeep*]!

Chimel: Well, you're so old that when you were born, the Dead Sea was only sick!

Korderas: Oh yeah, you're so fat, when you clip your cell phone on your belt, you get charged for roaming!

Chimel: You're so ugly, when you were born, your mother fed you through a straw!

Korderas: You were so poor, when your dad put out his cigarette, your mom said, "Hey, who turned off the heat?"

I think you all get the idea. This was just about an everyday thing. We would pick our spots to perform and our act got over. It wasn't well received by everyone but the majority of those that witnessed our back-and-forth insults enjoyed it. One person who really took pleasure in our verbal battles was Teddy Long. It kind of became a running joke for all three of us because whenever Teddy was around the both of us, we would turn to each other and begin the verbal attacks. Teddy would just sit back, listen, and laugh his butt off. Of course this was all done in jest. We never got angry at one another. To this day, Tony Chimel is still one of my very good friends.

Probably one of my favourite moments spent with my friend Tony Chimel was on the very first "Tribute to the Troops" trip we made for the WWE to Iraq. *WrestleMania* is generally considered the biggest show of the year, the Super Bowl of sports entertainment, but the most gratifying show that the WWE superstars and Vince McMahon do every year is the Tribute show. December 2003 was the first of the annual events. John Bradshaw Layfield made the suggestion to Vince about going overseas to perform for the military personnel. JBL had made several trips to visit the troops on his own and thought that bringing a live show to the troops would be great for morale. Vince loved the idea because he and JBL are huge supporters of the Armed Forces.

No one was forced to take part in this venture. I remember my direct boss Steve Taylor asking me if I would be willing to go on the trip. I told him it would be an honour for me to go. Of course the jokes began soon after that I would be the lone Canadian representative going to Iraq. Canada did not send troops to Iraq to aid the United States in the war effort. They did send peacekeeping troops to Afghanistan, but not Iraq. I quickly pointed out that Chris Benoit was also from Canada but it was brought up that he was living in Georgia; therefore by default I was the only Canuck representative. I had heard there were a few of the ring crew guys that didn't want to go. They even told me personally that they wouldn't go. To be honest, I don't blame them for not going but for me, this was a once in a lifetime opportunity and there was no way I was going to pass that up.

The long journey to the Middle East began in Nashville,

Tennessee. After taping TV in the Music City, those of us going on the trip boarded a bus and made our way to the military transport plane that would take us to our first stop, Mannheim, Germany. If I am not mistaken, the aircraft was a C-17 that carried the crew and all our equipment. They modified the interior to accommodate us. The insides of these planes have several different configurations. On this flight, there were a number of passenger seats put in for the majority of us. Those of us not fortunate enough to land one of the coach class seats had to settle for the jump seats located all along the side of the plane's fuselage. I was one of them. The jump seats were extremely uncomfortable, but not as uncomfortable as being in an active war zone.

With the talent and crew aboard, we were ready to depart. Of course it would not be a boring flight, that was for sure. Almost from takeoff, there were shenanigans for what felt like the entire flight. If it wasn't the boys ribbing each other, it was the crew having a laugh at some poor soul's expense. It was all done in fun and no one got hurt in the process. No one got angry either. Oh wait, I take that back. One person was upset about being the victim of a prank. Something you don't want in a confined space like an airplane is an angry giant. The Big Show became an unwilling participant in what was probably the funniest moment on the long flight. Here's what happened.

Before we left the States, we were briefed on the how the C-17 would be set up on the inside. Realizing that the trip might be more uncomfortable for the larger-than-most Big Show, his wife purchased an air mattress for him to use on the plane. There was enough space for Show to inflate the mattress and lie down. So that's what he did. While the big guy was taking a nap on his brand new inflatable bed, an unknown individual decided that Show was a little too comfortable. This mysterious person took it upon himself to use a small knife to poke a hole in Show's bed. As the bed quickly deflated, the assailant disappeared from the scene. The second Show hit the hard metal floor, he confronted JBL. As Show read him the riot act, JBL denied having any involvement. He just didn't sound believable because he could not stop laughing, which only served to infuriate the angry giant even more.

JBL would most often get blamed for episodes that the office found to have gotten a little out of hand. Yes he was generally right in the middle of the fray. He liked having a good time. Now to be fair, in this incident, JBL did not do the deed to Show's mattress. He will tell you himself that he had been fined a few times for, let's just say, having too much fun. Sometimes for things he had no part in. JBL joked that he wished he could pay his fines with his credit card so he could accumulate airline points. Now whether or not he took part in the planning, I don't know. What I do know is I'm almost sure he didn't do it. I was not a witness and I don't want to falsely accuse anyone but as I heard, it was a certain Chairman who got the better of the Big Show. If I were the Big Show, I would rather cuss out JBL instead of the boss. There was more tomfoolery, but I'll save those stories for another time.

Finally we landed in Germany. The USA has a large base there and that's where we were going to refuel and spend a few hours. Once we arrived in Germany, we were escorted to a facility that housed a bowling alley, a bar, slot machines, and a restaurant. It was a place where military personnel could get a little R&R. For us, it was a great place to unwind. We were fed well and given pretty much the run of the place. Bowling, video games, slot machines — what an awesome place. While we spent those few hours there, many servicemen and women dropped in to see the WWE superstars. All the boys were gracious in posing for pictures and signing autographs for everyone who came to meet them.

It was now time to head back to the plane for the four-and-a-half-hour flight to Iraq. After I had once again gotten settled in on the plane, my thoughts turned to our destination. What was it going to be like? None of us, with the possible exception of JBL, knew what to expect. One thing I didn't expect was how landing in Baghdad was anything but routine. On the contrary, landing in Baghdad, especially for military planes, is done with great care. As we began our approach to Baghdad, the plane started to bank left, then right, and they shut all the lights off inside the plane. It was descending in a zigzag kind of motion. I don't know if anyone else in our group knew why but I sure didn't. Once we were on the ground safely, I asked one of the servicemen on the plane why we descended in such a manner. He replied that they land like that so that the enemy on the ground cannot zero in on planes with anti-aircraft weapons. *Holy shit!* As incredibly shocking as that statement was, it didn't fully sink in until much later. Then we disembarked from the plane. The military presence was astonishing. There were armed U.S. army personnel everywhere.

The first thing they had us do was to put on camouflage flak jackets and helmets. Looking around at the faces of our crew, you could tell that they were a bit uneasy. The soldiers assigned to guard us did their very best to make us feel at ease and they succeeded for the most part. There was just no way to fully shake that uncomfortable feeling. Once again the Big Show was the centre of attention as there was no flak jacket nearly large enough to fit him. The hilarity of the situation eased the tension a little.

It was great that we didn't have to wait for our luggage because they were bringing all our bags to where we were staying. Then we made our way to where we would be housed for the duration of our stay, Camp Victory in one of Saddam Hussein's palaces. Trust me, it sounds much more glamorous than it actually was. Even though there was marble and gold throughout the massive structure, all of the furniture had been removed, leaving only the odd table, chair, or vase.

We were divided into two groups — all the talent stayed in one massive room while all of the crew stayed in another huge room. Chimel, Brian Hebner, and I stayed in the crew room. Other than one king-size bed in each room, we were all given cots to sleep on. No one complained, but we all eyeballed each other, wondering who would have the grapefruits to take the huge bed. The WWE's set engineer, Jason Robinson took it upon himself to sleep in the king bed. Only thing was, Jason was in all likelihood the smallest member of our crew and when he jumped into that bed, you became aware of resentment from a few of the guys. Any bitterness that the guys felt for Jason quickly dissipated when we got an unforeseen visitor to our room.

It just so happened that there was a power play in the talent room. They also had only one king bed and several cots, just as we had. I have no idea how they figured out who would take the bed but for some reason the largest man in the group did not end up with the bed. The Big Show wandered into our room to check and see if there was room for him there. He walked over to see little Jason curled up in the huge bed and that's when we were all awoken by the big guy. He basically took over the bed by kicking Jason out of it. I can't say I blame Show for taking the bed. Hell, the guy is seven foot and almost five hundred pounds. I really don't think there was a cot strong enough or big enough to handle him. We didn't have a choice, so Show ended up in our room. No one would have complained either, but Show has a tendency to be rather loud even when he sleeps. It was surprising that his incessant snoring did not give our position away to the enemy. Just kidding, Show, but you were killing us, with not only the snoring but also passing gas all night long. It felt like we were the victims of chemical warfare. All that being said, Show was always fun to be around. He's a good-natured guy with a good sense of humour, so having him in the room with us was fun.

On the night before the big event, I experienced one of the coolest moments in my life. Let me begin by saying that when the United States Army is stationed on foreign land, they abide by the laws of the country they are in. For example, while in Iraq, the men and women of the U.S. military could not drink alcohol because it was illegal for Iraqi citizens at that time. Booze was available for civilians; you just had to go back to the airport to buy it. Chimel and Hebner got a ride to the airport and picked up two cases of Corona and some Cuban cigars. That evening, Chimel and I, flanked by an armed staff sergeant, stood outside of Saddam's palace, sipping a Corona and smoking a Cuban cigar while in the far distance we could hear gun and mortar fire. It was a surreal moment that neither one of us will ever forgot. For us, it was too cool to put into words. A definite highlight of the trip for sure.

It was now show day and all of us were pumped for it. That was until we got some last-minute instructions from the special ops people. They gave us a crash course in what to do in the unlikely event of an attack by insurgents. Everyone kind of went numb for a few seconds. We could not believe what we were hearing. There was a chance we might get attacked? As much as the special ops guy tried to assure us that the chances of an attack during the show were slim to none, the thought of it would not go away for a while. As I got to the ring and looked out into the sea of soldiers, any fear I had going out there quickly disappeared, at least for a few minutes.

During the match between Eddie Guerrero and Chris Benoit, two helicopters flew directly over us in the middle of the match. All three of us stopped dead in out tracks, not knowing that the stunt was planned by our director. Unbeknownst to any of us, he arranged for the Hueys to do a fly-by during the match. It gave us a bit of a scare, but we got back to business. The troops loved every minute of it, and we were all proud to bring a small piece of home over to them.

After the show was over, the boys hung around, greeting as many of the soldiers as they could. We on the crew went to work tearing down the set and packing it all on pallets to be loaded on the plane. We were leaving that night and had a timeline we had to follow. With so many of the troops pitching in to help, we were done very quickly and went over to a nearby building to shower and prepare for the flight back stateside. I can't begin to describe what an honour and a privilege it was to take part in such a worthwhile venture. To this day, there are a few servicemen I still keep in contact with whom I met on that three-day trip to Baghdad. Those memories will certainly last a lifetime, not to mention the chance I got to pick up some souvenirs along the way. Among the trinkets I brought back with me was Iraqi money with Saddam's face on it, a couple of commemorative coins given to me by the troops, a camouflage bucket hat, and the *piece de resistance*, a bayonet knife from a Russian-made rifle that was taken from an Iraqi insurgent. I was afraid I would not be able to get that last item back home, but somehow the weapon went undetected by baggage handlers at Atlanta's Hartsfield airport and I managed to bring the keepsake home with me.

The two items that I treasure most from this trip came to me a few weeks after returning from this life-altering experience. I received two letters, including one from the Chairman himself. Vince McMahon thanked me for my participation on the gruelling tour. He mentioned in the letter that the joy we brought and the smiles we put on the faces of the soldiers made the trip worth every minute we spent there. He was absolutely right.

The second letter that arrived at my home was from the United States Military. The return address on the envelope was USAF and said *Pentagon OFFICIAL BUSINESS*. My first thought was that it had something to do with the souvenirs I brought home from the trip. I was worried that I had broken some kind of international law and the United States government was coming for me. It was actually a personal thank-you note from Arthur J. Myers, Director of Services. He was the man in charge of bringing the WWE to Iraq. At first I felt relief and then pride. It was a commendation letter thanking me for my involvement. It is something I value greatly and it continues to hang on my office wall.

On a side note, I also got to go on the second annual WWE Tribute to the Troops, this time at Camp Speicher in Tikrit, Iraq. That second trip to Iraq was just as rewarding as the first. There were two main differences on this trip. First the weather. A misconception about Iraq is that it is always warm there. That couldn't be further from the truth. The temperature at night dipped to 20 degrees Fahrenheit. It may have been chillier than that, which is far too cold, even for a Canadian.

The other major difference from the previous year was the accommodations. This time around, we stayed in a large tent. We slept on cots just like in 2003. Thank goodness they gave us space heaters. Another small change this year was the toilet and shower building. It was a bit of a walk over to the where the head (toilet) and shower facilities were located. Not a big deal. At least there was running hot water. It may sound like I wasn't happy to be there, but nothing could be further from the truth. I was glad to make a second trip to entertain the troops and would have gone every year if asked. I have been very lucky throughout my career to be able to take part in some timeless moments in wwe history. My two trips to Iraq to take part in the Tribute shows were by far two of the most fulfilling events I have been blessed to do.

Thank you to the wwe for allowing me to experience these life-changing trips and a special thank you to every single man and woman who puts on a uniform in service of their country.

CHAPTER 10

Tales from Inside the Ring

It has been said many times, especially by people in the wrestling business: what happens on the road stays on the road. That's where Chimel and I adopted our car rule from. Not every road story is a dirty secret that becomes a skeleton hiding in someone's closet. The vast majority of these tall tales are really quite harmless and actually pretty funny. I may not recall every tiny detail but I'll do my best. They say the mind is the first thing to go — sounds about right to me, but here goes in no particular order.

Where do I begin? Do I start with stories from inside the ring or outside the ring? I've talked about out of ring stuff so far, so let me give you some of my accounts from inside the ring. I will give you more from outside the ring but for now, let's focus on mishaps and fun from between the ropes.

One of the things I get asked about a lot is my time as a "scab" referee. Let me start from the beginning. Prior to getting married, I spoke with Jim Ross about taking time off for my honeymoon. JR, who was head of Talent Relations at that time, was my direct boss for my refereeing duties. Steve Taylor was the ring crew boss and I had to get clearance from him as well. They were both very receptive to the request and gave me two weeks off. They told me to relax and enjoy my time off. So, in September 1999, I married my wife, Audra, in Toronto.

We spent two amazing weeks in Spain on our honeymoon. Even more amazing to me was that I wasn't thinking about wrestling. No TV, no Internet — I was wrestling-free for the whole trip.

When I returned to work, I had no idea about what had transpired while I was away. Apparently all the other referees had gone on "strike" in protest of being abused and taken for granted by the wrestlers. As soon as I arrived at the arena, the jokes began. My co-workers were greeting me with cries of welcome back, followed by, "Why are you here? Aren't you on strike?"

Confused, I went into the production office to get to the bottom of this. That is where I learned about the most recent storyline involving all the regular WWF referees. Tom Prichard, Harvey Whippleman, and Steve Lombardi were handling the referee chores while the labour dispute was ongoing. Not for long as a brief exchange between Triple H and me sparked a chain of events that would put me in the forefront of this angle as far as the refs were concerned.

Here's how it happened. As I was walking down the hall towards catering, I bumped into Hunter and he said, "Hey, Corduroy, welcome back!" Corduroy was his nickname for me. "Too bad you're out a job with this strike. I guess you picked a bad time to come back." Then he chuckled at the joke.

I laughed and replied, "Yeah, wouldn't it be funny if when they show the other refs picketing outside the arena, I come strolling up unaware of the strike and ask what's going on?" Hunter looked interested, so I continued, "The other refs explain the situation and I tell them I just got married and can't afford to go on strike and try to walk into the building. Just then, the refs stop me and beat me with their signs and the next time they show the striking refs, I'm looking a little worse for wear and have reluctantly joined the rest of them in protest."

After hearing me out and finding my little scenario funny, Hunter turned to JR, who was walking down the same hall, and said to him, "Hey, JR, listen to this idea Korderas has." He then repeated the scene I had just told him to JR, who thought there was something there that could be used on TV. Then they both said they would talk to me later and walked off. I wasn't sure where this was leading but a storyline idea had been sparked by me.

Later on that day, I was filled in on the newest development in the referee strike. I would be the only regular referee to cross the picket line and would continue to officiate matches, much to the ire of my compatriots. This would go on for a week or two with everything coming to a head at the Unforgiven pay-per-view event. I would referee as if nothing was amiss. The main event (at the PPV) was a six-pack challenge match for the WWF championship featuring Triple H, Mick Foley, the British Bulldog, Kane, the Rock, and the Big Show. I would be the assigned official for the match and Stone Cold Steve Austin was designated the special enforcer on the outside keeping an eye on the proceedings. What was even cooler was that I got to do my first interview on *Sunday Night Heat* right before the PPV. Lillian Garcia asked me why I didn't join my fellow refs and strike with them and how I felt about reffing the six-pack challenge. That one-minute bit made me more nervous than being in the ring in front of 70,000 people. This was different because when you are a referee in a match, you are not the focus of the match. The referee is important but he is invisible in the ring. My explaining why I was not out there picketing with the rest of them made me appreciate the good talkers that much more than I already did.

It was now match time and all was going smoothly. Stone Cold was keeping a careful eye on the match from the announcer's table while sipping a "Steveweiser." The six men in the match were giving their all as the live crowd was very much into the match.

As the match was winding down, the striking referees entered the arena, walked down to ringside, and began to berate yours truly. I was somewhat distracted by the shouting but kept my composure and reffed on. After a flurry of activity, Big Show gave Mick Foley a choke slam and covered him in a pin attempt. Like any good referee would, I slid into position and began to count. The crowd counted along: "One, two —" Before I could hit the canvas for a three count, the striking referees grabbed my legs and dragged me out of the ring. An argument ensued; then, suddenly, Earl Hebner threw a punch at me. It was a working punch, but I think Earl was being a little too nice because the blow landed squarely on my chest and nowhere near my face. I bumped anyways as the remaining officials pummelled me while I was on the ground.

It really wasn't that bad until one referee decided to go into business for himself by kicking me as hard as he could in the back, in the butt, and even dropping down and punching me in the groin area. I was genuinely hurting, all from one individual. None of the other punches or kicks thrown by the other refs even registered. I didn't know at the time who the culprit was, but I was going to find out. In the meantime, Stone Cold came to my defense and beat up the refs who took out their frustration on me. Austin cleaned house, as they say, and took over for me as the official of the match.

The next day, we were in Greensboro, North Carolina, for *Monday Night Raw*. As is customary, the day after a pay-per-view, the tape of the previous night's event was available for viewing. I couldn't wait to check out the footage to see who the culprit was who had left me bruised and hurting. I popped in the tape and fast-forwarded to the moment in question. There he was! Busted! Playing it back, I was more surprised that Mike Chioda didn't break his foot from kicking me so hard. At one point he was kicking so hard that he nearly fell over as he whaled away. I knew right there and then that a "receipt" was coming his way. I wasn't sure when but one was coming.

That night's *Raw* proved to be a challenging one for me. Before the show, all the referees were called into Vince's office. We were not in any kind of trouble or anything like that. We were shooting a pre-taped segment for the show. The premise of the pre-tape was that Mr. McMahon had settled the dispute between the striking referees and the talent. After the first take, Vince looked at me and said to writer Vince Russo, "Didn't he get beat up by all the other refs last night? He doesn't look beat up to me."

Russo said that we didn't have time to alter my appearance to look beat up. The solution, they decided, was to put my left arm in a sling. That was suggested by Vince McMahon and would end up being the extent of my injuries. I guess he thought it would be funny to have me referee a match on *Raw* that night while in the sling. I was assigned to D-Lo Brown versus Chaz and when they found out I was wearing a sling on my arm, they changed up the match a little bit. Suddenly there were many more pin attempts added, which meant I would have to get up and down on the mat frequently and quickly, all the while selling my left arm. They were getting such a kick out of watching me struggle to get up and down, they were almost laughing during the match. They later confessed to me that they purposely added those extra near-falls as a rib on me. But the real rib had begun a few hours earlier when McMahon had me wear that damn thing. They all got me on this night but that's all right. I don't mind harmless pranks being played on me and if can make people laugh in the process, that makes it even more worth a minor inconvenience.

Before I forget to mention it, I did get Chioda back a few months later. It was during *Monday Night Raw*. All the referees had to run down to the ring to break up a brawl. When we got the cue to go to the ring, I let the other refs go first through the curtain. I then strategically positioned myself behind Chioda as we ran down the ramp. Once we got to the point of no return, I made my move. Everything had to be timed just right. The second Mike was about to dive under the bottom rope and enter the ring in dramatic fashion, I gave him a little nudge from behind, sending him crashing chest first into the side of the ring. Not only was I laughing at this point, but one of the cameramen found humour in it as well. Chioda was so mad and he shot me the dirtiest look imaginable. It didn't bother me in the least; I got me some payback for Unforgiven. Now I was a happy camper.

Playing an important role in the referee strike angle was a great thrill for me. Two years prior to this storyline, I almost became a prominent figure in a scenario that would have had me side with a fellow Canadian. It was shortly after the infamous "Montreal Screwjob." The Survivor Series 1997 was without a doubt one of the most unforgettable in modern wrestling history. I was there and witnessed it first hand. I'll get to that topic later.

After Bret "The Hitman" Hart left the company, the fate of the remaining members of the Hart Foundation was in doubt. Davey Boy Smith followed his brother-in-law Bret to wcw. Jim Neidhart also departed the wwf. Owen Hart stayed behind. It was rumoured that Vince would not grant Owen Hart his release. Whether that is true or not only they knew for sure. What I do know is that Owen made his shocking return at the In Your House DX pay-per-view the month after Montreal. Owen appeared almost out of nowhere and attacked the Heartbreak Kid, Shawn Michaels. Before Triple H or anyone else from D-Generation X or security could intervene and help Shawn by stopping the onslaught, Owen escaped through the crowd and vanished. The live audience was going nuts. They could not believe what they had just seen. Bret's younger brother was back and on a mission.

The plan was for Owen to take out his frustration with the way his family had been treated on the ones responsible, DX. Attacking Shawn was the first shot taken in the war. The next step for Owen was that he was going to try to capture Triple H's newly acquired European championship. He wasn't going to do it alone either. The idea was for Owen to have his title match with Hunter. Earl Hebner, the infamous referee from the "Montreal Screwjob," was to start the match as the official. Somewhere in the match, and it wasn't discussed how, I would run down and cause Hunter to lose the European title. Essentially, I would be a willing accomplice in restoring the Hart family name, with Owen leading the charge.

Sometimes, ideas do not go as planned, and this one got derailed before it had a chance to get rolling. To backtrack a little, Commissioner Sgt. Slaughter forced Shawn to defend the European title against Hunter. Shawn let Hunter pin him, thus becoming Euro champ. This took place on the December 22, 1997, edition of *Raw* from Lowell, Massachusetts. The January 26, 1998, *Raw* emanating from the Nassau Coliseum in Long Island, New York, was where the master plan would unfold. That was the starting date and location for the Canadian Invasion. That wasn't really what it was called — Canadian Invasion just has a cool ring to it. The plan was made, everything was set in motion, and then it happened. Two days before all this was scheduled to go down, Triple H suffered an injury at a live event in Hamilton, Ontario. Somehow, Hunter dislocated his patella. I didn't see it, but he said it occurred when his and Mick Foley's knees collided and his kneecap ended up on the side of his leg.

In true Triple H fashion he finished the tag match and was helped to the back by his partner HBK. I'm not sure who or when, but someone popped his kneecap back into place and he wrapped his knee. When I saw Hunter two days later in Long Island, I knew the match was not going to happen on that night. He had a brace on his knee and needed crutches to get around. As much as Hunter wanted to continue with the storyline against his better judgement, it was decided that the plan would be altered. Goldust subbed for Triple H in the match with the championship still on the line and lost the European title to Owen Hart. The original plan had been scrapped and I was no longer pegged as Owen's cohort. There were rumblings of adding other Canadian members to the group but we'll never know now. The "Canadian Mafia," as all the Canadians were dubbed, and of which Owen was the leader, might have been great. But then again it might not have been. We will never know

now. It's just the nature of the business. Plans change all the time; you just have to work with the hand you are dealt.

At the time I was kind of disappointed that it didn't happen but as I thought more about it, I felt better the way it ended up. I wasn't happy Hunter got hurt, in case you read it that way. I was glad I wasn't a rogue referee because once that angle runs its course, you might not be needed any longer. I'd rather be the anonymous referee the boys can trust in the ring and out who has a long career. Notoriety was never as important to me as it was to others. I simply loved being in the ring doing what I believe I do best. Don't get me wrong — it's nice to be recognized by the fans, but it was the recognition from my peers that meant more to me than anything. At times I wonder what would have happened if the intended story came to fruition. Regardless of the consequences, I would have loved to team up with Owen in the battle against DX. Who knows, maybe other Canadian wrestlers would have joined our cause. What a crew that would've made. Owen, myself, Edge, and Christian, *hmmmm*! I can now only imagine what that ride would've been like. With Owen at the helm, it definitely would have been one wonderful journey.

Fast-forward a few years to March 23, 2001. To many, that may have been the most historic day in pro wrestling. That night marked the end of the Monday Night Wars as the WWF bought their rival and main competitor WCW for what many considered a bargain price. I have heard several different money figures thrown around when discussing the purchase price, but I only know it was a great deal. Then on March 26, 2001, history was made again as the final episode of *Monday Nitro* aired for the final time alongside *Raw*. It was truly the end of an era.

The WWF absorbed most of the WCW's talent contracts with the purchase, thus nearly doubling their roster of not only wrestlers but also referees. Three of the WCW's refs were brought on board. Nick Patrick, Charles Robinson, and Billy Silverman were the refs who joined our roster to not so welcoming guys in stripes. Let me clarify that last statement by saying not all the WWF refs minded the additions to our squad. I surely didn't mind because I was always confident in my work. At the risk of sounding conceited, in my mind I believed I was one of the company's better referees and wasn't worried about being replaced at that time. A few of the other referees didn't share my sentiment. They questioned the reasoning behind bringing these guys over when in their minds, the extra baggage was not needed.

Another thing that didn't sit too well with my referee brethren was that there was a fourth WCW referee who was added to the mix. Brian Hebner, the son of longtime referee Earl Hebner, was hired by the WWF and added to the roster as a WCW referee. The other refs could not understand why the company would hire more referees. They believed we had more than enough already, so why bring others in? I did get their point. I didn't agree with it but I recognized the concerns they were expressing. For me, I was glad these guys still had a job and would have hated to see them out of work.

On a personal level, I made some new friends in the process. Nick, Charles, and Brian were now part of our family and we got along great. Nick Patrick is very knowledgeable about the wrestling business and I learned a lot from him. His father is Jody Hamilton, who wrestled as the Masked Assassin for many years. Charles is just a fun guy to be around and who was generally in a good mood. That was likely one of the main reasons we became very good friends. Brian was like the wild little brother who needed to be reined in sometimes. Not in a bad way most of the time. Let's just call it youthful exuberance. His was an uphill battle to be accepted by most of the other refs mainly because they felt he hadn't paid his dues and the only reason he was there was that his dad was the senior official. All that being said, Brain was a good young referee.

What was cool about the WCW/ECW Invasion angle was that the referees had a rivalry as well. There was even a locker room dust-up between both ref camps. It was a fun little side story that culminated with a match between Earl Hebner, the wwf's senior referee, and Nick Patrick, who was wcw's senior official. All the other referees from both sides were at ringside for the match, which Earl won of course. Eventually, the wcw brand was done away with and their refs joined ours and we were one big happy family.

We could debate for days about how the whole WCW/ECW Invasion storyline was not handled properly. The numerous missed opportunities to capitalize on potential dream matches the fans wanted to see was a major complaint. Many have said, "I would have done this" or "I would have done that." Naturally you can make such bold statements when you know there is no way to change what already happened. It's easy to say after the fact when there's no one to answer to. Sometimes you've just got to go with the flow. For me it was new talent and new friends to work with.

Buying wcw was not the biggest surprise move by the top brass at Titan Tower. In my humble opinion the most shocking move by the wwf/e was the night Eric Bischoff was introduced as the general manager of *Raw*. It was kept a secret all day long and less than a handful of people knew he would be the new gm of *Raw*. As far as I knew, none of the talent was aware of his hiring. Vince wanted everyone's reaction to be genuine. That's exactly what he got from the boys, particularly those who worked for him at wcw. Some were not happy to see him there, while others just couldn't believe Vince could work with his arch-nemesis.

All the doubts were put to rest when Vince McMahon and Eric Bischoff hugged it out on live tv. Vince is first and foremost a businessman and he saw money in hiring Eric for an on-air role, and that's what he was: an on-air talent and that's it. I'm sure he pitched ideas to creative, but he was not an official member of the creative team. At least not that I was aware of.

From my point of view, I thought it was brilliant. Appointing his most hated real-life business rival was genius. It made the despised Mr. McMahon character appear to sell his soul for ratings. As controversial as the Bischoff hiring was to the fans, it almost seemed even more of a questionable move in the eyes of the boys backstage. I had heard stories from many who worked for him in wcw and most of the stories were not flattering. I can only speak of the Eric Bischoff whom I met in 2002 as the *Raw* GM. He seemed friendly enough and was approachable. We didn't interact very much but he was pleasant. As for his on-screen character, he played the evil general manager very well and was good on the microphone. All in all, I think Eric Bischoff was an asset during his time in the wwe. Even though some were not happy he was there in the first place, they have to admit that the *controversy* did *create cash*. (Pun intended.)

CHAPTER 11

The King of Harts: Owen

"In this business you make a lot of acquaintances but very few friends. Owen was one of those friends." Those were the emotional and very heartfelt words of Jeff Jarrett less than 24 hours after the tragic and unfortunate accident that took the life of Owen Hart.

What I would like to do right now is to tell you a little about the Owen Hart I knew and, for the first time ever, describe the events of that day and my feelings. I first met Owen Hart in the late 1980s — I believe it was 1988. He had just begun wrestling in the wwf as the Blue Blazer, a masked superhero-like character. Right from the beginning, you knew that Owen was special, not only in the ring but outside of it as well. I generally consider myself a very good judge of character and when Owen and I first met, it was the little things one might notice that told me he was down to earth and genuinely a good guy. Owen had this calming quality about him. He made everyone feel at ease. I was no different. We got along very well right from the very beginning. Maybe it was because we were very close in age, or the fact that we both had an unusual sense of humour. It could have been simply that we were both Canadian and there seemed to be a different camaraderie among the Canucks in the WWF. It sort of exists even to this day. The honest truth is, sometimes you just can't pinpoint one particular thing that makes people friends and, in Owen's case, there were just too many reasons to like the guy.

It has been said many times by many people that no one has ever heard a bad word spoken about Owen Hart. I know they say that about a lot of people but, with regards to Owen, that is an absolute truth. Another thing Owen is very much famous for is being one of the greatest if not the best practical joker, or as we say in wrestling "ribber," ever. His ribs were the stuff legends were made of. The thing about the ribs Owen played on people was that they were not malicious or mean-spirited. No one ever suffered any personal injury and to the best of my knowledge no personal belongings were ever damaged as a result of Owen's pranks. What I liked most about Owen's ribbing was that no one — and I mean no one — was immune. Everyone from me all the way up to Vincent Kennedy McMahon has been an unwilling participant in his shenanigans.

I remember after a particularly long evening of television tapings, I became the victim of one of Owen's harmless pranks. I was in my hotel room, watching television but still half-asleep. It was almost one a.m. when the phone rang. The person on the other end said he was calling from the front desk claiming that there was a problem with my credit card. I asked what the problem was, but they said I needed to come down to the front desk to clear up the situation. So I put on a pair of shorts and a T-shirt and made my way down to the front desk. When I got there, the fellow behind the desk asked me if he could help me. I said yes and explained who I was and the whole conversation on the phone and while I was explaining myself I could see that he had this confused look on his face. After I was done explaining why I was there, he informed me that no one from the front desk had called my room and that everything seemed to be in order regarding my credit card. I didn't clue in to the fact that I had been had at first, but when Owen showed up moments later claiming that he had fallen victim to the same phone call I put two and two together. He got me. As we stood in the lobby laughing about the situation, I saw other wrestlers making their way to the front desk after apparently having received the same phone call I had gotten. I looked at Owen as he smiled like the Cheshire Cat in Alice in Wonderland. Apparently, he was a busy man. At least I wasn't the only one to fall for his hijinks that night.

Even the boss has fallen prey to Owen's tomfoolery. Years ago there was a pay-per-view match involving Hunter Hearst Helmsley and Henry Godwin. This particular match however was to take place in a hog pen. So early that day not only did the crew have to build the ring as usual, they had to help construct the structure they were to wrestle in. Now, the WWF does not carry their own hogs and pigs with them. The animals had to be rented — I have no idea where one would rent these animals for the day but those in charge found some. Early that afternoon a truck arrived to deliver the farm animals that were going to be roaming freely in the pen while the match was taking place. The production manager was looking for somewhere to temporarily house these pigs when, lo and behold, who should appear but none other than the prankster himself, Owen Hart. With everyone at the production meeting, including Mr. McMahon and all the agents, Owen took it upon himself to help find a place to store the pigs. With the swine in tow, Owen directed the delivery fellow down the hall and into a room. With the pigs securely in the room, Owen escorted the delivery guy back to his truck. No one saw the sign on the door that Owen cleverly concealed. It read *Vince's Office*. Once it became evident, everyone was laughing and terrified at the same time. What if Vince thought that the crew had put them in there? As everyone discussed what the next move was going to be and whether someone should move the animals out of Vince's office, the production meeting let out. As the Chairman made his way down the hall towards his office, the guys considered running but decided to stay within earshot just to hear his reaction. Mr. McMahon entered his office, and you could only imagine the incredibly shocked look on his face. A few seconds later he burst out of his office half-smiling, screaming for Owen. No one said anything to him; he just knew who it was and actually had a good laugh about it. Even Vince McMahon appreciated Owen's sense of humour. Fortunately, or maybe unfortunately, I was not present while all this was taking place. I was busy doing other chores and nobody let me know what was going on. I had to hear about it after the fact like most of the boys did. Regardless, it was still a classic Owen ribbing at its best.

Owen Hart's ability to make all of us laugh was not restricted to ribbing his co-workers outside the ring. On the contrary, he got just as much enjoyment out of making us laugh in the ring as well. One classic example of this occurred in Germany. We were in Oberhausen and it was a tag-team title match — Jeff Jarrett and his partner Owen Hart versus Edge and Christian. Yours truly happened to be the referee for this contest. There was nothing out of the ordinary at the beginning of this match; in fact, the heels began to get some serious heat on a babyface Edge. Then all of a sudden the serious nature of the match took a 180-degree turn and hilarity ensued. Like any good heel, Owen decided to reach into his tights and pull out a foreign object and proceed to use it on his opponent Edge. All this occurred behind the referee's back — once again, that would be me. Edge sold like he got hit with a brick. Owen then went to the corner and climbed up to the bottom rope, yes that is right, the bottom rope, and came off that bottom rope with a big splash on Edge's lower legs and proceeded to cover his legs. Since Edge's shoulders were down I started counting. Edge barely kicked out at two and three quarters. Then Owen proceeded to cover Edge with his crotch directly in Edge's face. Edge then kicked out a little stronger this time. After Owen had used the object several more times, again behind my back, the time was right for me to call him out on it. Owen had hidden the object under his arm and despite my repeated request for him to raise his arms, he refused to do so. I told him that I would begin my five count and if he did not raise his arm I would disqualify him then and there. At this point I still did not know what the object was. I began to count, and when I got to four Owen raised his arms and a single red napkin floated harmlessly to the canvas. I couldn't believe it. I looked at Owen and there was that smile again. I looked at Jeff, then I looked back at Christian and Edge, and it became a laugh-fest. I usually pride myself on the fact that I am very good at not cracking up in the ring. That night I didn't have a prayer. From that point forward it became known to us as the Foreign Napkin Match.

If there is one thing in my career that I've been asked about more than any other, it has to be regarding the day Owen Hart passed away. This will really be the first time that I talk about this day in detail. I've touched on this subject in the past but feel that now is the time for me to finally tell people how this tragedy affected me personally.

May 23, 1999, Kansas City, Missouri, the Kemper Arena — not only a day I will never forget but also a time that changed my life and that I think about almost daily. Let me start from the beginning of that day. I arrived at the arena at ten a.m. with the rest of the crew to begin setting up for the Over the Edge pay-per-view being held later that evening. Kemper Arena is a difficult building to load-in because there are no loading docks to unload the 13 trucks. We had to ramp or forklift everything out of the trucks and push all the equipment into the arena. Yes, we basically dumped the trucks outside of the building. All that said, everything was running quite smoothly that day. As the day progressed, the talent began arriving to the arena. It was business as usual, nothing out of the ordinary. All the other referees and I were waiting for the production meeting to end in order to find out which matches we had been assigned to. I was in catering having lunch when I found out that I would be refereeing the Intercontinental title match between the champion, the Godfather, and the challenger, the Blue Blazer a.k.a. Owen Hart. I found Owen and the Godfather in the locker room to let them know that I would be working their match later that night. They said that was great and that they would fill me in on the details of the match a little later. There didn't seem to be anything different or unusual with regards to Owen's attitude or demeanour, at least nothing that I noticed. My day went pretty much as expected. I carried out whatever duties I needed to do before finally sitting down with the guys in my match to iron out the specifics and what they needed from me. That is when I first discovered that Owen would be making his spectacular entrance descending from the rafters of the arena. To be honest with you, I didn't really think much of it as Owen had performed this stunt before. Was he nervous or apprehensive about the stunt as others have claimed? I can't say for sure. I didn't really notice anything out of the ordinary. I do know that right after that he went out to the arena to practice being lowered from the rafters. I don't know how many times he practiced it; I was running around at the time performing other duties.

As far as the finish of the match, it was to involve a masked mini-me version of the Blue Blazer. The company had brought in a Mexican mini-wrestler to portray the Blue Blazer's side-kick, dressed just like the real Blue Blazer. He would be involved in the finish and help the actual Blue Blazer become the new Intercontinental champion. It was meant to be very comedic, just like Owen's entrance was meant to be funny. He was to be lowered toward the ring where they would stop him about five feet above the canvas and kind of leave him there dangling. He would then, in a very funny way, flail his arms and legs, trying to somehow make it all the way down to the ring. When the time was right, he would pull the quick-release located on his harness and tumble into the ring, once again all for comedic effect.

It was now showtime. The pay-per-view was running smoothly with nothing out of the ordinary going on. The IC title match was approaching. Right before that match was a Hardcore Title match with Al Snow defending the title against Hardcore Holly. After the match ended, I made my way to the ring and began helping the crew remove some of the debris left in the ring after the hardcore match. On the video screen, they were playing a pre-taped interview Kevin Kelly had conducted with the Blue Blazer. I was now in the ring holding the top rope with my left hand while kicking pieces of broken table out of the ring, slowly moving towards one of the corners. I had my head down as I was doing this and heard someone yelling something at me. I didn't pay much attention to it as I assumed it was coming from the crowd. Just then, I felt something hit me in the head while at the same time the top rope was pulled out of my hand, snapped back, and jammed the fingers in my left hand. Almost simultaneously, I heard a loud bang in the ring. My first reaction was to duck and cover my head. Then I thought, *Holy shit, the top rope broke while at the exact same time, some idiot fan threw something at me.* I really didn't know what the hell was happening. It felt like ten things were happening all at once. As I looked around, I saw the top rope intact. What I was stunned to see though was Owen Hart lying in the corner of the ring, flat on his back. My first reaction was to run over and call to him. I repeatedly called his name and got no response whatsoever. Looking at his face, even through the mask, his eyes were wide open, but you could tell that something was drastically wrong. I started to panic, ran over to the timekeeper, Mark Yeaton, and began screaming for help. Panic turned to fear as I waited for help to show up. It seemed to take forever although it was probably just a few seconds for EMTs to arrive. As the medical staff began what I can only assume was checking for vital signs and so forth, it finally dawned on me what must have happened. The only explanation was that Owen had fallen. I knew just by the way they were frantically working on him that the situation was not very good at all. One thing I did notice as they worked feverishly on my fallen friend was that there was a baseball-sized wound on Owen's left forearm. It almost appeared as if the flesh had been removed with an ice cream scooper. The odd thing about it was that the wound was not bleeding. There was very little blood around the damaged arm. Again after what seemed like an eternity, they placed him on a stretcher to take him to a waiting ambulance. I picked up his Blue Blazer cape and followed them to the back. I don't know what made me pick it up. I suppose it was a reflex. As they wheeled Owen through the backstage area, there was a broad range of emotions — some were crying, others were praying, but most definitely all were very concerned and confused. I stood outside dismayed as they loaded him in the back of the ambulance and watched them drive away. One of the production people gave me a cigarette to smoke with the hope that it might settle me down. I was shaking uncontrollably as I puffed away on the cigarette. I was an emotional wreck. Just then I was approached by John D'Amico, one of the production managers for wwf. He insisted I go to the hospital to get checked out. I told him I didn't need to go and didn't understand why they were insisting I go. He then explained that it was a company policy and for precautionary reasons I had to go. I left the pay-per-view for the hospital where they checked out my head and neck as well as my hand. Everything turned out to be fine with me physically.

While I was sitting in the examining room waiting to be discharged, still in my ref clothes, someone — I think it was one of the nurses — asked if I was with the wrestler who was brought in to Emergency. I responded yes, and asked how he was. That is when they told me that Owen did not make it. Owen Hart had passed away. It is hard to explain the emotions that I was experiencing right there and then: sadness, shock, disbelief, as well as what seemed like hundreds of other thoughts. The first thing I did after somewhat collecting myself was to call my fiancée, Audra, to let her know what had happened and for her to call my family and to let them know that I was all right. That is when it really sunk in and I broke down on the phone. Audra was able to somewhat calm me down. I didn't want to hang up the phone. She understood I had to go but before I said goodnight, I told her that I loved her very much; then I hung up the phone. After being discharged, I walked into the waiting room; there was John D'Amico. John stayed and waited for me at the hospital and was a great comfort to me in a very difficult time. He drove me back to the arena to pick up my clothes. After that, I don't recall anything else that occurred that night. I honestly do not remember travelling to St. Louis for *Monday Night Raw*. I don't remember flying, driving, or anything — all I know is that I somehow got there still feeling the emotional effect of this night.

Walking into the arena in St. Louis, I had mixed emotions. I didn't really know if I wanted to be there after what had happened. I was also conflicted about whether or not we should proceed with the show. Either way, I eventually felt I needed to be with my road family, the guys and girls I travel and work with weekly. The first person I ran into was the Undertaker. He asked me if I was all right and if I needed anything. I told him that under the circumstances I was doing about as good as can be expected, and he replied that if I needed anything to let him know. What a great guy he was and still is to this day. I thanked him and immediately after ran into Triple H. He pretty much echoed what the Undertaker had said and also mentioned that if I needed anything to let him know. That is when I made my way into the production office, where Vice President of Event Operation Steve Taylor was. He immediately came over to me and with tears in his eyes gave me a big hug and said that he was glad I was all right. Neither of us could control our emotions. He also stated that if I needed anything to let him know. Mark Yeaton, Tony Chimel, and the rest of the production office staff reflected on how much time we really spend together and what we actually mean to one another. Jim Ross was the next person I saw, and he immediately wanted to know if I was okay and whether or not I needed to take some time off. After all, he was the head of Talent Relations at the time. I told him thank you but I think it would be best if I didn't take time off. He said it was entirely up to me and if I thought I needed to, to let him know. I know it is very much a cliché to say that the WWF was like one big family. That day in St. Louis, it was never more evident to me that we were a family, a family trying to cope with a terrible tragedy.

Here is where things got a little more intense for me. I was sitting talking to Jerry "The King" Lawler, and he informed me of something that really hit me very hard. He told me that he had actually witnessed the last 15 or so feet of Owen's fall and that his immediate thought was, "Oh my god, he is going to land on the ref." He then told me that it was Owen's hand or foot that had hit me in the head. I don't remember which, as I was dumbfounded by what I had just heard. He also said that if I had been standing one foot closer to that corner I was moving towards, Owen would have landed right on top of me. I was blown away by what I had just heard. This new information put me in kind of a daze for the rest of the day.

Later that afternoon, Vince McMahon held a meeting with everyone. You could see he was visibly shaken. In true Mr. McMahon fashion, though, he put on a brave face and proceeded to address everyone who was there that day. Talent, crew, office staff, anyone who was a part of the WWF family was at the meeting. With incredible sorrow in his voice he told us all that we were going ahead with the show tonight and that it would be a tribute show in honour of Owen Hart. While attempting to keep his emotions in check, Vince said that Owen would have insisted that the show go on. Never before have I, or possibly anyone else outside his family, observed him in this state. Mr. McMahon said that no one was being pressured to wrestle on the show; it was all up to them. Storylines were going to take a back seat for the evening. Vince also informed everyone that they were setting up a special room for anyone who wanted to go in and leave a video tribute to Owen, which would not only be aired that night but would also be sent to his family. It was impossible to air everyone's tribute on TV as not only wrestlers but officials and the entire crew were given the opportunity to send their condolences to the Hart family. I took advantage of that and expressed my condolences to the Hart family as did everyone else. To this day I can't bring myself to sit and watch the *Monday Night Raw* tribute show for Owen, which I still have on tape. It is just something I couldn't bring myself to do. Maybe after writing about this chapter in my life, I will be able to bring myself to sit down and finally watch it.

The funeral for Owen Hart was held in his hometown of Calgary, Alberta, Canada. The entire WWF roster and most of the crew were in attendance, all at the expense of the company. I believe that everyone would have attended regardless of whether or not the company paid for the travel out there or not. That is how much everyone thought of and loved Owen Hart. What was incredible to see was that it seemed like the entire city of Calgary was in mourning. The local and national news in Canada were covering the funeral as if it were for a head of state. To us, though, Owen was more important than any head of state. It just goes to show everyone how much Owen was loved not only by his own family, but how deeply he touched all who knew him personally, at work or through their televisions. He was a true inspiration on how one should conduct themselves not only in their professional lives, but also how we should conduct ourselves in our personal life and show respect to everyone.

I really thought that writing about my friend would allow me to open up more and come to grips with the emotional and mental trauma I went through after that day in Kansas City. Instead, it brought those old feelings back and made it more difficult to express my thoughts. I did my best to convey to you those feelings. I believed I had moved on. I guess the wounds heal but the scars still run deep. It will be something I will deal with for the rest of my days. I'm fine with that because I had the privilege to have known this fine young man.

Owen Hart touched the lives of everyone he came in contact

with. I felt honoured, humbled, and extremely lucky not only to have known and worked with Owen, but also to have considered him a friend. Of my friend I can only say this: I miss you very much and think about you often. And to be totally honest, when I do think about some of the things you have pulled over the years, even through the sadness it always makes me smile. Thank you, my friend, for all the memories, your friendship, and for making me smile still to this day. God bless Owen Hart.

CHAPTER 12

More Travel Woes

If you constantly have to travel as part of your work, whether by land, sea, or air, you invariably will have both good and bad days trying to get to a destination. When I hear my friends from outside the wrestling business or anyone else talk about their terrible travel experiences, 99 times out of 100, I believe my tales of travel woes have them beat. To tell you the truth, there has been more than one occasion where I thought, "This is it. We're going down." Some of you may think I am exaggerating. I wish I were, but I have witnesses. The first near-death experience I would like to share with you I have named "The Real Flight from Hell." It was not the other "Flight from Hell" that was widely reported on and blown out of proportion by many Internet wrestling sites. Rather, this flight almost left those of us on board scattered across Siberia.

Before I get into the details of the flight I'm referring to, let me give you a quick rundown of the more famous plane ride that was the talk of the wrestling world. The reason I said that everything was blown out of proportion was because I personally did not witness anything I would consider too crazy. Yes, as reported,

Curt Hennig did try to take down Brock Lesnar and yes, they did brush up against the emergency exit door, but they didn't hit the door as hard as some claimed. I was sitting with a few guys playing cards right near the emergency exit door and saw the whole thing. There was no way that door was going to open just by bumping into it. We didn't know this at the time so everyone reacted quickly to break things up, fearing that the door might accidentally open.

With that minor skirmish settled, the other happenings on the flight were mostly out of my view. The stories began making the rounds after we landed at Bradley Airport in Hartford, Connecticut. The serenading, wooooing, hair cutting, and whatever else were things I didn't want to know about. Jack Doan, Chad Patton, "The Coach" Jonathan Coachman, played cards pretty much the entire flight and kept out of trouble. Was there some rowdiness on the plane? Sure! Did things get a little out of hand? Maybe a little. Was anyone hurt during the festivities? Not really (that I know of). The only casualties were a certain clump of hair and some hurt feelings. Other than that, whatever else occurred is all hearsay to me. I can speak only to what I saw and that was not a whole heck of a lot.

Back to the flight I was referring to: the Real Flight from Hell. We began this overseas trip by boarding a different charter plane than the ones we were accustomed to. The WWE has used everything from 757s to sports charters where all the seats are business class to regional jets for shorter trips. For longer hauls, though, they usually request a larger aircraft. The plane we were flying on this trip was an older model Boeing 727-100. I do not claim to be an expert on airplanes but as soon as we boarded, I could tell that this one was somewhat primitive by today's standards. Okay, maybe not primitive but definitely not a newer jet. The pilots greeted us as we got on the plane, which was nice but raised a few eyebrows. Let's just say that the two men piloting the aircraft were very very experienced. Fine, they looked like really old guys. I nicknamed them Jack Lemmon and Walter Matthau. The stars of *Grumpy Old*

Men were flying our plane. Little did I know at the time but that extra experience would actually come in handy later on.

The crew had settled in for the first leg of our trip to Southeast Asia. There was one catch to having chartered this older airplane; we needed to make more frequent fuel stops than we normally would on a newer or bigger plane. The first stop was on the west coast — either Seattle or Portland, I don't remember which. From there we made a second refuel stop in Anchorage, Alaska. We spent the night in Anchorage because by law, the pilots can only fly for a certain number of hours before taking a mandatory rest period. The next morning, we re-boarded the plane and took off to our next pit stop, to once again refuel in Petropavlovsk, Russia. The airport in Petropavlovsk was not very big and, from what we were told, it was mainly used by the Russian military. As we made our approach to this remote area on a peninsula located on the coast of the Bering Sea, the mood on the plane began to change. We have all had to deal with turbulence on many flights in the past, but this time it was different. We were informed over the P.A. system to take our seats and fasten our seatbelts tightly. We were already seated because the plane had begun to shake. The shaking got progressively worse as we attempted to land. I say attempted to land because our first try had to be aborted and the pilots took us back up in the air to circle and try again. We were landing in a blizzard and, by all accounts, the pilots could not make out where the runway was, causing them to abort the landing and make a steep climb.

You could see fear begin to creep into the faces of the superstars on board as we tried to land for a second time. The shaking got worse as the plane was bouncing left, right, up, and down. I don't know how to explain this but the plane was also twisting. What I mean is the right side wing would dip down low while the left side wing would go high up. Then it would be the reverse. If it wasn't for the fact that I was terrified, I would have vomited. Coming in for landing attempt number two, wind shears and whiteout conditions made it impossible to land for a second time, and we again had to abort the landing and pull up.

Now panic was beginning to take over. There was no screaming or yelling. There was an eerie silence on board. Sitting near the back of the plane, I could hear the flight attendants crying. I don't blame them one bit because I couldn't help thinking that we were not going to make it and that we would all perish, in Russia of all places. I thought about my wife and my family. I honestly believed we weren't going to see our loved ones again and I began to pray. I do not think I was the only one praying as we tried for the third time to get the plane safely on the ground. The next effort to get us down fared no better than the previous tries. The plane continued to shake violently as everyone held onto the armrests with white-knuckled fingers. The seat back of the chair Big Show was sitting in broke and he fell into Brian Hebner's lap. Despite his calls for help, he was ignored by all. With the third landing attempt aborted, the pilots now had no other option but to get us down on the next try because we were dangerously low on fuel. One way or another, they were going to land the plane. This was going to be the final approach.

It was more of the same. As we got closer to the ground, the pilots fought the wind shears and extreme turbulence amazingly well. We heard the landing gear and braced for the worst. The plane was coming in at a 45-degree angle to the runway. In what seemed like a split second before we hit the ground, the pilots righted the plane and we touched down. You could feel the whole plane shimmy and slide as the pilots applied the brakes. As we began slowing down there was a sense that everything was going to be all right, but we felt we weren't out of the woods just yet. Once the aircraft came to a full stop, there was no cheering. Instead everyone very nearly had tears of joy. We then taxied to the refuelling station and the Russians refuelled the plane.

I truly believe to this day that the many years of combined experience of those two pilots saved us that night. I wish I knew their real names because they saved all our lives. For now I will thank Jack Lemmon and Walter Matthau for the great job they did keeping that plane in one piece and getting us safely down. They are true heroes.

We were on the ground for about an hour and a half. The Russian authorities would not let us off the plane for some reason. I figured it was no big deal, we could sleep on the plane and leave when the weather cleared. I was wrong again. For some unexplained reason, the local military informed us that we were not allowed to stay and had to depart as soon as we were refuelled. None of us understood why they didn't let us wait for the storm to subside before making us take off. Well, no one was going to argue with the guys carrying the AK47s, so we prepared for takeoff.

As you can imagine, we were all uneasy about the decision to leave but we had no choice. We were ordered to go. The pilots took us out and lined us up on the runway. As they revved up the engines, I prayed once again. With the blizzard making things that much more difficult, we started down the runway. As we picked up speed, the plane started to shake and even seemed to skid a bit on the ice. Miraculously, Jack and Walter managed to get us in the air and on our way to our next stop in Japan. Again a sigh of relief overtook the plane as the guys carried on deep discussions about our brush with death. Some made light of the experience as a way to lighten the mood. Hell, at that point we all needed a laugh or two. Once again, a huge thanks to Jack and Walter, my two favourite pilots of all time.

Perth, Australia, was where we ended this international tour, and we once again boarded the plane and reunited with our pilots Jack and Walter. We took off without incident, and flew until we got to the eastern coast of Australia, where we made an unscheduled landing in Cairns because of a mechanical problem. This time we had no trouble landing. We got off the plane and made our way into the terminal to wait for the repairs to be done. There were two odd things about this stop. First, we found it strange that there were no people in the terminal building except for a few who were working. They opened up a coffee shop/snack bar for us, which was nice of them. Still we wondered why there were no travellers in the terminal. The funny thing was that I never bothered to find out why we were the only travellers there. I was more concerned with the mechanical status of our plane.

The second thing I found strange was our ring announcer Justin Roberts in tears being helped into the terminal by two of the boys. As it turned out, Justin "fell" while going down the airplane stairs and sprained his ankle. At least that was the story I heard. Those steps are quite steep, and you have to be very careful when using them. Oh, enough about him, we had more important matters to deal with. We couldn't get a straight answer from anyone about the mechanical problem. In my mind, the confidence level in our airplane was disappearing quicker than an order of red beans and rice in front of Tony Chimel. We all liked Jack and Walter but not so much the plane.

After several hours of uncertainty, we were told that the problem with the plane had been fixed and we were again ready for the trip home. Everyone boarded including a limping ring announcer. We buckled in and off we went. With every refuelling stop on the way back to the States, we all held our collective breath and crossed our fingers that there would be no repeat of previous trouble or that new problems would arise. Thankfully, nothing like that occurred, and we made it back physically unscathed, but emotionally it was a different matter altogether. That landing and takeoff in Russia rattled the whole group. Some more than others but all of us were left with a bad taste in our mouths. If you were to ask anyone who was on that flight how bad it really was, I think they would all tell you it was the most terrifying in-flight incident they have ever been a part of. That is, with the exception of Ric Flair and JBL, who were both involved in plane crashes. I can't imagine what it was like to have been in a plane crash, survive the ordeal, and then come so close to being in another one. One thing I did forget to mention was when we all feared the plane was going down, a lot of the guys were looking to Ric Flair to see how he was reacting. I couldn't see Ric from my seat but I did see many looking in his direction. I kind of understand it but wondered, *What can Ric do from his passenger seat? He's not flying the darn plane.* I guess if he seemed to be calm maybe they thought that would keep them calm as well. Just thought I'd throw that little tidbit in.

When you look back at that harrowing experience, the media dubbing that other flight from the UK to the United States the "Flight from Hell" doesn't seem appropriate. That's the way I see it. Without a doubt, the Flight from Hell was that flight that nearly crashed in Russia.

As bad luck would have it, that was not the only aviation incident I had the misfortune of enduring. One thing you have to learn is to try not to think that the law of averages will catch up with you. On one unforgettable flight in Europe, I thought the law of averages had indeed caught up with me and the boys. This time it was a commercial flight, not chartered. We were heading to Zurich, Switzerland, from Frankfurt, Germany, on Lufthansa Airlines. As usual, the flight was uneventful until we began our descent into Zurich. There was an abnormal amount of turbulence, which rattled many of the passengers including wrestler Jamie Noble, who was sitting across the aisle from me, and fellow referee Mickie Henson, who was seated in my row by the window.

Jamie confided to me that he was very nervous about the excessive shaking and wondered how I was staying so calm. I had him fooled. On the inside I was having flashbacks of landing in Russia a few years before. I mentioned to Jamie that I was a little nervous but after the Russian ordeal, this was a cakewalk. I really didn't believe that, but I was just trying to put Jamie at ease. That's when he confessed to me that he didn't remember the landing in Russia because he slept through the whole thing. I didn't press the matter any further, and we sat back worrying about the situation we found ourselves in at the time.

The plane was on its final approach and the landing gear was engaged. All of a sudden, the engines sounded like they were thrust into full throttle, and we climbed very fast. Just as that happened, Mickie pointed out the window and made us aware of another plane we had narrowly avoided while coming in for the landing. That plane banked hard to its left as we climbed hard. Apparently, that other aircraft was taking off from the very runway we were supposed to land on. After circling, we again made our approach into Zurich and landed safely, although many of us were pretty shaken up. The show went on as scheduled that night. Of course the dominant conversation for the rest of the tour was that near-miss while landing in Zurich. I could get into the semantics of the term "near-miss" but I don't want to turn this into a George Carlin bit. Let's just leave it at this: we had a near-collision. Bit over!

All kidding aside, coming that close to disaster not once but twice affects people in many ways. While those two incidents were probably the most frightened I had ever been in my life, it really did not have a life-changing outcome for me. It's hard to explain but for some unknown reason, particularly after the second near-disaster, I had no fear of flying afterwards. It was almost as if any fear I previously had of flying was scared out of me. I now possessed a strange sense of composure anytime I flew after that day. I never bothered to question why I felt that way; I just embraced it and continued living the dream.

Travel woes were not only restricted to air travel. We drove practically every day from one town to another and sooner or later something happens that makes you think twice. Some of those moments are downright scary while others are just annoying and more of a pain in the butt than anything else. Sometimes it's more the guys you are travelling with who get under your skin.

One tour we were on began with a live event in Cape Girardeau, Missouri, if I'm not mistaken. It was early Saturday morning and I boarded a plane in Toronto and flew to St. Louis to meet with the guys I was travelling with on this tour. On this trip it was me, Tony

Chimel, WWE athletic trainer Larry Heck, and Hornswoggle. Yes, we added a fourth to the car. Actually, Hornswoggle made it three and a half people in the car. He hated when I would say that and he'd respond with a kick to the lower shin or a straight punch to the groin. I was not the only one who got his jabs in on the little guy. We all cracked on him but he held his own with the comebacks. Now for a smaller person, Swoggle had more luggage than both Chimel and I combined. Larry was the trainer so he had his equipment bag, which was large and took up a lot of truck space. As always, I took the initiative and started packing the rental car. I managed to get most of the bags in the trunk but a few smaller bags would have to go in the back seat with Larry and Swoggle.

Everything was business as usual. Arguing over what radio station we were listening to, one-liners about how old Chimel and I were, short jokes, and taking shots at Larry's ankle- and knee-taping abilities were all par for the course. We were all laughing it up pretty good when just outside St. Louis, we got a flat tire. The rear driver's side tire just deflated, so I pulled the car over on the shoulder of the highway and we all got out of the car. Larry called the rental car company, and they said it would take several hours before they could get anyone out to where we were to help. We couldn't wait that long so he asked them if we could put the spare on and drive back to the rental car location and get a replacement vehicle. They said no problem, so we started pulling all of our luggage out of the trunk to get to the spare.

Larry and I thought that with the four of us assisting, it would take no time at all to change the tire. What were we thinking? As Larry and I got busy making the necessary repairs, Chimel was preoccupied with a phone call while Swoggle's attention was directed at large trucks that were passing us on the highway and trying to get them to honk their horn. Not to mention it was cold out and our fingers were frozen and numb. We managed to put the temporary spare on, loaded the bags in the car, and drove back to exchange vehicles. All the way back Larry and I berated Chimel and

Swoggle for not being any help. We might as well have been talking to the flat tire; we would've got a better reply. All they did was try to justify their actions by saying they just would have been in the way and that Larry and I had it handled. They probably would not have been much help anyway, but the least they could have done was offer to help. Anyhow, we got back and they upgraded us to a minivan, which gave us more room. This ordeal was minor compared to others, but I just wanted to show that not all of our travel woes that we encounter on an almost weekly basis are of a life or death nature. Some are comical while others end up being very scary. They created memories that will stay with me forever. Some have also been forgotten but with the right prodding they will be remembered as well and be told one day.

Speaking of flat tires, I just remembered another situation travelling with the Punjabi Giant, the Great Khali. Khali was really a nice guy but the language barrier caused some problems at times. He did not drive, so every week someone would be assigned to chauffeur the big guy to get him from town to town and more importantly, to the shows on time. When Khali was on *Raw*, Marty Elias was assigned to him. Marty would tell us all horror stories about driving him all over town at all hours of the night. When Khali was drafted to the *SmackDown* brand, the office asked me if I would take on the duties of being his driver. The offer included a rental vehicle as well as the hotel all paid for by the WWE. You see, at this time I was no longer on the production/ring crew. I was now considered talent and responsible for those expenses myself, so the added perks suited me just fine. I was going to miss travelling with my regular partners. Those guys were fantastic as far as allowing me to ride with them. For example, Chimel and Larry were employees of the company and had their cars and all hotels paid for. In return for doing the driving, they let me ride with them and also stay in one of their rooms. We would play cards and usually the loser got me for a roommate.

Anyhow, back to my new travel companion. As I said, Khali was a good guy and we got along very well. We sat down with Howard Finkel, who at this time was working in the Talent Relation department, and he thoroughly explained that my duties were only to get Khali from point A to point B and that's it. That was nice of him but more often than not, I went a little beyond those duties. I was fine with it, plus the Great Khali paid for many of my meals so it was well worth it. He never took advantage of the situation and treated me with respect. I learned that first-hand on one particularly long drive from Las Vegas, Nevada, to San Diego, California. It was a Monday morning the day after a pay-per-view in Vegas. We had the entire day to drive to San Diego because there was no *SmackDown* live event scheduled for that day.

We slept in a bit and didn't get on the road until about 11:00 a.m. It was a nice sunny day as we headed west on I-15 towards California. Driving through the desert is boring and the big man was not very conversational so singing along with the radio was occupying my time. Then it happened: we were struck by the tire gods. The rear passenger tire was flatter than a Tony Chimel mattress. I pulled the sports utility vehicle over on the shoulder approximately 15 miles from Barstow, California, and called the rental car company, who were no help whatsoever, so we got out to change the tire. Since I had never owned an suv, my first order of business was to locate the spare. I deduced that I would find what I was looking for under the back of the hatch. That's exactly where it was, so we unloaded our bags, got out the lug wrench and jack, and got ready to start.

We ran into a major snag with the spare. Since it was located on the undercarriage of the vehicle, it was bolted on and we could not for the life of us figure out how to release it. After about 15 to 20 minutes of trying to figure it out, my brain finally kicked in and I went to the glove box to find the manual. Leaning on the suv as I thumbed through the manual, I felt the whole vehicle shaking. I walked to the back to see what was causing the trembling. As I got closer, I saw a pair of long legs protruding from under the back of the suv. Khali had taken it upon himself to try to dislodge the spare tire forcefully. Lying flat on his back, he was pulling on the spare relentlessly, and I truly believe, given another few minutes, he would have gotten the damn thing off.

I stopped him from causing any more damage and helped him get to his feet. We were going about this all wrong. There was a release on the inside of the storage space in the back of the suv. With that figured out, I proceeded to change the tire. A 15- to 20-minute operation lasted over an hour, mainly because I didn't think to read the owner's manual from the get-go. After tightening the last lug nut, we repacked the suv and made our way to San Diego without any further problems. It was comforting to know that my giant friend was there to help me. He was really very helpful. I didn't get all the complaining others did when they were asked to drive him from town to town. Maybe it was because we became good friends and I actually liked riding with the big guy. There was a bit of a language barrier at first, but it wasn't long before we understood each other. It even got to a point where guys would ask me to relay messages to Khali whenever his on-screen manager Ranjin Singh wasn't around to translate. I didn't speak Punjabi; I just repeated it to him in English. It may have been the delivery, I don't know. But for some strange reason we were able to communicate with one another. Some of you may not believe it, but I miss the big guy.

Travel woes are not reserved for cars and airplanes. There have been some real horror stories when it comes to hotel accommodations. Over the years, I have had the displeasure of staying in some really terrible dives. I could compile a list of rat traps and fleabag motels, but I would rather tell you about what Tony Chimel and I have named the worst hotel we have ever been booked in. First let me say, in this case worst doesn't refer to cleanliness. It's much more than that. I'm talking overall experience.

The winner is the Owl Hotel in Saitama, Japan. The hotel was not unclean; it was a combination of things that made for a rough stay. We had travelled to Japan for the first ever *Raw* and *SmackDown* television tapings held in the land of the rising sun. Filming took place in the Saitama Super Arena, which is a magnificent facility. When we arrived in Tokyo, we were informed by our international liaison Lynn that due to an error when booking rooms for the trip, the Tokyo Dome Hotel was filled to capacity. She had made arrangements for eight of us on the crew to stay at a hotel much closer to the venue in Saitama. It would have been nice to stay with everyone else in Tokyo, but we were fine with the plan. They loaded us and our luggage in a minibus and took us to the other hotel. Lynn had to go with the larger group to the main hotel to ensure everyone checked in without any problems.

When we arrived at our hotel, the red flags went up almost immediately. The driver dropped us off and left without making sure we got our rooms. Then the young woman at the front desk did not speak any English. It took us awhile but we finally all got checked in and took turns taking the tiny elevators to our rooms.

On a side note, I had lost a card game before we left the United States and because of that, I had to carry the "Bull Horns" in a makeshift case for JBL's limousine for TV. It was kind of a rib on me as the horns were one long piece and the case was about five feet long.

Now, back to the Owl. After squeezing into the lift with my bags and horns in tow, I got to my floor and was about to put my key in the door when Chimel popped his head out of his room. He didn't look very happy, that's for sure. He asked me if I had been in my room yet. I looked at him and answered sarcastically, "Yes I have, but my room is so small, my bags don't fit in the room."

He laughed and said with a scowl, "So your room is like mine then?"

What? Something was not right here. Before I could get my key in the door, Richie Posner, who was head of the "Magic" department at TV, popped his head out and surveyed the situation. Now I was curious and hurried to open the door to my room. I will say this, it wasn't the cleanest room I'd ever stayed in but not bad. It was definitely the smallest room I would ever spend a night in. Without exaggeration, I had not enough space for my luggage. I had my smaller bag on the tiny desk and my bigger bag on the floor behind the door. There was no room for the horns so I had to try to convince the non-English-speaking lady at the front desk to lock them up in a room down there. Lucky for me there was a businessman in the lobby, and he translated for me.

With the horns taken care of it was time to go back to the room and really see what we had to deal with. Here's the room layout. As you walked into the closet, I mean room, on the left was the bathroom. It was so small that if I needed to sit down on the toilet, I could not close the bathroom door because my legs were in the way. There was a stand-up shower that was tiny too. The bed was a step past the bathroom on the left as well. It was a small single bed with a solid mattress, not to mention my feet hung over the end. I felt like Andre the Giant in that bed.

The other thing that made me suspicious of my surroundings was the coin slot on the ten-inch screen television. That's right, my laptop screen was bigger than the TV in my room. Too bad there was no Internet access, at least none that I could access. Well, at least I had a good view — *not*! I opened the window and all I could see were old buildings and laundry wires everywhere filled with hanging clothes. It was not exactly ideal conditions to say the least.

We all got together and decided that since we had the rest of the day to kill, we would go scout the area for something to eat. After sampling the local cuisine, we went back to the hotel and played cards in the lobby. Usually we play in someone's room but I think you can guess why that was not an option.

The next morning we made our way to the arena. It was a setup day which meant the stage, lighting, and ring would be put together and the first of two TV tapings began the next day. We finished our duties rather quickly and before we left to go back to our cubicles at the Owl, we mentioned our rooms to Lynn to see if she could do anything about getting us into a better hotel. She tried with no luck so we made the best of it for at least one more day. When others asked us how bad the rooms were, Chimel and I got into full Rodney Dangerfield mode.

"The room is so small, when I put the key in the door I broke the window."

"That hotel is so bad, they stole my towel."

"The hotel was so bad, room service had an unlisted number."

"I called the front desk and asked them to send up a larger room."

It was our way of stressing our point with humour instead of sounding like whiny schoolkids. It didn't work that day but the next day, Chimel had an ally who would resolve the hotel dilemma.

Shane McMahon was at the TV tapings in Japan and when Chimel saw him in the production office, he immediately explained our hotel plight to him. Now Chimel and Shane go way back to when Shane was learning the business from the bottom up. When he was setting up rings, Shane was on Chimel's ring crew. Upon hearing about our hotel conditions, Shane made sure that the matter was handled right away. Before you knew it, we had a driver take us back to the Owl Hotel, grab all our stuff, and take us to the Tokyo Dome Hotel to stay with everyone else. I can't speak for the other guys' rooms but mine was large. A king-size bed, a big chair, a nice TV, and a bathroom that was bigger than the entire room at the Owl. Oh, and my favourite amenity was the heated toilet seat. You read that right, a heated toilet seat. Not only was the seat heated, the toilet also acted as a bidet. The control panels on the side of the seat made it feel like you were in the captain's chair on the Starship *Enterprise*. The difference between the two hotels was night and day.

It's experiences like that that make great stories to tell your grandkids. As much as I disliked that Owl Hotel, it was kind of fun having to deal with the obstacles presented to us. Hard times are sometimes fun times.

CHAPTER 13

Montreal from My Vantage Point

Whenever I speak with wrestling fans, especially those who were fans back in the '90s, one question almost always comes up: "Were you there for the Montreal Screwjob. Was it a work or was it real? What was the reaction like backstage?" There are many more questions but these are the ones most often asked. The Survivor Series 1997 in all likelihood spawned more debate and became the most infamous moment in professional wrestling or sports entertainment history. The events of that evening are still talked about. I can remember it as if it just happened. We all knew that Bret was leaving the company for the competition in a month or so. He and Shawn had well-documented disagreements in the past. These two even came to blows in the locker room one night in Hartford, Connecticut. So everyone was curious how things would play out on this night.

I guess people either don't remember the entire match or just forgot that I was involved in the early part of the match. As Shawn Michaels and Bret Hart battled all over the arena in Montreal, we followed them everywhere. Our main duty was to keep the fans away from the boys as they fought all over the building. It was part of the match. So, to answer the question about being there that night, yes I was there. After our little part was done, we retreated back to the Gorilla Position and waited for the finish of the match. The finish as it was told to us by Pat Patterson was that the match would end with a non-finish. Members from both D-X and the Hart Foundation would get involved and the match would be thrown out. Pat would send us, the referees, to the ring at the right time to break up the brawl and restore order.

Watching the match unfold on the monitor, I was preparing myself for when we would be sent to the ring. Also at Gorilla were Owen Hart, Jim Neidhart, Davey Boy Smith, and Hunter Hearst Helmsley. They were also waiting for their cue to go to the ring. A funny thing happened on the way to the finish, though. Well, it was not funny but it was definitely unexpected.

Earl Hebner, who was the referee for the match, had just taken his planned ref bump. With the referee down and out, HBK applied Bret's own finishing maneuver, the Sharpshooter, on him. Here is where things got bizarre. I heard someone in my earpiece say, "*Okay, Earl, get up. Get up now!*" I looked over to the microphone that the producers use to communicate to the referees and the instructions were not coming from there. I can only speculate that whoever told Earl to get up was in the production truck or ringside. Either way, the call didn't come from Gorilla that I saw. Earl then made his way to his feet and acted as if he was checking to see if Bret would submit to the Sharpshooter. Without waiting for the Hitman to reply, Earl called for the bell. He then bolted out of the ring to where his brother Dave was waiting in a car with all of Earl's clothes in the parking garage. Earl jumped in and they sped off.

It must be noted that Bret allegedly refused to lose the title to Shawn in Montreal. I say allegedly only because I was not privy to those discussions, but it has been made public knowledge that Bret wanted to relinquish the title the next night on TV from Ottawa,

Ontario. I'm not sure about those details but you can read Bret's book if you want to know the back story to what transpired.

Everyone in Gorilla began to freak out wondering what had just happened. It took a few seconds but you could see in the faces of some of the guys that they realized what they had just seen. It took me a little longer to clue in but suddenly, I too understood what went on. It was a plan devised to get the WWE title off of Bret without his co-operation. Shawn did a great job of acting as if he had no part in what went down. Of course years later we found out that he was fully aware of the plan. Bret's focus was not on Shawn, rather, the main target of his displeasure was Vince McMahon. Bret spat in Vince's face. As everyone left ringside and headed backstage, Bret remained in the ring, lashing out by destroying the announcing position.

In the back, I along with many others was unsure of how to react to what we had just witnessed. It was a moment that those of us who worked on the crew didn't have a lot of time to digest. We had to get right to work and disassemble the ring and go to Ottawa for *Raw* the next day. The ride to Ottawa that night was quieter than usual, but there was some talk about it. No one sided with Bret or the company. Believe it or not, we were more concerned about Earl and how he was handling the whole thing. Then the discussion turned to "What would you do if you were in Earl's shoes?" I could not answer that question, truthfully. Unless you are put in that position, how could you know what you would do? For people who say that they would have refused to do it if they were in Earl's shoes, I say that's easy to say when your job and the ability to provide for your family could be in jeopardy. As much as I love the wrestling business, my family comes first and always will.

No one knew what to expect the next day in Ottawa. There was talk that many of the boys would boycott *Raw* that night in protest of what went down in Montreal. A few did but returned to work soon after as they were under contract and faced potential legal action if they did not return. Rick Rude left the company and became the first wrestler to appear on wcw's *Monday Nitro* and *Monday Night Raw* on the same night. It was a taped episode of *Raw* airing that night, making it possible for Rude to accomplish the feat.

While things worked out fine for Rick Rude, Earl Hebner was dealing with his own dilemma. He told us how terrible he felt about his role in the Montreal Screwjob and that he had contemplated quitting his job. In his mind, he had betrayed a friend. Several locker room veterans sat down to speak to Earl to let him know that they did not blame him for what happened. He was just following orders. It was just what Earl needed to hear. They ended up convincing him that he should stay with the company and that he had their support.

The biggest news to come out of the Ottawa live *Raw* was the famous interview Vince McMahon did with Jim Ross. Vince defended his position and explained to a worldwide television audience his side of the story. I thought it was a bold decision by the boss to go on TV with a black eye and reveal to everyone things that the public normally don't get to share. Listening to the interview as it aired on TV, I was amazed when Vince first uttered the words, "Vince McMahon didn't screw Bret Hart; Bret screwed Bret!" Amazed because as soon as I heard him say it, you knew that it was only the beginning of a master plan the boss had. That one line would be the catalyst for turning Vince into Mr. McMahon, the most hated heel in the industry. It was the shot in the arm the wwf needed in their ongoing ratings war with wcw. We took the lead in the ratings and never looked back. In my humble opinion, Vince McMahon may have had this idea of being the "Evil Owner" for a while. The circumstances that night in Montreal were the perfect storm of events that allowed him to present the Mr. McMahon character to the world.

The day after the Ottawa *Raw*, we were in Cornwall, Ontario, to tape the following week's *Raw*. This was the day Vince McMahon held a meeting with all the talent to explain his reasoning for what had transpired two days prior. We all sat back and listened to the

Me with the world's greatest tag team,
Shelton Benjamin & Charlie Haas, in Iraq.
Personal Photo

Chris Benoit & me getting ready for
a helicopter ride while in Iraq for the
first Tribute to the Troops.
Personal Photo

The Big Show & me outside one of
Saddam Hussein's palaces, which
served as our accommodations in
Iraq. Personal Photo

Sitting in the back of a Humvee going to the barracks. Personal photo

About to paint the ring steps in Iraq. Personal photo

Me with John Bradshaw Layfield & Charles Robinson in Iraq. Personal Photo

Tony Chimel & me at Camp Victory, Baghdad, Iraq, before the Tribute to the Troops show. Personal photo

Eddie Guerrero & me in Iraq. Personal photo

Vince McMahon & me at the Atlanta airport after returning from Iraq. Personal photo

Tony Chimel, Brian Hebner, me, & Charles Robinson on our way to the WWE Hall of Fame ceremony in Detroit, Michigan. Personal photo

I "bet" you can guess who this is. Couldn't resist. Yes, Charlie Hustle, Pete Rose. Personal photo

Jermaine Jackson & me backstage in Anaheim, California. Personal photo

The gang is all here: Scott Armstrong, Mickey Henson, Jack Doan, John Cone, Charles Robinson, Chad Patton, me, Marty Elias, & Mike Posey. Absent was Mike Chioda. Photo courtesy Charles Robinson

Hanging with Buzz Sawyer, circa 1983. If I looked like that today, I would be on the No Fly List. Personal photo

The Air Canada Centre, October 2002. Lesnar versus Palumbo. Photo by Steve Argintaru

Virgil & me at Maple Leaf Gardens.
Photo by Steve Argintaru

The refs (Jack Doan, Mike Sparks, me, & Mike Chioda) give Will Sasso a hand after he got "stunned" by Stone Cold Steve Austin.
Personal photo

John D'Amico, Tony Chimel, & me having lunch on a patio in Port Elizabeth, South Africa, circa 1997. Personal photo

Me, Gavin (Overseas Ring Coordinator), & Chimel after setting up the ring at the soccer stadium in Johannesburg, South Africa. Personal photo

Dustin Runnels (Goldust) & me in South Africa, 1997. Personal photo

Me & Tony Garea in South Africa, 1997. Personal photo

Putting finishing touches on the ring.

Personal photo

Working through the "pain."

Photo by Steve Argintaru

Having trouble keeping a straight face.

Photo by Steve Argintaru

Trying to tell Gunner Scott who leads this dance. Photo by Steve Argintaru

Mike Sparks, Dave
Hebner, me, & Tim White
in Richmond, Virginia.
Personal photo

The WWF crew on tour in
South Africa posing in front
of our "vintage" charter
plane. Personal photo

Ron Bleggi (pyro guy),
Larry Heck (WWE trainer),
John Cena, & me golfing
in Scotland. Personal photo

boss. I can't speak for anyone else, but from my perspective, he had no choice but to do damage control with his talent. I can't tell you if the boys bought his explanation or not but to me it really didn't matter if he was being truthful or not. I needed my job so I wasn't going anywhere or saying anything. As terrible as I genuinely felt for Bret, for me it was business as usual. I didn't have the luxury of making a statement by not showing up for work. The thing that surprised me the most was how much the Screwjob was referenced and replicated for so many years afterwards. That day will live in infamy in the history of pro wrestling as quite possibly its most controversial moment.

For years afterwards, I couldn't help thinking about that day and the repercussions. Then a very different idea emerged in my overactive mind. What if the entire scenario was an elaborate plan? What if the chain of events as they unfolded were carefully mapped out by Vince in an attempt to get the end results he got? This may be a conspiracy theory but there are a few things I found strange when I think back on it.

First off, according to Bret, he spoke with Earl Hebner the day before Montreal and told him that he felt WWF might ask Earl to screw him in the match at Survivor Series. Why would he even think that? Either Bret was tipped off or he has keen ESP.

Second, Bret was wearing a microphone all day every day for the documentary someone was filming about him. Everybody knew the cameras were around and that everything might be caught on film or audio. This would put most people on their best behaviour. So when Bret went into Vince's office to discuss the finish of his match, he had his mic-pack conveniently turned on as he talked to the boss. The crew picked up the entire conversation and recorded it. I believe Vince knew it was possible Bret was wired. Therefore Vince either made an uncharacteristic error in judgement or he just didn't care that Bret or, more accurately, his film crew might have been recording them.

Last but certainly not least is why any boss would send a

commodity as valuable as a Bret Hart to the competition, especially when the competition is beating you every week in the ratings is beyond me. I don't consider myself a businessman the calibre of Vince McMahon but to me, Vince telling Bret to go ahead and negotiate with the "enemy" makes no sense. Then I thought it could be a long-term plan put together by both Vince and Bret. Maybe I'm way off base or maybe it is true that when you have been in the wrestling business for a while, you tend to believe everything is a work. So let me present to you what my overzealous imagination thinks may have happened.

DISCLAIMER: I have no inside knowledge of what really occurred. This is all just speculation, conjecture, and more than likely just some fantasy booking on my part.

Let's just say that sometime in the second half of 1997, Vince held a meeting with Bret and Vince told him about the company's apparent financial problems. What if the two of them mapped out a strategy that would see the boss screw the loyal employee? The loyal employee ends up working with the rival promotion while the boss becomes this evil villain who needs to be stopped. In the meantime, the evil boss sells shares to turn the family business into a publicly traded company generating enough cash flow and assets to keep his organization afloat. Fast-forward three years and once the employee's very lucrative contract with the competition ends, he returns to his original company to exact revenge on the boss who screwed him. Now that would draw money! Why things didn't play out this way one can only guess, but you have to admit, it really is a pretty good story. I do know better than to think what happened was anything other than genuine. I truly believe that Bret was an unwilling participant and it took him 13 years to finally find some sort of closure. Hopefully after all the times the Montreal Screwjob has been mentioned and rehashed in the last 15 or so years, we can all finally put the matter to bed. If those directly involved can move on at last, so should the rest of us. I definitely have.

CHAPTER 14

More Tales from
Inside the Ring

Professional wrestling is a business that most who are in it take very seriously. That does not stop the boys from having a little fun. Not all of the laughs take place away from the ring. Some of that fun takes place inside the squared circle. There are countless times when I struggled to keep my composure and hold in my laughter. There were a few instances when it was impossible for me to hold it in. As I stated earlier, I take great pride in my ability to stay in serious referee mode. It didn't always work, mainly because some guys just had a knack for getting me to break.

Owen Hart was the master at getting everyone to crack up. Besides the foreign napkin story, there was another encounter I had with Owen in the ring that made me burst out laughing. He was wrestling a young man by the name of Carl LeDuc. Carl was the son of Paul LeDuc, one of a pair of famous wrestling brothers from Quebec. At this point in time, Carl had very little wrestling experience. His WWF debut match was an opening match. He faced off against and defeated Justin "Hawk" Bradshaw, who later became JBL. I'll get back to Owen, but I just remembered Carl's first ever

WWF wrestling match, which took place at the Montreal Molson Centre in August 1996 in front of a huge crowd. I was assigned that match and went to find JBL to see what the he wanted in the match.

John asked me if I knew anything about this kid. I explained to him that I had never met the kid before that day but I would go find him and bring him to John to go over the match. JBL introduced himself to the young fellow and asked him what his finish was. Since he was going over in his hometown, JBL wanted to make the kid look good. When young Carl answered that he did not have a finish, JBL asked him another question, "Just out of curiosity, how long have you been working?"

Carl's answer was, "I've been working about three weeks."

JBL was very interested and had a follow-up question, "Who trained you?"

Carl replied that his dad gave him some pointers but he was mostly self-taught. The look on JBL's face was priceless. He looked over at me and smiled. He looked back at Carl and asked him, "So, what can you do?"

I wish I could remember what the answer was but by this point, I was scratching my head in disbelief. I couldn't understand for the life of me why anyone would allow this very green rookie to take part in a WWF event when he was blatantly not ready for it. Finally JBL just asked if he could perform a small package. A small package is a simple roll-up pinning maneuver. Once again the young man's response raised more eyebrows when he said he did not know how to do the move. A clearly flustered JBL looked at me and said, "Jimmy, put me in a small package."

I hesitated for a moment, and he repeated what he said. I'm not a wrestler but after so many years in the ring, I knew how to apply most of the basic moves. I small-packaged JBL and held him there for a few seconds. When he asked Carl if he got that, he said, "I think so." JBL then said to him not to worry about a thing and to listen to him out there. He would tell him the right time to hit the finish. Carl agreed and I didn't see him again until we were in the ring. Carl's entrance was the best part of his performance that night. He did not belong in any ring, let alone a WWF ring and JBL introduced him to the world of pro wrestling. JBL didn't kill the guy or anything like that but he was a bit snug and the kid was definitely feeling every blow. After a few minutes of agony, JBL ended the debacle by literally putting himself in a pinning predicament and pulling Carl on top of him. I counted to three and the Molson Centre erupted in a chorus of boos. As much as Quebecers love to cheer for their own, they are also intelligent enough to recognize what they see.

In the backstage area, a frustrated JBL greeted the young man, shook his hand, and asked him if everything was okay. To his credit, Carl shook JBL's hand, said everything was fine, and thanked him for the match. I will give him credit for not bitching about the solid chops and forearm shots he took. Now that was not the funny part I was talking about but it leads to the next evening in Ottawa when Carl would face none other than the notorious ribber, Owen Hart.

The WWF officials decided to have Carl wrestle Owen mainly because they felt Owen would take it easy on the kid. The only instructions the agents gave Owen was not to let the youngster run the ropes. In other words, do not throw him into the ropes or run a spot that required Carl to bounce off the ropes because he didn't know how. Owen agreed and went on his way to get ready. Once again I had the great fortune of refereeing. After I got the finish from Owen, it was time for the match.

I called for the bell and right away I could tell that the prankster had something up his sleeve. They locked up and Owen told Carl to grab a headlock. Carl did what he was told. It looked a bit awkward but he applied a headlock. So far so good, or so I thought. Then I leaned in to hear what the next spot was. I almost burst out laughing when I heard Owen say, "Okay, I'll shoot you off and then criss-cross spot."

For those who are unfamiliar with that term, it refers to a spot in a match where one wrestler runs back and forth bouncing off the ropes while his opponent does the same thing, only the other way. So one guy runs north-south in the ring while the other one runs east-west. It was one of the funniest things I had ever seen in the ring. As Carl would run towards the ropes, he would come to a near stop, turn around, lean against the ropes, and start running at the other ropes. It made him look absolutely horrible. Owen in the meantime was running the ropes like he was in slow motion, then running backwards, moving as if he were running on the moon. It was hilarious and I roared with laughter. The rest of the match was very simple and ended mercifully when Owen finally finished the match with the Sharpshooter. Owen did it again: he made the entire locker room laugh.

Another superstar who could get me to burst out laughing was David "Fit" Finlay. Fit was not only one of the toughest men I have ever met but one of the best in-ring performers I have ever had the pleasure to work with. He has to be one of the most underrated wrestlers ever. He did like to have his fun as well. He had a great sense of humour outside the ring but his antics inside the ring had me laughing on more than one occasion. Usually, those laughs involved the shillelagh Fit carried with him to the ring. No one was safe and Finlay knew how to discreetly cause minor pain whenever he wanted. He could also leave lasting marks, as some of our very own security people found out the hard way.

One instance that stands out in my mind concerns Todd Harris, who was one of the WWE's security personnel. Todd was a really good guy and loved to have fun with the fans. Part of what made him good at his job was that he knew how to defuse situations with his good-natured attitude. One thing Todd learned very quickly was that you never turn your back on Finlay, especially when he has a shillelagh in his hand. This one evening, I was standing in the ring with Finlay and his shillelagh waiting for his opponent, Kane. As Kane entered the ring, he looked right at Finlay and then turned his attention to something behind Finlay. It was Todd comforting a female fan who was pretending to be afraid of the Big Red Monster, Kane.

Fit turned around to see Todd's head buried in this girl's ample cleavage. Fit looked at me, looked back at Kane, and said, "Watch this!" In a flash, Fit slid under the bottom rope, walked over to Todd, and promptly tapped him on the top of the head. By tapped I mean it was a good knock on the noggin. Todd screamed like a little girl as he tried to run away from what became an onslaught of shillelagh shots. Before jumping out of the ring to try to save poor Todd, I turned and saw Kane with his hand covering his face. You could clearly see from how his shoulders were heaving up and down that he couldn't control his laughter. Once again I burst out laughing as I went to save Todd. I eventually convinced (wink, wink) Fit to re-enter the ring. I slid under the bottom rope into the ring and froze. There I was, on my hands and knees right at Finlay's feet, looking directly into the shillelagh. Finlay looked down at me and said, "You are so lucky we have a match or this would really hurt."

That's when he tapped me on my follicly challenged head. It hurt but it was nothing compared to the beating our security guy took. For the rest of the tour Chimel, who was a frequent target of Fit's shillelagh, and I joked that the wwe needed to hire extra security for their regular security.

Todd was not the only security guy to get pummelled by the dreaded shillelagh; Jimmy Noonan felt the wrath of Finlay after he directed some derogatory comments at the Fighting Irishman. We were on a tour of Spain when, after a match, Noonan made a comment to Finlay about not being fast enough to get him with the shillelagh. Once he uttered the words "old man," Fit chased Noonan up into the arena seats. We couldn't see from our vantage point what happened but when Noonan returned backstage, he had several noticeable lumps on his clean-shaven head. Again we were laughing our asses off. Noonan claimed he would never doubt any of the boys' claims again. Those were just a few of

Finlay's many hilarious encounters. He provided so many happy moments for not just me but for everyone. I miss Fit. Not only was he an agent and my superior, he was a friend and a real stand-up guy. His advice and guidance helped me so much; I will always remember that. The wrestling business needs more Fit Finlays as far as I'm concerned.

As funny as some things were, there were other cases where you didn't laugh. Sometimes what you were witnessing made you cringe. One such time was during the infamous tag-team match between the Johnny Grunge and Rocco Rock collective known as Public Enemy against JBL and Faarooq (Ron Simmons), the APA. Public Enemy was new to the WWF, having just arrived from ECW. Their gimmick was that they put their opponents through tables. In this match with the APA, I honestly do not recall what the planned finish was, but it didn't go as scheduled; that I do know for sure. What I remember most from the match was that right from the beginning, JBL and Faarooq walked to the ring with a look of utter disdain on their faces. As soon as they hit the ring, they tore into Public Enemy as if those guys owed them money. It was not a wrestling match, it was a brutal beating. In fact, it was the most brutal beating I have ever personally witnessed.

The APA not only punched, kicked, and clotheslined the living shit out of these guys, they hit Public Enemy with chairs, tables, ring steps — even the timekeeper's table was used as a weapon. I was like a deer in the headlights. I could not believe the punishment they were dishing out. After JBL hit one of those guys with one of the most vicious chair shots I have ever seen, Gerald Brisco yelled into my earpiece, "Jimmy, are you going to ring the bell anytime soon and end this thing?" That's when I called for the bell to end the match but that didn't stop the pounding the APA was administering. There was no way I was getting in the way of JBL or Faarooq. Obviously something had set these two off and Public Enemy paid the price for it.

The only version I heard about what caused the annihilation

was told to me by JBL. As he explained it, the two teams had worked the finish for the match and everything seemed fine. While I was standing in the ring waiting for the teams to come down, as JBL tells it, just as Public Enemy's music began, they turned to JBL and said they didn't like the finish and were changing it, then went through the curtain towards the ring. A stunned JBL looked over at Faarooq, who asked what PE had said. JBL repeated what he had heard and Faarooq just said, "So they don't want to do the finish, huh? Well okay, we'll change the finish for them" or something along those lines. A furious APA marched to the ring and unleashed their assault. The bottom line is, two guys got their asses handed to them and after the match they walked into the Gorilla Position, shook the APA's hands, thanked them for the match, and left. I'm not here to judge whether or not what happened was justified. That decision is left to those involved. I'm just telling you what happened from my viewpoint. It was another memorable moment for this kid from Canada, but not the last one for sure.

There was another Royal Rumble memory that stands out for me personally. The date was Sunday, January 30, 2005, the place Fresno, California's Save Mart Center. The ending of the Royal Rumble match was memorable for many reasons. The first reason was because of the controversial ending. The final two men left in the ring were *Raw*'s Batista and *SmackDown*'s John Cena. At this time in their careers, they were both very popular fan favourites. They were arguably the two most popular superstars on their respective brands. As these two beasts battled to eliminate each other, something unexpected happened. Batista had Cena in a position to Batista Bomb him over the top rope to the outside. Cena hung onto Big Dave and they both tumbled over the top rope to the floor, landing simultaneously. For the record, this was not the planned finish for the match. In fact, Batista was supposed to hang onto the top rope and only Cena was to be eliminated. This unexpected turn began a chain of events that could not have worked out any better if you had planned the whole thing.

Let me explain. Batista and John Cena crashed to the floor at virtually the same time. Jack Doan, being the ranking *Raw* official at ringside, immediately signalled that Cena hit the ground first and Batista was indeed your winner. Batista was slated to win all along so Jack just raised his hand. Fellow *SmackDown* ref Charles Robinson was not convinced that Cena had landed first and was not comfortable about going along with Jack's decision. As Charles and I were discussing what we should do, we heard in our earpieces that on the replay, which they had reviewed several times in the back, it was inconclusive as to who hit the ground first. Someone said in our earpieces for one of the *SmackDown* refs to raise Cena's hand. Charles was closer to where they landed than I was so I assumed he would go ahead and raise his hand. But "Little Naitch" kind of hesitated and looked at me, which I took as him wanting me to raise Cena's hand. Only thing was, John wasn't aware of what we were doing and instinctively jumped back into the ring and raised his arms triumphantly in the air. I followed him in the ring and raised his hand, signalling that Cena was the winner of the 2005 Royal Rumble. Jack raised Batista's arm again, which led to a battle of the arm raising. All this was what you might call "impromptu" as all of us refs continued debating over who we thought had won: *Raw* refs calling Batista the winner while the *SmackDown* refs sided with Cena.

While we continued our disagreement, we could hear again in our earpieces that they were frantically looking for Eric Bischoff and Teddy Long, the *Raw* and *SmackDown* general managers respectively, to come out to help settle the situation. I guess they thought the competing general managers would make for good TV. Since they were not found in a timely fashion, the Chairman himself burst out from the Gorilla Position and stormed his way to the ring. As Vince McMahon got closer to the ring, his pace quickened and he dove under the bottom rope to get in the ring. One little problem though, as Mr. McMahon entered the ring, he hit his knees on the metal portion of the ring and when he attempted to stand up, he tore both his quadriceps muscles and fell backwards on the seat of his pants, where he remained for several minutes, all the while telling us how he wanted us to proceed.

Once we got our instruction, we all cleared out of the ring, except for Big Dave and John of course. Even Vincent Kennedy McMahon left the ring and slowly made his way backstage, not wanting any help. We had no idea how severe the boss's injury was at the time because he managed to make it to the back on his own. I can only imagine how much pain he was masking. The boss does not ever want to show any weaknesses and on this night he did not. Meanwhile, back in the ring, John Cena and Batista went into overtime. They had a very brief exchange before Batista finally eliminated Cena to become the 2005 Royal Rumble winner and go on to *WrestleMania 21* to face Triple H for the world championship. As for John Cena, he didn't do too badly for himself either as he went on to win the WWE title from JBL, also at *WrestleMania 21*.

When playing this match back, I can't help but remember how calm we all were under such extenuating circumstances. Not once did I or any of the other refs feel like we didn't have the matter under control. Sometimes things happen for a reason. The spontaneity made for good drama. That pretty much says it all. To this day, not many people know exactly what happened that night. Now you all know why this is my all-time favourite Royal Rumble moment. So much happened in such a small time frame that, like I said before, this could not have come off any better even if we had planned it that way. Whenever I talk to people about that match and finish, they all say the same thing. They all thought it played out as planned and never realized that we flew by the seat of our pants that night. A job well done by all.

Dark matches were always a good source of entertainment, not only for the fans but for the boys as well. For those who don't know what dark matches are, when the WWE holds a televised event or taping, they have matches that are just for the live audience. They are not aired on TV. Now the pre-show type of dark match generally features non-contracted talent and is essentially a tryout match for these guys who are trying to get signed by the company. Most of the time, we would alternate who would referee these dark matches and no one complained. Then something happened that changed that attitude in a hurry.

It all started innocently enough when Gerald Brisco asked the referee in the ring to do jumping jacks. The dark match had not started yet and the ref (I believe it was Brian Hebner) just looked towards the camera with this confused look. Gerald repeated his demand and the ref performed the jumping jacks. We all heard him and rushed to the Gorilla Position to watch Brian in action. It was pretty funny but that was not the end of it. During the match, Gerald told the ref to do a cartwheel. Again the ref looked puzzled but Gerald said to him that if he didn't do a cartwheel, not to come back to Gorilla. Right there in the middle of the dark match, the referee did a cartwheel. We all laughed our butts off. It was the worst thing we could have done, especially in front of Gerald, because he made absolutely sure that we all had an opportunity to perform a cartwheel for him. This went on for quite a while. All of us had no choice but to do what we were told.

Then a new player entered the fray. It was my turn and I was refereeing a dark match fully expecting to hear Brisco telling me to do something out of the ordinary. Then I heard a familiar voice tell me to do a forward roll. It wasn't Gerald but the voice was unmistakable. It seemed that Stone Cold Steve Austin had caught wind of what was happening during the dark matches and decided he wanted in on the action. Not wanting to upset the Rattlesnake, I did a forward roll. Then he told me to do a baseball slide into the three count. The guys hit their finish and I slid in to count like I was stealing second base. He must have left the microphone on in the back because I could hear everybody in Gorilla laughing.

Every week it was the same routine. One of us refs would work the dark match and the others would gather at Gorilla to watch and laugh. Stone Cold became a regular, joining us when he could, providing he wasn't doing a pre-tape or something but he was there more often than not. Then one week it all came to a crashing halt. Vince McMahon stormed up to the Gorilla Position and angrily asked Brisco, "What the hell are my referees doing out there? I look at the monitor in my office and the ref does a cartwheel — this stops *now!*"

With that, the era of dark match cartwheels, jumping jacks, forward rolls, etc. was over. It was fun while it lasted but it was not the only time that the WWE made a referee the butt of a joke. I fell victim to the shenanigans. It all had to do with the annual Thanksgiving Day–themed show and an inflatable pool full of gravy. That's right, I said gravy.

Thanksgiving Day marks an important time of the year. For those living in the United States of America, Thanksgiving means that there are certain traditions you can count on. Giving thanks for all we have, gathering with family and friends, turkey dinner with all the fixings, the Macy's parade, and, of course, all-day football. In the WWE, it is no different. They have their own annual customs that the WWE universe has come to expect.

The crew and stage hands will usually dress as pilgrims. There is a large banquet table set up somewhere with an enormous feast placed on it which could probably feed the entire WWE roster. *Okay*, maybe only 25% of the roster but it is still a lot of food. With all that food you just know that it is inevitable that a food fight will occur. No one is immune from being splattered with flying turkey, cranberry sauce, biscuits, and mashed potatoes. Oh yes, I almost forgot about the *gravy!*

The date, November 22, 2001; the place, the Crown Coliseum in Fayetteville, North Carolina. I was assigned a match that I had never participated in before. I was scheduled to officiate the women's title match between the champion Trish Stratus and Stacy Keibler. I had refereed many ladies' matches before so at first I didn't think anything of it. Then they informed me that this match would be the first ever gravy bowl match. *What the heck is a gravy bowl match?* I thought. As it was explained to me, the participants would begin the match at the previously mentioned banquet table. It would start off as a food fight and spill into a large inflatable pool filled with gravy, where the match would finish.

The only thing I thought to ask was, "Where am I going to be while this match takes place?" I was told that I would not have to enter the pool during the match. I was to remain on the outside and help the ladies out of the pool afterwards. That's when my Spidey senses started to tingle. I had a sneaking suspicion that I was in for a little surprise.

Watching the crew set up the gravy bowl/pool was enlightening. Not only did they fill it with freezing cold water, they dumped an enormous amount of powdered gravy mix and began to stir the concoction with rowing oars. Don't ask me where they got the oars. The more I surveyed the situation, the more I thought about my IFB pack. The IFB pack is a small receiver refs carry in their back pockets with a wire that runs up on the inside of the ref's shirt and is attached to an earpiece so the producer can communicate with us. If by some happenstance I were to somehow make my way into the pool, how would I keep the IFB dry?

Always trying to be proactive, I went to see Richie Posner. Posner was in charge of the "special" projects, and I'll just leave it at that for now. I explained the issue I was having with keeping my receiver dry and, as usual, he had a brilliant idea. Richie walked over to one of his road cases, opened a drawer, and pulled out two condoms. You read that right, two condoms. He suggested encasing the IFB inside the two condoms, I suppose in case one broke, and tying off the end tightly so that no liquid could seep in if I were to get wet (pun intended).

It was now time for the match. Me and my double-bagged IFB were ready. Trish and Stacy began the match by throwing food at each other. I totally forgot to mention the pies earlier but they were abundant as well. Eventually, the ladies made their way towards the pool and, lo and behold, into the gravy bowl they went. If I was sure my wife would never read this story, I would comment on having the best seat in the house, so let's just say two beautiful and very wet divas in tight clinging dresses . . . sorry, drifted off there for a second, but I'm back now. After splashing around in the gravy for a few minutes, Trish put Stacy in a modified camel clutch. Stacy tapped in the gravy and the match was over.

Of course, being the gentleman I am, I first assisted Trish out of the pool and raised her hand, declaring her the winner and still women's champ. I then went over to help Stacy out of the pool. I gave her a helping hand. She took it and stepped out. She then turned to me and began screaming. Just as I was about to say something, Stacy reared back and shoved me as hard as she could. The only problem was that the gravy-filled pool was now behind me. In I went, looking like a guy who fell off the back of a speedboat that just hit the gas. I wonder if George Clooney has to deal with this sort of thing.

As I struggled to get to my feet, another thought popped into my head. Not only was my referee uniform soaked, my ref shoes were now drenched and weighed what felt like 20 pounds each. It was going to be really tough to get my shoes dry but I had to get the smell out of my ref clothes as well. As I turned to exit the knee-deep liquid, I noticed that my referee brothers and others were gathered and having a grand old time laughing at my expense. Never one to disappoint, I pretended to have trouble getting out of the pool and took a pratfall landing back into the gravy. Everyone popped big time for my little gag. After doing a little backstroke, I made a second try to exit the pool and took an even bigger bump back in the gravy. Everyone was now in stitches. Everyone that is except Gerald Brisco. That was when I discovered that my IFB was still working. Mr. Brisco sounded annoyed when he said, "All right, Jimmy, that's enough, let's go. We have a show to finish!" I finally got out of the pool and made my way to the locker room. I took off my wet clothes and shoes, put them in a large Ziploc bag, showered, and prepared to help with dismantling the ring.

The next morning it was off to the airport to catch the flight home. I normally do not check my bag and just carry it on the plane. This time, there was no way I was bringing my luggage on board. The odour from my wet clothes and shoes was lingering. Even with them sealed in the Ziploc bag. I could not subject the other passengers to the stale gravy aroma emanating from my carry-on bag. I also don't think that two showers and my Cool Water cologne were enough to mask my own distinct fragrance. I may have been just a little funky that morning. At first I felt terrible for my fellow passengers but that changed when I remembered that I had been subjected to some nasty-smelling flyers plenty of times and I didn't think my funk was all that bad. Let them deal with it.

From that day on, the mere smell of gravy just turned me off. It took several years for me to get over my dislike for gravy. I don't mind it so much these days but every once in a while, I have flash-backs whenever I go swimming.

CHAPTER 15

Tales from Outside the Ring

While the ring provided me with countless fond memories, the road and my dealings with the cast of characters I was surrounded by made for some of the best times for me. So much happened in my 20-plus-year career, you might say the comedy just writes itself. I'd like to tell you some of those stories. I don't know where to start. Why don't I just give you whatever pops into my head? It likely will not be in chronological order but does that really matter? I think not, so here goes.

The first thing that comes to my mind is golf. That's right, golf. It is the one activity that I truly enjoy more than any other, besides being a part of wrestling of course. Thanks to wrestling and in particular the WWE, I have had the great pleasure of golfing around the world. Some of the places we have golfed are Scotland, South Africa, Australia, Europe, and of course all over North America. The person I golfed with the most was Larry Heck, the WWE's athletic trainer. Larry and I are good friends and share a passion for golfing. Whenever we had a day off on the road, we would arrange to hit the links. We were frequently joined by some of the WWE superstars. Booker T is a huge golf enthusiast and joined us many times. He is quite good as well. I know what many of you are thinking. Many of you might find it hard to picture professional wrestlers golfing, but everyone from Spike Dudley to the Big Show has joined us for a round.

One member of the roster who joined Larry and me many times was JBL. In my opinion, and I hate to admit this, JBL is probably the best golfer of the WWE. There was one small concern whenever anyone golfed with JBL, he liked to have a few "pops" while he played. He also bought enough "pop" for everyone, so it would have been inconsiderate to not accept his generosity. Okay, he didn't really twist our arms to drink, but by the time we got to the turn, JBL was restocking the cooler. The other thing JBL liked to do while we golfed was play drinking games. For example, if one of us had a two-foot putt, JBL would shout, "If you miss that putt, you have to chug a beer." Now 99 times out of 100 I make that putt. Unfortunately once there are consequences involved, other than costing me a stroke, I will invariably miss an easy two-footer.

It wasn't really fair to us normal humans because JBL's tolerance level to beer was at least five times that of Larry's and mine. The other thing that astonished us humanoids was the more that JBL drank, the better his golf game got. It was uncanny how much farther and more accurately he hit the ball. I hate to out him like that but it is the stuff legends are made of.

The WWE also does some charity golf tournaments that benefit so many worthwhile causes. I had the great fortune of participating in the Road to Summer Slam 2005 golf tourney with all proceeds going to Ronald McDonald House in my hometown of Toronto. Whether it's golfing with John Cena in Scotland, the Undertaker and Big Show in Australia, or Booker T and JBL all over the United States, I got to experience the sport of golf unlike anyone else I know, besides Larry Heck of course. Combining my two passions, wrestling and golf — it really doesn't get much better than that. It really made me feel like the luckiest man on the planet.

Not all of my non-ring memories revolved around golf alone. Some happened at the arena, just not in the ring. I had so much fun being the voice of Kaientai on a few occasions. It was a last-minute thing I was not prepared for but had to do. You see, Shoichi Funaki and Taka Michinoku were the two remaining members of the Japanese faction. As part of their ring entrance, they would stop at the top of the ramp and deliver a promo. Only it wasn't Taka or Funaki speaking. Both knew limited English so their voice was dubbed for the promo by Brother Love himself, Bruce Prichard. It was done in a way to mimic how English was overdubbed in classic kung fu movies where the actors' mouth and spoken words are not in sync. It was actually quite funny as Taka would begin by berating their opponents before handing the mic to Funaki who would move his lips for several seconds before Bruce uttered the word *indeed*!

It was a running gag they did every week on the WWE's syndicated show *Velocity*. At one TV taping for *Velocity*, Kaientai were about to make their entrance but Bruce was nowhere to be found. Brisco sent a few refs to search for him with no luck. They finally located Bruce but he was producing a pre-tape and could not go to Gorilla to do the voice. Now the show was being held up so Brisco called an audible. He told the truck to hit the music and sent the Japanese duo out. He then handed me the microphone and said, "You do the voice!" I was reluctant but Brisco was very insistent so I agreed to do it. He gave me the cue and I began talking. I had no idea what I was saying but I did my best dubbing voice and threatened the guys in the ring with bodily harm, I think. Then Taka handed the mic to Funaki and I gave the best *indeed* I could and it was over. After the match, Funaki asked who did the voice. Brisco told him it was me, and Funaki thanked me for doing it. He said he liked it but maybe he was just being nice. Bruce then came to Gorilla and asked who did the Kaientai voice. Everyone pointed to me as if I had taken it upon myself to fill in for him.

Bruce commented on how terrible it was and said that he hoped I never got another chance to do it again. Thanks for the high praise.

As luck would have it, I once again had an occasion to provide the voice for Kaientai in Bruce's absence and once again was told how bad it was by Brother Love. I just couldn't win so I tried to avoid Gorilla whenever Kaientai were about to go on but it didn't help. They would call me on my earpiece so there was no escape. I performed the voice only a handful of times and, all kidding aside, I had a blast doing it. I was allowed to say anything I wanted (within reason) and really enjoyed it.

Sometimes I contributed in other ways. When Curt Hennig first arrived in the WWF (at that time) he was Mr. Perfect. He did everything perfectly. So one day at a live event, I overheard Jack Lanza tell Curt that Vince wanted him to come up with a name for his finishing move. Curt told Jack that his finish was called a Fisherman's Suplex. Jack acknowledged that but then said that Vince wanted a catchier name for it. As this conversation was going on, I was listening and also watching the match in the ring. Bob Orton Jr. was just about to deliver his finisher, the Superplex. Suddenly it hit me. I turned to Curt and said to him, "Hey, Curt, I couldn't help overhearing you and Jack talking about a name for your finish and I wanted to throw a name out there to see what you think. How does PerfectPlex sound to you?"

He absolutely loved the name and told Jack about it immediately. Jack agreed it sounded right. Vince had the final say but he was confident he would like it as well. He did and Curt has always credited me with coming up with the name of his finish. What can I say; even a blind squirrel finds a nut once in a while. That was my early claim to fame. Thanks to Curt Hennig for being a good buddy. He's definitely another superstar who is missed terribly.

Curt Hennig was not the only superstar from that era who provided me with memorable moments. The Macho Man Randy Savage was one of the most charismatic and memorable superstars of all time. His relationship with his then wife, Miss Elizabeth, was the subject of many rumours. The word going around the locker room was that Randy was very protective of Liz, maybe a little too protective at times. I was always someone who never entirely believed everything I heard. Was Randy overly protective of his wife? Maybe so but I could understand how he felt. I can only assume he felt uncomfortable having his beautiful wife around the boys. No offence to the boys, but I might be a little apprehensive myself if I were in his shoes. Then I got to experience Randy's over-active imagination first hand.

It was some time in 1988 or 1989 at a live event in Guelph, Ontario. It was another one of those days where it was business as usual. I set up the ring, got a bite to eat, and waited for the guys to arrive. Randy and Liz would generally get their own dressing room if availability would allow it. If not, Liz would change with the other girls in the female locker room. On this day, they had their own large room all to themselves. Then Randy called me over and asked if I would do him a favour. Of course I said yes and he brought me into his and Liz's room and said, "I've got to go some-where for a few minutes. Jimmy, would you mind watching the door and making sure no one comes in?"

Again I agreed to his request and he left the room to do what-ever it was he had to do. I sat nervously right beside the door as Liz sat on the opposite side of the room. We exchanged pleasantries and chatted about the weather. We were just making small talk, but I felt uncomfortable and I think Liz did as well. After a few more minutes of awkwardness, Randy came bursting through. He quickly surveyed the room, seeing me still sitting by the door and Liz still sitting on the other side of the room. He seemed relieved and thanked me for helping him out. I waved goodbye to Liz and told Randy it was not a problem. He held the door open as I left and when the door closed, he locked it immediately. Don't get me wrong. I'm just telling you what happened that day in Guelph. My intention is not to paint Savage in an unfavourable light. Randy was a great guy who treated me well and taught me so much. I always enjoyed working with Randy. I just couldn't help wonder what he thought I would try with his wife. Did he really think that I would hit on her? That's the impression I got when he stormed into the room. I liked Randy and we did get along very well but that was a day I'll never forget. Babysitting Liz while Randy took care of business was one of the most awkward moments I have ever experienced.

Well, at least he didn't give me a big chop or hit me with a spoon. How's that for a segue? One of the most common moves used in a wrestling match is the "knife-edge chop." It's when one wrestler hits the other with an open backhanded slap to the chest. It often leaves a reddish handprint on the person's chest. As a referee, I have never had the misfortune of taking a chop to the chest in a match. Notice I said in a match. It doesn't mean I haven't been chopped outside of the workplace. I've chopped in a bar, on the golf course, even on a plane. Most of those were given by my old buddy JBL. But the hardest chop I have ever been on the receiving end of was in Ireland and not from JBL.

We were on one of our European tours and had two shows in Dublin. I don't remember the name of the hotel we stayed in but after the first show, some of the guys got into party mode. The bar had closed for the night but the hotel staff was more than happy to continue serving us drinks. We moved the "party" into the lobby and it lasted into the wee hours of the morning. One of the games the guys were playing had two guys cut a deck of playing cards. The guy with the high card gets to chop the guy with the low card. I was not a part of the proceedings. I was just an innocent observer laughing at the guys getting their chests chopped. Brian Hebner and Tony Chimel were willing participants and feeling the effects of the game. Then Brian looked over in my direction and challenged me to join the game. I wanted no part of it but I could not back down either. I had been sitting there drinking and watching for a few hours now so I felt I had to get involved.

Right from the start they had me cut the deck with our fearless leader Fit Finlay. Not a guy you want to lose to in a game like this. Of course I lost and had to take a chop from Fit. Before he did it, the elevator doors opened and the Big Show walked out and over to us. It was now about six a.m. and Show was heading to a media appearance. He could not believe we were still up playing that stupid game. Then Fit had a brilliant idea. He decided to pass the chop to the Big Show. I wasn't too sure which would be worse but I went ahead, lifting my shirt to expose my chest. Then Show said something that scared the hell out of me. He said, "You may want to move that crucifix or it might get embedded in your chest permanently."

I moved my cross and prepared for the worst with my eyes closed. Nothing could have prepared me for what I felt next. Now, I have been in car accidents, been thrown around by many a superstar, but never have I been hit as hard as when that giant paw made contact with my chest. The impact sent me across the lobby and had it not been for a strategically placed sofa, I might have ended up at the front desk checking out for good. It was by far the most painful thing I had felt without breaking anything. Big Show just thanked everyone for letting him play and left for his appearance. I, on the other hand, had to be helped up and the imprint on my chest stung so bad, it hurt just to breathe. Once everyone stopped laughing, we noticed that the restaurant had just opened for business. So we did the only thing we could after a night of zero sleep and shenanigans: we ate breakfast. We eventually got a few hours of sleep and then got ready for show number two in Dublin. Visitors of Ireland have fond memories of the beautiful rolling hills, the scenery, and the great people they meet. I will remember Ireland as the place where I got a gigantic hand smashed into my chest. I think if you look very closely, you can still see the outline today.

The chopping game was not the only form of amusement the guys had. Thanks to Fit Finlay, we were introduced to the Spoon Game. Here's how it is played. First, a veteran wrestler would be chosen to face a rookie or one of the newer guys. Both guys would get on all fours facing each other. Then, they would get a table-spoon and place the handle in the rookie's mouth, leaving the bigger end exposed. His counterpart would lower his head and the one with the spoon in his mouth would hit the other guy on the top of the head as hard as they can with the spoon. Of course they can't use their hands. They would take turns hitting each other on the head with the spoon until one of them would give up. Sounds simple, right? Well, this game was not on the up and up.

After the new guy took his best shot, the veteran wrestlers would sell the hit as if it was quite painful. To be honest, you do feel the spoon, but you can't really hit that hard when it's hanging out of your mouth. Then the spoon gets passed to the seasoned pro. The rookie then lowers his head, preparing for the impact, and that's exactly what he gets. While this unsuspecting newbie has his head down, another vet uses a much larger spoon or in some cases a ladle, and cracks the kid on his head. You can only imagine how much pain the young man would be in. The funny part is that the victim of the game never wants to quit after only one shot to the head and continues to "play."

This process is repeated, sometimes for several rounds. Eventually the first-time player would give in as those of us who watched the festivities busted a gut with laughter. After questioning the "professional spoon player" about how he could hit so hard, he was let in on the secret. The reaction was always priceless but they were always good sports and the boys would buy him a few rounds. It really is one of the funniest things I had ever seen. Thankfully, I was never asked to play. I was only a spectator and much preferred it that way. The Big Show's chop was bad enough, but at least it was only a one-time thing. Trust me, one time was more than enough.

Even the boss likes to have a little fun now and then. At some TV tapings, the WWE hierarchy holds talent meetings. These meetings are on a variety of subjects and last about a half-hour or so. On days when there is a meeting, someone puts up signs all around the backstage area from catering to every locker room so all the talent knows about the meeting, its time and location. On this particular day, I was helping hang the signs backstage. I thought hanging the signs a little higher would make them easier to spot so I jumped up on a road case to hang it high. As I reached up while standing on the wheeled case, somebody thought it would be funny to shove me from behind into the wall. Almost taking a huge bump off the platform, I quickly collected myself and turned to give the culprit an earful.

Who did I see staring at me but the Chairman himself, Vince McMahon. Instead of the outburst of profanity I was planning, I fell silent. Then Vince said to me in a stern voice, "You were saying?"

Almost mimicking his very own hard oh my god gulping swallow, I followed that up with the immortal words, "Good to see ya, boss. How's it going?"

He laughed and replied, "I'm doing good, pal. Carry on." I could hear laughing as he walked down the hallway. There are times when I think, *What if I had said what I was going to say? What if I had turned around and pushed the person back?* It's a good thing flying off the handle is not one of my trademarks. I rarely get angry. If I had been really angry that day, this scene may have turned out much differently. Instead, I got another tale to tell the youngsters.

CHAPTER 16

The Referee's Role
& My Colleagues

I can't tell you how many times I've heard people say, "What's the big deal? All you have to do is just stand there and wait until the end of the match and count one, two, three." That is how many view the job of a pro wrestling referee. Those who have never been in the ring will never understand how involved the referee is in a wrestling match. There are even some within the industry who do not totally grasp the concept of being a ref.

When I first started refereeing matches, I had no idea there was so much to learn. I, like most people, was not aware of all the little things that came with the job. Unlike many of the refs today who learned their craft on the independent circuit or a developmental system, my training was on the job. I'm not saying one way is better than the other; it's just a different time and era. That was how things were done when I started.

Trying to define the role of a wrestling referee may be a good place to start. Obviously, he is not like a referee in any of the major sports you watch on television. The biggest question is how much of a presence he should have in a match. Some say he should be invisible in a match. While this is partially true, there is a fine line a referee has to walk while working in the ring. The focal point in any match is the wrestlers, the superstars that the fans pay to see. The referee is more of a supporting actor. His main role is to enhance the match and the story the wrestlers are trying to tell in the ring. He should not be invisible but at the same time, he should not be a distraction. I believe that the referee should act naturally in the ring and treat each match as if it was a true contest. Be a *referee*! Don't act like one because then you will not appear genuine. Fans can tell the difference.

Squared Circle Training, which is a wrestling school in Toronto run by head trainer Rob Etcheverria, better known as El Fuego, asked me if I was interested in running a referee camp for those who wanted to learn the craft. In May 2010, I, along with fellow veteran referee Harry Dee, held a month-long camp teaching the finer points of reffing. To my knowledge, they were the first classes dedicated to refereeing taught by referees. One of the things I did when preparing for the classes was make a list of what pro wrestling referees should know and learn. Here's what I came up with. This is in no particular order but rather a guide or outline of dos and don'ts.

Always conduct yourself in a professional manner, whether at work or in public, especially if you are working for one of the major companies. How you are perceived by others is very important because in this business, perception becomes reality. If you come off as arrogant, even if you are not, you will be labelled that way and it will affect your relationships with the talent. So, in a nutshell, be respectful of everyone — don't be a dick!

When you are in the ring, you must appear confident at all times. If you are officiating a match and appear to be tentative or hesitant, no one will buy you as an official. Again, perception is reality. If you look in command and authoritative in the ring, people will believe it.

When enforcing the rules, treat both the heels and babyfaces the same. You don't want to seem to favour one or the other. You should be impartial at all times, unless of course they are planning to use you in a storyline or angle. Otherwise, play it straight.

During a wrestling match, there will be certain counts that the referee will have to make, not only pinning attempts, but also other instances where a count is utilized. A five count will be administered when the wrestlers are on the ropes, in the corner, or when an illegal hold is being used. A ten count will be used when one or more participants are outside the ring. Regardless of which count the ref is making, the counts should be rhythmic and consistent. Any variation in the cadence of the count is noticeable by the fans. This really applies when counting a pin attempt. Nothing bothers me more than when a referee has a different cadence for near-falls and the actual finish. Slowing down or speeding up the counts is a common problem with many referees I watch. I'm sure I've been guilty of doing this also but I make a conscious effort not to do it. This is one of my biggest pet peeves.

I always treated every match as if it was an actual contest. Treat it like a shoot. Always look as if you are doing your job. Stay busy in the ring without being a distraction. Don't be distracted by fans at ringside. Your focus should be on the action in the ring.

Your movements as well as your facial expressions in the ring will help tell the story. Your movements in the ring should be natural. That goes for facial expressions as well. No over-the-top motions or looks will help. If the ref portrays his role correctly, his involvement is mostly subtle, but very important in order to help the wrestlers get across what is going on in the ring. This also goes for body language. Exaggerated motions and movements in the ring are not only distracting, they look ridiculous. You are the authority figure in the ring, not trying out for *Dancing with the Stars*.

This may sound contradictory, but when enforcing the rules, be vocal and use body language to show what rules you are enforcing. Be vocal so the fans close enough to hear you as well as the TV cameras can pick up what you are admonishing the wrestler for. Also, by pantomiming at the same time, those who cannot hear your admonishment will know what rule you are enforcing. This can be done subtly while at the same time visibly to those in the farthest areas of the arena.

Ring positioning is one of the most important aspects of being a pro wrestling referee. This does not only mean staying out of the way, it also includes being in the right spot at the right time throughout the match. A good referee will talk to the guys he's working with and find out what the game plan is, and ask questions if he doesn't understand something. Never go into a match blind. Know what is expected of you.

Again, positioning is important when TV cameras are involved. Always be aware of them and do your best not to get in the cameraman's way. This includes blocking the wrestler's face when they are selling a move or a hold. Do not position yourself where the talent's face cannot be seen by the fans or TV viewers. Stay to the side but not so far away that you look like you are not doing your job. This also comes into play when you have to relay messages from one talent to the other. Know how and when to assist the wrestlers in communicating with each other and how to make it appear to be something else you are doing. You can simply pass on something while appearing to enforce the rules. Of course you will not be as vocal in this case. The last thing you want is for the first two rows in the audience to know what you're going to do next.

There are so many other things that could be listed here, but most are things learned through experience and over time. The most important thing to know as a wrestling referee is that you never stop learning and that the business continues to evolve which means the role of the referee will evolve with it. If he portrays his role correctly, his involvement will help the wrestlers get across their story in the ring.

During my time in the WWF/E I have had the privilege to work with some of the best referees and the greatest wrestlers in the world, all of whom have contributed in helping me become confident in my abilities. I feel my body of work through the years has consistently improved. It is said that you can have a good match without a good referee but a good referee can make a good match so much better. This is very true and I believe that I fit into that category. Those who know can tell you it takes three to tell a good story in the ring.

I get asked a lot of questions by many fans about my time in the WWF/E. Questions such as how has refereeing a match changed over the years, especially with the addition of the earpiece? What's the difference between working on TV versus non-televised events? What is the pay like? What is it like to referee the different types of matches and their unique challenges, as well as the dangers that may be present?

Let me start with how things were when I began refereeing. For me it was more about not making any mistakes and getting the finish of the match right. It was a long and slow process to get comfortable enough to not overthink my every move in the ring. I was very critical of my work in the ring and constantly asked my peers for advice. With their help and guidance, I developed and improved into a very confident and competent referee. That is not conceit; it is confidence. Once I gained valuable experience, I began to understand the storytelling aspect of a wrestling match. I understood there was psychology in putting a match together that made logical sense to the fans watching. Also very important in my opinion is how the babyfaces and heels react to the official. The referee is to be respected as he would be in any other sport and treated that way. Most every talent knew how to toe the line regarding how they dealt with a referee. They respected the referee.

Fast-forward a decade or two and things have changed to a certain degree. The way I look at it is referees are not being uti-lized correctly at times these days. I don't know if it's so much that the referees aren't being trained properly, or a lot of the newer, younger guys in the business aren't utilizing the referees properly.

Heels nowadays just blatantly do things in front of the referee, for example, something as simple as choking. The way I see it, putting a count on someone while he's choking doesn't get any heat on the heel. If you do it behind the referee's back, and everybody in the building sees it, and the heel does it in a creative way where the referee doesn't look like a total buffoon by not seeing it, then it makes sense and it gets some heat. But to just blatantly do it in front of the referee, that's not heat. Heels cleverly cheating out of sight of the official is a lost art and rarely done in today's pro wrestling. I always enjoyed working with guys like William Regal and Dave "Fit" Finlay. They knew how to best incorporate the referee in their matches. No matter how much they broke and/or bent the rules, they always had respect for the referee and made it very apparent to the audience. There were others but those two were the masters.

Speaking of pet peeves, another one that I have is in tag-team matches. Referees are often getting buried and made to look a little dumb in these types of matches. I have had this happen to me many times. Sometimes you just have to do what you are told but that is no excuse for making the ref look bad. I recall a tag match I refereed that featured Paul London and Brian Kendrick taking on Deuce and Domino on an episode of *SmackDown*. As often happens in a tag-team match, the heels (Deuce and Domino) were cheating and at one point drew my attention away from Paul London who was being choked on the ropes by the illegal man behind my back. As this was going on, Brian Kendrick entered the ring, also illegally, and drew my attention away from his partner. It was my job to get him out of the ring before I could turn my attention back to the match. All of this may sound like it took a long time to occur, but in reality the whole scenario was fairly quick. Not quick enough for the boss. Vince McMahon apparently blew a gasket. I say apparently because it was John Laurinaitis who came to us after the match and gave us all an earful. He said Vince was angry that they buried the referee and that the referee was to blame as well for letting it happen. He was so pissed off that he fined all of us. I was fined $250 while the boys were fined $500 each. We were all stunned. I wanted to protest but sometimes it's just best to suck it up.

The following Sunday at a pay-per-view in St. Louis, the other referees, led by Jack Doan and Charles Robinson, got a copy of the tape from *SmackDown* with the match I was fined for. They asked Johnny if we could have a meeting with all the refs to discuss the fine and what was done wrong in the match. The main reason given for the fine was that I was distracted for far too long and made to look bad. When we reviewed the tape, we counted how long I was distracted and it was less than five seconds. Johnny finally agreed that it wasn't as bad as they thought the previous Tuesday night, but there was nothing he could do about the fine because Vince was the one who apparently called for it. Even though I paid the fine, I felt somewhat vindicated. That's not the end of the story. The other WWE referees all chipped in and paid the fine for me. I tried not to accept the money but I was outvoted. That really shows how much of a brotherhood we really were.

Now this may or may not have anything to do with the fine I received, but I did get a bonus once. At the Unforgiven PPV in 2007, the *SmackDown* main event was a triple threat match for the world heavyweight championship. The champ, the Great Khali, was to defend the title against Rey Mysterio and Dave Batista. There was a problem getting Khali to agree to the finish of the match. He did not want to take a Batista Bomb off the second rope in the corner. He was not comfortable climbing the ropes in the first place, which I can understand given his lack of mobility. He didn't say so but it was believed he didn't want to take that finish. He didn't mind losing the match but not with such a big bump. I was at ringside and was fully aware of the situation, watching as the agents were brainstorming to come up with a suitable finish that would work for everyone.

Then it hit me. Sometimes I would get ideas for finishes. I was comfortable enough to pitch my ideas to the agents. I went to

Finlay, whom I felt most comfortable with, and laid out my idea. Mysterio would hit two 619s, first on Batista then on Khali. Khali would land in a seated position on the mat. Rey would springboard off the top rope, landing on Khali in a pinning position. Batista would not only break up the pin attempt, he would Batista Bomb Rey right on top of Khali. Then Batista would wait for both men to get to their feet, push Rey out of the ring, and hit Khali with a Spinebuster for the one, two, three, and become the new champ. Finlay liked the finish and had me explain it to the guys in the match as well as the other agents. They all agreed that my idea would work, and they used it for the PPV match that night. Arn Anderson, who is one of the most respected men in the business and one of the lead agents, came to me afterwards and told me, "Jimmy, you saved the day. Thank you for helping out."

I was so flattered that Double A would say something like that to me. After the match that evening, John Laurinaitis stopped me as I walked by and said, "Good job tonight, Jimmy." I wasn't sure if he meant the tag match I refereed earlier or the finish I came up with. I assume he meant the finish as I received a bonus in my pay that John said was for coming up with that finish. I don't know for sure, but I think it was John's way of making up for the $250 fine I got a few weeks prior. Either way, it was nice to get some props from your boss sometimes. And, by the way, the bonus was for exactly $250.

Refereeing different types of matches is all part of the job. The one that may surprise people as being the most involved are the tables, ladders, and chairs matches. I have been a part of many of them and the referee is very important. Not so much in relaying the time to the boys; it's more being constantly aware of what is happening in the match and making sure the ring is clear of debris so the guys can work more safely. There are usually huge bumps and big high spots and that is when the ref has to check on the talent and make sure they are not hurt. If you watch the TLC match from *WrestleMania X-Seven* in Houston's Astrodome, you can see many times during the match when I am moving ladders or tables or chairs to clear the playing surface, so to speak. You can also see yours truly check on the guys several times after big bumps. No one ever explained to me what to do during those matches. I would sit in when the boys talked over the match and reacted accordingly. I took it upon myself to be proactive in the TLC match. There was no standard set for these matches so we learned on the fly. I just did what came naturally, and it seemed to work. As always, my number one priority was the safety of the boys. I feel I kind of set a standard on how to officiate TLC or ladder matches as I was generally assigned those matches. On occasion, it was requested by the participants in the match that I be assigned. For me there is no bigger compliment than that.

Another question I get asked frequently is, "How much do referees make and how difficult was it for a Canadian to work for an American company?" Let me tackle the money question first. I never liked revealing exactly how much I got paid, even to my fellow referees. Everyone's contract was different. I was on the road over 200 days a year, travelling all over the world all on the WWE's dime and getting paid for it. When I worked on both the ring crew and as a referee, all expenses were paid for by the company. Flights, rental cars, hotels, and a per diem were all perks when doing double duty. Of course we were the first to arrive at the arenas setting up and the last to leave taking everything down. This was the not so glamorous side of wrestling most fans didn't see. People automatically assume that because we travelled all over the world, we got to sightsee everywhere we went. Although we did get to see some sights, most of the time we did not have the opportunity because we were so busy working. I always told friends that I could describe most airports, hotels, and arenas but not too many popular landmarks from the countries I visited.

Getting home after long trips was challenging as well. When I got home, all I wanted to do was relax and catch up on some much-needed sleep. Unfortunately, that did not happen too often. Don't get me wrong; for the most part my wife was fairly understanding of my needs. I understood her needs as well. Being home for two and a half days a week meant I had to cram a lot of husbandry into a short amount of time. While home, I wanted to spend as much time with my wife and family as I could, which meant I didn't get to see my friends very much, if at all. If I was lucky enough to get a week off, my wife wanted to take a trip to somewhere. I on the other hand was not in the mood to travel anywhere and preferred to stay home and relax. Most of the time, I sucked it up and Audra and I took a little trip to somewhere. After it was all said and done, those little trips were a nice break from the usual day's routine.

Things changed when I was no longer a part of the crew and became what we called a "full-time" ref. This meant that I would no longer receive the perks that went along with being a part of the crew. If you only refereed, you had the same expenses that the talent had with regards to travel. Flights were paid for but rental cars, hotels, and meals were your own responsibility. That's why the boys generally travel in small groups to split the costs of cars and hotels. I was very fortunate in that regard as I still travelled with Tony Chimel. Tony is an employee of the company and all his expenses are taken care of. Chimel, being the friend that he is, allowed me to ride in the car with him, I drove of course and he let my stay with him in his hotel room. Two beds of course. Sometimes, Charles Robinson or Larry Heck let me stay with them. This really helped me out as I didn't have to spend money on these things. They were all a tremendous help to me and I will never forget their kindness and friendship.

Being a Canadian working in the United States did present some challenges. When I first began working for WWF/E, it was under Jack Tunney. In essence, I worked for the WWF out of their Canadian office. I was paid by them, not the American office. This all changed when I began to work in the U.S. I needed a work permit to work there. The WWF/E took care of all the procedures in obtaining my work permit. They used their lawyers and took care of that end. They did all the leg work and all I had to do was pay the lawyer for his service. It was roughly $4,000.00 a year for my P-1, as it was called. It was a necessary expense if I wanted to continue my dream job.

With Jack Tunney no longer in charge of the Canadian office, Carl DeMarco took over the reigns as president of the Canadian arm of the WWF/E. I knew Carl from his days before he was friends with Bret Hart. He was a wrestling fan. He was known to us as Bret's driver because he took Bret everywhere he went. They were really good friends. Unlike Jack, Carl was never my boss. I didn't work for him. By the time he took over, the Canadian office was more of a sales office working on developing television and licensing deals for the WWF/E in Canada. My connection to this office was merely that as a friend and colleague to those who worked there. I will give Carl credit as he worked very hard promoting the brand all across Canada and represented the company well. He was also responsible for Canadian talent getting their breaks in the WWF/E. Edge, Christian, and Test are just a few of the superstars who got their opportunity because of Carl. Carl no longer works for the WWE as they essentially run the entire operation from their home base of Stamford, Connecticut. Carl is a good guy and we still keep in touch.

Having to cross the border from Canada into the United States and back every week was a bit of a pain in the butt. Having to arrive at the airport a minimum of an hour and a half before departure was a little annoying. It used to be the same routine every week. Get there early, line up to get my boarding pass, line up to clear U.S. customs, go through security, and then wait to board my flight.

I never really had any trouble entering the United States. I suppose the customs agents began to recognize me from lining up every week. Once they found out who I worked for, they were more interested in what was going on in the world of WWE. I never minded filling them in on the weekly goings-on. They were friendly enough and I just chatted whenever they wanted the latest lowdown. What I found was I got hassled more when returning to Canada. It seemed to me that I was constantly questioned by Canadian customs about where I had travelled to, why I was there, and what goods I was returning with. I felt like coming home always included a game of 20 Questions. Oh well, just another minor inconvenience that I had to deal with.

It took a few years but going through U.S. customs became a breeze. I purchased a NEXUS card. This card is issued to frequent travellers. To obtain one, any citizen of Canada or the U.S. who resides in either country and can pass criminal history and law enforcement checks may apply for a NEXUS card. NEXUS card holders are identified at land border crossings by presenting their cards for scanning and at airport kiosks by undergoing a retinal recognition scan, a process that takes about ten seconds. Needless to say, border crossing became very easy and I didn't have to get to the airport as early anymore. Between being able to print boarding passes at home and not having to line up at customs anymore, the airport experience was relatively easy from that point forward.

Before moving on with more stories, I would like to take this opportunity to mention and say thank you to all the other referees I have had the pleasure to work with during my WWE career. John Bonello, Jack Lotz, Gilberto Roman, Terry Yorkston, Dave, Earl, and Brian Hebner, Danny Davis, Danny Marsh, Mike Clarke, Goose Mahoney, Mike Posey, Marty Elias, Tim White, Jack Doan, Chad Patton, Teddy Long, Bill Alfonso, Mike Sparks, Mike Chioda, Chris Kay, Nick Patrick, Charles Robinson, Scott Armstrong, Mickie Henson. If I missed anyone, I do apologize as over a 20-year period, it is quite possible I may have. I really do want to thank you all.

One of my referee brothers I purposely left out was the late Joey Marella. Joey was the adopted son of WWE Hall of Famer Gorilla Monsoon, whose real name was Robert Marella. Joey began his career on the ring crew based out of New Jersey. His longtime friend Tony Chimel joined him on the crew and a few years later they were joined by Mike Chioda. Joey performed double duty as part of the ring crew and the referee team. He quickly made his way to the top, becoming one of the promotion's premier officials, refereeing many main event matches, his biggest possibly being the famed *WrestleMania III* encounter between Hulk Hogan and Andre the Giant, which drew over 93,000 fans to the Pontiac Silverdome.

On July 4, 1994, Joey was driving home to New Jersey after an event in Ocean City, Maryland. Bruno Lauer, better known to wrestling fans as Harvey Wippleman, was riding with him. At some point, Joey fell asleep at the wheel. The car veered off the road and crashed. Bruno was wearing his seatbelt, which in all likelihood saved his life. Joey was not and was killed in the accident. It was a terrible blow to his friends, but it was an even heavier blow to his family. His father was devastated and in my opinion was never the same. Gorilla passed away five years later at the age of 62. Some say he never quite got over the loss of his son Joey.

This was the first time that I had to deal with the death of a friend and colleague. None of us knew how to deal with the loss. These were uncharted waters for us on the crew. It could have happened to any one of us as we have all made similar long drives after an event. This changed our approach to night travel. We were told that if we were tired, not to continue driving. If your travelling partner was up to driving then fine; otherwise we were instructed to stop at the nearest hotel or motel and get some rest before carrying on.

As with any loss of a friend, it took some time to get over it. As terrible as we all felt, we also learned a harsh lesson about life in the world of sports and entertainment: the show must go on. Yes, we mourn our friends but we must also move forward. It is not meant to disrespect their memory but rather to honour their contributions to our industry. Some may not understand that sentiment but that is the nature of the business. This is how we pay homage to our fallen colleagues.

As a tribute to his best friend, Tony Chimel named one of his children after Joey, as did Joey's sister Valerie. We all remember him in different ways. I choose to remember Joey as the friend who helped pave the way for us referees who were also on the ring crew. He was one of the most recognizable referees of that era. I always found it funny that sometimes as I would make my way to the ring to referee a match, the fans would call me Joey. Dick Ebersol from NBC Sports labelled Joey and me the "Bookends" because he said we looked alike. I guess we did as the fans seemed to agree with Mr. Ebersol. I got a kick out of it but I think Joey wasn't too impressed.

I wish I were able to thank Joey for helping me along the way, at least for the early part of my journey.

CHAPTER 17

The Celebs

One of the perks of travelling and being a part of World Wrestling Entertainment is the celebrities you get to meet. Many people would be astounded at the long list of famous people outside of the wrestling business who enjoy and attend the WWE events. I'm talking celebs from sports, TV, the big screen, the music world — even politicians are frequent attendees to live events. The list is a veritable who's who in the world of pop culture. Some I didn't get to interact with very much, while others I had the pleasure of getting to meet and talk to.

I met the "Baddest Man on the Planet" the day after the 1998 Royal Rumble. *Monday Night Raw* aired live from Fresno, California. There was a definite buzz all day long around the venue as everyone waited for the arrival of Mike Tyson. When Tyson entered the arena, he looked like a kid in a candy store. Not only were the WWE superstars anxious to meet the heavyweight boxer, Mike Tyson himself was ecstatic to meet the "boys." He seemed genuinely happy to meet and say hello to everyone, including a young, balding referee from Canada.

The day seemed to go by very quickly; we were about to go live when I happened to bump into Tyson again. I was talking to Headbanger Chaz in a narrow hallway when Iron Mike walked over trying to squeeze by. He excused himself. As we made room for him, he passed by and thanked us. That wasn't good enough for one half of the Headbangers. Chaz has an odd sense of humour and is not afraid to say pretty much anything to anyone. As Tyson walked away, Chaz cavalierly said, "No problem, Mike. I didn't want to lose part of my ear." Thank goodness, Tyson just kept on walking and didn't acknowledge the comment. I was not entirely sure he heard it anyway.

I was shocked, chagrined, and stupefied. What the heck did he just say to Mike Tyson? I asked Chaz what was up with the "ear" comment. He looked at me with this surprised expression of innocence on his face and said, "What? He has done it before ya know." I have to admit it was funny but still, what if Tyson got really upset? Who knows what he would have and could have done? Chaz I'm quite sure can handle himself. I, on the other hand, might have had just a bit of trouble with Iron Mike. However, the first thing I remembered was that Tyson was a world-class boxer, not a sprinter. I was ready to test that theory if the moment called for a quick exit. I was fairly fast in those days.

Back to the main reason Tyson appeared on wwf television: his eventual confrontation with "The Rattlesnake" Stone Cold Steve Austin. Their interaction in the ring that night was off the hook awesome. When Austin flipped Tyson the double bird and Tyson retaliated by shoving Stone Cold, it was on like Donkey Kong. All hell broke loose. As we all tried to restore order, the crowd in the arena was going absolutely crazy. Everyone in the building was on their feet. Right then and there, I knew this was one of those special moments that do not occur very often and I was a part of it. A small part, but a part nonetheless. This was likely the incident, along with Survivor Series 1997, that catapulted the wwf past the wcw in the ratings war, where they remained until wcw closed their doors a few short years later. It was undeniably one of the defining moments in sports entertainment history and I was there.

Another celebrity I had the good fortune of meeting and interacting with was Drew Carey. One question that everyone constantly asks me is, "Did you keep any of the money you scooped up that Kane slapped out of Drew Carey's hand?" Before I finally tell you all the truth about this, let me paint the picture from my vantage point. Truth be told, even my *Aftermath Radio* co-host Arda Ocal hasn't heard the real story about this night, so this will be news to him as well. (I'll explain the *Aftermath Radio* gig later.)

As a referee in the Royal Rumble match, you have to be prepared for anything that can and might happen. We all knew that comedian Drew Carey was to be a participant in the match, but I was not fully aware of how involved he would be. As the clocked clicked down to zero while Matt and Jeff Hardy fought to eliminate each other, who should appear in the number five position but Drew Carey.

The Cleveland, Ohio, native was in no hurry to enter the ring. The Hardys managed to eliminate one another simultaneously, leaving Carey as the only entrant standing in the ring. As the time counted down to the number six entrant, Drew anxiously awaited the next superstar to enter. The look of utter fear in his eyes told the story as flames and pyro lit up the New Orleans arena and Kane walked confidently to the ring. Once inside, Kane raised his arms above his head and quickly brought them down and more flames shot out from all four ring posts. A terrified Carey extended his hand in an attempt to shake hands with Kane, but the Big Red Monster just stared a hole through Drew. Carey then reached into his pocket and pulled out several $100 bills. Kane slapped the money out of his hand, wrapped his extra large hand around Drew's throat, and was about to choke slam the future *Price Is Right* host.

This is where I leaped into action. Seeing all that money just lying there in the ring, and with all those photographers hovering around ringside, I decided that the only smart thing would be to scoop up all the cash. Raven, who was the next entrant in the Rumble, stormed into the ring, hitting Kane with a Kendo Stick and making him release Carey who, in the blink of an eye, jumped over the top rope, thus eliminating himself from the Rumble.

Here's where I've had fun with the story over the years. I have told people that I gave it back when the match was over. I've told others that I may have kept some of the cash before returning the rest of it. The actual truth is, and this is the very first time I am telling this, is that I was so concerned about what "the office" might think that I gave the money right back to Drew Carey as soon as he eliminated himself from the Royal Rumble. I didn't hold onto it, I didn't keep any of it, I just figured the sooner I gave it back, the less chance of me being blamed if it were to disappear. I could always put the blame on the millionaire comedian. In hindsight, I'm not so sure who they would have believed had the money gone missing. It would've been one hell of a trial. Drew Carey took the cash back, and it was out of my hands from there. I remember getting to the back after the match and Gerald Brisco asking me what I did with the cash I scooped up. I told him I gave it all back to Carey, and he nodded as if to say that was the right thing to do. That was the last I heard about the money.

Well, there it is. It only took 11 years for the truth to rear its head. I just couldn't live this lie any longer. I feel like a huge weight has been lifted from my shoulders. Well, maybe not, but it was fun letting fans think I might have copped a few dollars that night. For one night, people thought I was the bad guy. Probably not, but a guy can hope.

When celebrities attend a WWF/E event, they usually get an opportunity to visit backstage and mingle with the superstars. It's incredible to see how genuinely excited the celebs get when they meet the wrestlers and vice versa. I have to confess that with certain notables who came to our shows, I went out of my way to try to meet them. There was one time at *WrestleMania 2000* where I was accosted by a celebrity who was sitting in the front row.

One of the matches on the show was the Hardcore Battle Royal for the hardcore championship. It was not your traditional Battle Royal. This iteration of the match included some unusual rules. As far as I knew, it was a first. The rules were as follows: the match would go on for 15 minutes. The championship could exchange hands an unlimited number of times during the time limit. The final wrestler in possession of the hardcore championship, when the bell rang to end the match, won and would be declared the hardcore champion. I was one of the referees assigned to the match; Tim White was the other official working the match. I had a great deal of respect for Tim and I was glad we were working together for this match.

The match began and, as one might suspect, chaos and mayhem ensued. The participants fought all over the arena. They fought in the ring, out of the ring, and even all the way backstage. Falls counted anywhere in the building, so that meant Tim and I had to follow the action wherever it took us. At one point while I was standing at ringside during the match, someone began to heckle me with a barrage of insults. Normally I would ignore such comments, especially during TV or PPV events, but this person would not stop. After a few minutes of listening to this guy go off, I decided it was time to tell this guy to shut up. I turned around, fully intending to let this guy have it. Suddenly, I was face to face with none other than Michael Clarke Duncan. That's right; the big dude from the movie *The Green Mile* was the guy giving me the gears.

My frustration disappeared and I began to silently "mark out" over the fact that MCD was jaw-jacking me. He looked right at me, smiled, and extended his hand. I wasn't sure if it was a good idea to shake his hand while in the middle of a match but I didn't want to offend the big guy either. So I did shake his hand, very quickly mind you, and turned my attention back to the match. I was only distracted for a few seconds. Thankfully I didn't miss anything, considering the match was going on while I was dealing with my celebrity heckler. It was a cool moment for sure, but that wasn't the end of it.

After *WrestleMania* was over, some of the notables in attendance were invited backstage to meet some of the boys. One of those notables was Michael Clarke Duncan. As I approached him he broke out into a huge smile, shook my hand, and tried to apologize for hounding me during the Hardcore Battle Royal. I told him it was fine and that it was an honour to be heckled by a big star such as him. Again he laughed and put his rather large arm around my shoulder and said, "You're a good sport. Thanks for playing along."

Now I was laughing. He asked me why I was laughing and I explained to him that before I turned to see who was yelling at me, I was getting legit angry because it was getting under my skin and when I turned around to say something and saw him, I thought it was so cool and changed my tune. We both laughed and MCD gave me the guy-hug thing. I then told him that I'd love to hang out but I had to get to work on tearing down the ring. He said with a bit of a smirk, "No problem, dude. We'll do this again next time! Take care."

Walking back to get out of my referee gear, I couldn't help but think about my encounter with a Hollywood star and how cool he was. Another part of me wondered if we ran into each other at another wrestling show, would he even remember who I was? That question was answered the very next time we staged an event in Anaheim, California. It was a regular TV event and, just like every time the WWE is in the Los Angeles area, the stars come out to the show. Michael Clarke Duncan was indeed at the show and much to my surprise, he remembered me. He walked right to me, shook my hand, and started chatting with me. It was so cool because he is such a down-to-earth guy and he always had a smile on his face.

After our friendly chat, I had to go to work and he was escorted to his seat to watch the show.

After the show, I was outside the arena by the loading docks talking to my wife on my phone. I didn't notice MCD leaving the building and as he put his hand on my shoulder to get my attention, he asked me, "Who are you talking to?" I said I was talking to my wife and he held out his hand and said, "Give me the phone!" Looking puzzled, I handed him the phone and he began speaking to my wife, Audra. Only being able to hear MCD, I could tell that Audra had no idea who she was talking to. Even after he told her who he was, she did not believe him. I think Audra eventually caught on and became apologetic for not believing him in the first place. They conversed for a minute or two until MCD said to her, "It was really nice talking to you. Let me hand the phone back to your skinny-legged husband."

If it wasn't Michael Clarke Duncan calling me skinny-legged, I might have been offended. I didn't think my legs were skinny at all but I guess compared to his, they just may be. It's kind of weird but it didn't seem like I was interacting with a celebrity. That was how much of a good guy he is. It speaks volumes that someone so famous stays so grounded. Every time I got to see him at shows, he always made an effort to say hello to me and just shoot the shit. MCD is quite possibly my favourite celebrity meeting of all time. I was saddened to hear of his untimely passing in September 2012. He will be sorely missed by his family, friends, and fans.

The list of celebrities who have been a part of wrestling and *WrestleMania* is endless. From A-list celebs to the more obscure, here is a partial list of famous people I have met over the years minus the three already mentioned. I will try not to make it a Chris Jericho–type list with 1,004 wrestling holds. Here goes. Jermaine Jackson, Mr. T, Floyd Mayweather Jr., Vinny Pazienza, Pete Rose, Bob Uecker, Boyz II Men, Ice-T, Snoop Dogg, Kid Rock, Gladys Knight, Kim Kardashian, Raven Simone, Donald Trump, Vanna White, Dan Marino, Shaq, Tracey Murray, Jerome Williams, Ozzy

Osbourne, Leslie Nielsen, Mike Ricci, Doug Gilmour, Bruce Willis — I could go on and on, but I think you get the point. I have had the pleasure of meeting so many incredible celebrities that it's impossible to keep track of them all.

As it turns out, I just remembered another one. This time it was the day of *WrestleMania VI* in my hometown of Toronto. Among the celebrity guests that day were Steve Allen, Rona Barrett, Mary Tyler Moore, and singer Robert Goulet. Goulet was scheduled to sing the Canadian national anthem to kick off the show. One small problem though: Robert Goulet didn't know the words to "O Canada." Pat Patterson found me that afternoon and asked me if I knew the words to the Canadian national anthem. I was a bit perplexed but said that I did. He asked me if I could teach it to Mr. Goulet. I thought Pat was kidding, but he insisted it wasn't a rib and took me to meet the singing legend. It was somewhat intimidating meeting him without the added pressure of teaching him the anthem. After a few minutes of reciting the words, I had a brainstorm. "Why couldn't they just put the words up on the Jumbotron and Mr. Goulet could read them from there?"

Pat looked at the star and said, "Would that work for you, Robert?" Goulet agreed that was the best course of action. He said thank you, and I left his dressing room. Pat followed me out and thanked me for the idea. I was just happy I didn't have to sing for the guy, even though I can carry a tune. As for how the national anthem came across that night, putting the words on the big screen worked like a charm. Problem solved!

Sometimes when you meet celebrities, they can surprise you with their knowledge of the wrestling business. One such celeb was Freddie Prinze Jr. It was widely known by those in wrestling that Prinze was a huge fan of the WWE. In 2008 he was hired by World Wrestling Entertainment as part of the creative team. At the *SmackDown* tapings one day, I thought it would only be proper for me to introduce myself to him. I noticed he was standing by the ring and made my way over to him. I extended my hand. "Hi, Mr.

Prinze, I just wanted to introduce myself. My name is Jim Korderas and I'm one of the referees here on *SmackDown*. It's a pleasure to meet you."

As soon as I finished my greeting, he said, "First off, please call me Freddie and secondly, I know who you are. It's a pleasure meeting you, Jimmy, and I'm looking forward to working with you."

We chatted a bit about his love for wrestling and how excited he was to be a part of the wwe. How freaking awesome was that? Freddie Prinze Jr. knew who I was! Now that was definitely a boost to the old ego. How can you not be impressed that a Hollywood star knows who you are? After all, no one pays money to see the referee and most of the time we go unnoticed so it was nice of him to say he was aware of who I was and was familiar with my work. It's a nice little feel-good moment that I will always remember.

Of course there are many more celebs whom I have had the privilege of meeting and working with. But for me there are no bigger celebrities than the men and women I worked with about 250 days a year. The wwe superstars are some of the most recognizable figures in the world. They are on television in more than 145 countries and viewed by as many as 15 million people each week. I don't know of any other entertainment enterprise with that kind of exposure. I guess that means I also was viewed in those countries by that many people. Obviously fans recognize the Cenas and the Undertakers and the Triple Hs and not the referees. I never had any illusions about being a superstar myself. The only person who thought of me as a star was my wife, Audra. But it's still nice to think that you are seen around the world by so many people and that maybe, just maybe, they will remember you and appreciate your contributions.

CHAPTER 18

Viva la Raza:
My Friend Eddie

Every so often, someone comes along in the wrestling business who is so gifted, so talented, and so passionate that you cannot help but feed off the energy they bring with them each and every day, not only at work but in their everyday life. Eddie Guerrero was definitely one such person. Before I get into how much he influenced me and helped bring me out of my shell, let me tell you a little about my friend, the Eddie Guerrero I knew.

Eddie was born into the wrestling business. His father Gory Guerrero was a very famous wrestler, not only in Mexico but also in the Southern United States. Eddie's brothers Chavo Senior, Mando, and Hector also donned the tights and entered the family business, as well as his nephew Chavo Junior. Eddie had wrestled all over the world for every major promotion except for one, the wwf. Before he entered the wwf, it was rumoured that Eddie, along with his friends Chris Benoit, Dean Malenko, and Perry Saturn, were unhappy with the goings-on in wcw, where they were employed. Eddie and the gang apparently talked about leaving wcw but were unsure whether the wwf, which was and still is the number one sports entertainment company on the planet, would hire them. After all, the promotion up north was known as the "Land of the Giants" and since all of them were smaller in stature, they thought the WWF might not want to hire them. But then again, Chris Jericho, a wrestler of similar stature, had made the successful jump from WCW to WWF, paving the way for them.

This leads to a story that very few people know. It is however a true story about how I played a minor role in helping the WWF land Eddie and his gang, the Radicalz. It was a Sunday morning around Christmastime in 1999. The phone rang and woke me up at about nine-thirty a.m. Yes, I was sleeping in; after all I had the weekend off, so why not? I answered the phone and it was my friend Jeff Marek. Jeff is a radio and television analyst who covers NHL hockey; however at the time he was the host of a weekly wrestling talk show on the radio called *Live Audio Wrestling*. I had been on the show a few times, so Jeff and I had become pretty good friends. He's really a good guy and has a great respect for the wrestling business. Jeff wanted to know if he could ask me a hypothetical question. I told him of course, ask away. He then followed with this scenario: "What if there were four wrestlers who worked for this certain company and they were very unhappy and wanted to quit?" It was early. I wasn't fully awake yet, but I still kind of clued in to who he was talking about. After all, it was no secret that those four wrestlers were very unhappy in WCW. We even heard the scuttlebutt in WWF.

"Okay," I replied.

Jeff continued, "And these four wrestlers don't know if the other major wrestling company would have any interest in them."

Now I was fully awake and I said to him, "Are we talking about the four guys I think we are talking about?"

"*Yes!*" he said emphatically.

This was unbelievable. I thought for a few seconds as this was absolutely out of my area of expertise and definitely not part of my job description. At this point, I definitely knew who Jeff was talking about. I also knew that he was good friends with Chris Benoit and that he knew the others as well. I told Jeff to give me a little time to make a call and I would phone him back. A hundred different thoughts were running through my head. *Did this just happen? Should I get involved? Is this considered some form of tampering with talent under contract to another company? What's my next move? Who can I call?*

I searched the numbers on my cell and decided to call Michael "P.S." Hayes, who is an influential member of the creative team. I got along well with Michael and felt comfortable with him, so I figured he would be a good place to start. I called and when he answered, I said, "Hello, P.S., it's Jimmy Korderas."

You could tell he was a bit puzzled because I very rarely if ever called anyone from the office unless it was truly important.

"Hey, Jimmy, what's up?" he answered, sounding a little curious.

I proceeded to explain the phone call I had received from my friend. I told him that this was surely outside my area of expertise with the company and asked him what I should do next. Even though I didn't mention any names, Michael knew as I did who we were all talking about. He told me not to do anything just yet and he would get back to me. I began to worry. I started thinking that maybe I'm getting the wwf in hot water. Maybe they would not appreciate my involvement in this situation. One thing I did know was that I was in way over my head and should just let those who deal with this sort of stuff handle it.

Just then my phone rang again, "Hi, Jimmy, it's Bruce Prichard." *Holy crap!* Why was Bruce calling me? Now I'm really thinking that I'm in big trouble. Bruce was one of Vince McMahon's multitasking right-hand men. He was a writer, agent, and producer as well as an assistant with Talent Relations.

Trying to sound calm, I said, "Hi, Bruce, I'm assuming that P.S. gave you a call?"

"Yeah, he did. What's going on?" he asked.

I explained the whole thing to Bruce. After I was done giving him the lowdown, Bruce asked me if I was sure we were talking about the four guys we all assumed we were talking about. Right then I thought, *Why is everyone asking the same question; of course it is the same four guys we are all talking about. You would think by now we would all have it figured out.* Then he asked me if my friend could be trusted. I assured Bruce that we were talking about the same four individuals and that I had no reason not to trust my friend.

Bruce then said, "All right then, give your friend my pager number and have him call me and leave his number and I will contact him."

I called Jeff back with all the info I had been given. We had a short conversation about wrestling in general and how things were getting very interesting. We then wished each other well and hung up the phone. I didn't hear another thing about this until a few weeks later. On the January 31, 2000, *Monday Night Raw* in Pittsburgh, Pennsylvania, the Radicalz debuted attacking the New Age Outlaws, Road Dogg Jesse James and the Bad Ass Billy Gunn. The place exploded as these four outsiders jumped over the security barrier and soundly manhandled these established wwf superstars. Eddie, Chris, Dean, and Perry were now members of the wwf family and I like to think that I had a hand in bringing them into the fold. Okay, a small hand, but a hand nonetheless.

For me the best thing to come out of these new arrivals was that I developed a close relationship with Eddie, Dean, and Chris. Don't get me wrong, Perry and I got along fine, it was just that he kind of did his own thing, marching to the beat of his own drum.

When I first met Eddie Guerrero, it's not like we became instant buddies. You could sense that he was maybe a little overwhelmed by his new surroundings. It is understandable that there would be an adjustment period. I can't speak for the atmosphere he was subjected to in the wcw; all I can tell you is that in the wwf at that time, it truly felt like we were all on the same team. I believe that Eddie and the others were a little apprehensive, not being sure how well they would be accepted. I also believe that the uncertainty they felt regarding their acceptance by the WWF locker room was quickly put to rest. Despite the rivalry between the WWF and WCW, in my mind there was never really any heat between the talents. After all, the boys are the boys and they will always have each other's backs. That being said, the Radicalz were now a welcomed addition to the WWF roster.

Back to Eddie. One night after a television taping in Austin, Texas, I believe, I went to the locker room to get changed into my "tear down the ring" clothes. The only two guys there were Chris and Eddie. They were slowly getting dressed but seemed to be having a conversation. I excused myself for interrupting and said I would only be a minute while I quickly got dressed. They both said not to worry and to take my time, that I wasn't interrupting anything important. Before I began to change, I thought this would be a perfect opportunity to spark up a little conversation. After all, it was Eddie Guerrero and Chris Benoit sitting right there, two wrestlers I very much respected. I began by asking them what their take was on the WWF and how the change of scenery had been going for them so far. They agreed that they were both pleasantly surprised at how receptive everyone here was and seemed to want to continue our friendly conversation. I knew plenty about their careers but not a whole lot about them. They also knew nothing about me other than that I was a referee, so I guess they figured now was the time to find out who and what I was all about.

They began asking me questions about how long I had been with the company, how long I had been refereeing, and so forth. I was amazed that they were truly interested in not only my role with the company but me personally. We were sitting across from each other just chatting like old friends. I really had not realized how much time had gone by and I totally forgot that I was in a bit of a hurry to head out to ringside to help tear down the ring. That is until Tony Chimel popped his head into the dressing room door and asked me what was taking so long and that they were almost done and about ready to load the ring truck. Laughing, I apologized and told him I would be right out. Eddie and Chris both apologized for holding me up. I told them not to worry about it and that it was about time that Tony did some work around here and that my back was sore from carrying him for so long. They popped on that one and told me that they very much appreciated my hard work and that they truly respected me because they could tell that my passion for the wrestling business was genuine. I thought, *Wait a minute, this is kind of odd. Here are two guys that I respect the hell out of telling me that they respect me very much.* I was blown away. I thanked them and told them that I hoped we could have more conversations like this. They said most definitely we would. Leaving the locker room the only thing I could think was, *Wow, how freaking cool was that?* Right then and there I knew a friendship was in the making.

Over the next few months not only did I have the opportunity to work in the ring with Eddie Guerrero, I also had the privilege of getting to know him on a personal level. That is when I discovered what a great guy Eddie really was. As I said earlier, he treated me with the utmost respect as he treated everyone who worked for the WWF. He was so humble and grateful that there were times when he would come down to ringside as we were assembling the ring and begin to help out. We would all tell him that it was not necessary and that we had plenty of help. Besides, he had already more than paid his dues and did not have to help us. He would always tell us that this was not his first rodeo and that he had set up many rings before and that he knew what he was doing. We didn't argue with him as we knew he was speaking the truth but that wasn't the point. So all of us on the ring crew would get together and physically get Eddie to stop helping. Of course this was done in a playful manner because we all knew if he wanted to, well, you can fill in the blanks.

Unfortunately for Eddie, he suffered a setback to his career when he was released from the WWF in November 2001. It's no secret that

Eddie had a substance abuse problem at that time. This is well documented in his book. His closest friends were all very concerned for his well-being as were his family. He and his wife had separated while Eddie worked very hard on getting his problem under control. I felt terrible for my friend and was hopeful that he would get the aid and support that he needed. Eddie fought his demons and got the help he so desperately wanted. During this time, Eddie turned to the Bible and, through his faith, reconciled with his family and was ready to return to where he belonged, the WWF.

Eddie returned to the WWF in April 2002. Our friendship pretty much picked up where it had left off. I say pretty much only because there was something a little different about Eddie. He was appreciative of the opportunity he had been given and was even more focused and determined to succeed. As anyone who has gone through the struggle that Eddie Guerrero faced can tell you, it is a daily fight when battling those demons that haunt them. There were many times when Eddie would just sit next to me and share some of the things he was finding conflict with. He told me that sometimes he just needed to express his thoughts without someone judging him or trying to offer advice. All I would do was listen, I mean really listen, and offer words of encouragement. I also stressed to him that anytime, day or night, he was more than welcome to call me and I would be there to help. Even if it was just to let him vent. Don't get me wrong here. I don't want to make it appear that I was Eddie's best friend. After all, Chris, Dean, Rey Mysterio, Chavo, and JBL were all his closest friends. Not that we didn't have a special bond as well — I just want people to understand our relationship. We were good friends and as a good friend will do, he also offered me some great advice.

Here's a quick story demonstrating how big a heart Eddie had and how he gave back to his fans. Fast-forward a few years to the day after Eddie realized his dream of becoming WWE champion. It was February 16, 2004, and we had a live event scheduled for Stockton, California. Eddie had just finished wrestling in the main event, a six-man tag match. After the match was over and the boys were back in the locker rooms, Charles Robinson and I began to dismantle the ring. All the fans had been cleared out of the building, all except for one young boy in a wheelchair and his mother. The building security was trying desperately to get them to leave but the boy was crying. I wanted to find out what was going on so I walked over to where they all were and right away knew the young boy in the wheelchair was a special needs kid. He wanted so badly to meet his idol, Eddie Guerrero.

The security guard was having none of it and when his mother tried to explain to the boy that it was not possible for him to meet his hero, the kid just fell apart. Watching all this unfold, I decided I would try to help the situation. I told the security guy and the boy's mother to wait two minutes and I would see what I could do, no promises. I yelled to Charles that I would be right back and ran to where Eddie was changing. Fortunately, Eddie had not begun to change. He was engaged in a conversation with the others in the room. I excused myself for interrupting and whispered to Eddie what was going on out in the arena. Before I could finish, he snatched his WWE title, got up, and said, "Show me where they are."

I led him to where the boy and his mother were. It was an incredible sight to see. Watching Eddie interact with this kid was magical. He spent about 15 minutes with the youngster chatting, asking him how he was, and giving him encouragement. It was truly an amazing moment that really no one but a few of us was privileged to witness. It is a memory that I vividly recall to this day, a reminder of how much Eddie gave back to the fans.

One of the things Eddie did for me was to help me bring out my creative side as it related to the wrestling business. For a long time, I had ideas for adding to existing storylines and spots for matches as well as some ideas for match finishes. The problem was I didn't believe it was my place to suggest certain things to the wrestlers. Right or wrong, I wasn't sure how my input would be interpreted by the guys who actually performed what I wanted to recommend to them. I just couldn't bring myself to do it. Then one day Eddie was going over a match at ringside during a TV taping. This was the beginning of the Latino Heat character and involved his mantra "Lie, Cheat, and Steal." As I listened in on the ideas being bandied about, Eddie noticed that a big smile had come over my face. He looked at me, smiled, and said, "Why have you got that big smile on your face? What are you thinking?"

"Something just popped into my head; you don't want to hear it, though," was my reply.

His smile almost seemed to disappear. "Look, if you have an idea, I want to hear it. Never think that you can't say anything to me. Some guys may not appreciate it but I am open to everyone's ideas. We all work together."

I told Eddie that from then on whenever I had an idea pertaining to him, I would tell him about it and he could decide if he liked it or not. He actually used a few of my suggestions with a slight "Latino Heat" modification to it. I can't describe how good that made me feel. Eddie Guerrero liked and implemented one of my ideas into his character. We often had conversations about different ways to utilize his Lie, Cheat, and Steal motto. Sometimes he would use them and sometimes he wouldn't, but he always genuinely appreciated my input. He also told me that he could see that I had passion for the wrestling business and had good ideas. He said that I should not be shy and to present my ideas whenever I had them. After that day, my confidence got a huge shot in the arm. I learned quickly how to introduce an idea to the boys without appearing to be a smartass. Most of the boys welcomed my input whether they used the ideas or not, while only a few didn't respond to them so well.

There was one scenario I talked to Eddie about that he liked and told me that I should tell someone about it. The idea was a finish to a tag-team match that would incorporate the Lie, Cheat, and Steal persona that was now synonymous with the Guerrero name. Eddie was one half of the tag-team champs with his partner

Tajiri. His regular partner was his nephew Chavo Guerrero. Chavo was only three years younger than his uncle Eddie and they were more like brothers. Chavo had recently injured his arm and was on the shelf for a while, hence the substitution with Tajiri.

Back to the finish I had come up with. At *SmackDown* TV, I approached road agent/producer Dean Malenko. Dean was easygoing and we had a good rapport. I had become very comfortable talking to him about anything, especially presenting ideas for matches or storyline-related material. In this instance, my idea was for the heels, in this case Charlie Haas and Shelton Benjamin, to be getting the better of Eddie during the match. Eddie would then make the "hot tag" to Tajiri, who would come in the ring and clean house. There would be several near-falls and eventually Charlie and Tajiri would be the only ones in the ring as Eddie would take out Shelton on the outside. Here is when it would get interesting. Charlie ends with his finishing move, the Haas of Pain, on Tajiri. The referee is asking Tajiri if he wants to give up. The referee's back is to the timekeeper's table. Eddie, seeing an opportunity, walks over to the timekeeper's table, grabs the bell hammer, and rings the bell and runs away. The referee turns to argue with the timekeeper, asking why he rang the bell when he did not call for it. While they argue, Eddie sneaks in the ring with one of the tag titles. As he is about to nail Charlie with the title, the ref begins to turn around. Before he turns completely, Eddie tosses the belt to Charlie and lies on the canvas as if he had been hit with the object Charlie was holding. The referee would see Eddie on his back and Charlie holding the incriminating evidence and call for a disqualification of Haas and Benjamin. Once again, Latino Heat would have Lied, Cheated, and Stolen his way to victory.

After I explained this whole scenario to Dean, he said he liked it a lot and would present the idea to Vince McMahon. If Vince liked it, Dean said he would take credit for it. If Vince didn't like it, he would tell him that it was my idea. Funny guy! After the agents' meeting that day Dean came to me and said that Vince loved the idea and that they were going to use it on TV that night. The match went off without a hitch. I did not officiate the match; instead I watched it in the Gorilla Position. The timing of everything was executed perfectly. Everyone in Gorilla applauded after the match. The Big Show, who was in Gorilla enjoying the match, looked over to Dean and said, "What a great finish; good job, Deano."

As Dean stood up he pointed over to me and said to Show, "That was Jimmy's finish. He came up with it."

Show looked at Dean and then he looked over at me and smiled. He gave me a high five and said, "Good job, Jimmy. Not bad for a Greek." Show's wife is of Greek descent so he ribs me with Greek jokes all the time.

Vince and Stephanie McMahon were also in Gorilla watching the matches. Both of them looked over and nodded their approval. What a moment for me. Kudos from the bosses and the boys was a real badge of honour for me and I owe it all to Eddie for giving me the courage to speak up.

Another great honour for me was when I was given the opportunity to referee the match between Eddie Guerrero and Rey Mysterio at *WrestleMania 21* in Los Angeles, California. This bout was going to open the show — a very important spot on the card, especially for an event of this magnitude and importance. It sets the tone for the rest of the evening, and the opening match is counted upon to get the audience engaged. The choice of putting this match on first seemed logical. Both Eddie and Rey were hugely popular with the fans, making this an interesting and fun match-up that would deliver excitement. I must admit, the nervous energy exhibited by all three of us demonstrated how important *WrestleMania* is. It is like the Super Bowl of sports entertainment and that is exactly how we treated it. The nerves seemed to get to Eddie a bit more than Rey or me. Let me explain.

The story going into the match was that Eddie had faced Rey a few times recently but had been unable to score a victory. As the match progressed on this night, Eddie would attempt to pin Rey several times unsuccessfully. With each failed pin attempt, Eddie's frustration would grow. Now the agent for this match was Dean Malenko, a close friend of both men. As the agent, Dean had a direct line to the referee, in this case yours truly. I'm not sure if it was Dean himself or possibly Vince McMahon, but someone was not happy with the frustration, or lack thereof, shown by Eddie. A few times during the match, Dean would tell me in my earpiece to "tell Eddie to show more frustration!"

Like any good referee, I did just what he told me to do. Unfortunately for me, Eddie didn't appear too thrilled to be hearing me relay Dean's message. The look on his face the first two or three times I told him what they wanted was really quite scary. I made sure to let him know that the instructions were coming from elsewhere and not from me. That didn't seem to matter as I still got the cold stare.

As the end of the match neared, Eddie tried one more time to pin Rey and gain a victory over his friend. Once again, his pin attempt failed: Rey kicked out at two and three quarters. Eddie sat there dumbfounded for a moment. Right then and there Dean repeated the same thing he had told me several times before in this match, "Tell Eddie to show more frustration!"

I leaned in closer to Eddie so I could relay the same message as before. This time, I got a completely different result. I had barely begun to speak when Eddie, clearly and legitimately frustrated with being told the same thing over and over again, turned to me in the middle of the ring and angrily shouted, "Shut the fuck up!"

Stunned by what I had heard, my first thought was shutting the fuck up! I was not offended or anything like that. I completely understood where he was coming from. Here you are performing on the biggest show of the year and you have someone constantly telling you what to do. Meanwhile, you have this idea in your head and you want to execute the game plan your way. The last thing you need are distractions.

The match had ended as planned and we made our way back-stage. Eddie and Rey hugged and thanked each other for the match. This is customary in wrestling, to thank your opponent and ref-eree. It is a show of respect and gratitude. As I went up to Eddie to thank him for the match, the first thing he did was apologize for swearing at me in the ring. Before he could finish his apology, I cut him off and said there was no need to apologize and that I totally understood why he had said it. I know he felt bad, but after a few minutes we all had a good laugh about it with Rey as well. It did provide me with a *WrestleMania* moment I will never forget.

Once again, it was time for me to present another idea I had for Eddie regarding his eventual split with his tag-team partner Rey Mysterio. At this point in time Rey and Eddie were the tag champs but would eventually lose the titles to the team of MNM. The plan was for them to have a falling out and develop their own rivalry. The tension between the two was already well documented and now the time was right for them to go their separate ways — but not before they had engaged in a heated feud. How the split would finally happen was what I had been thinking about.

After weeks of minor dissension, the split was going to happen in England, where the WWE was taping their TV that week. Two or three nights before that tapings, we were in Ireland. Eddie and I had a long conversation about many things. After an evening of playing cards with the regulars and having a few pops, I made my way to the elevator, heading to my room. Eddie had just come out of the restaurant and headed to the elevators as well. In his hand he had a can of Coke Classic. We rode up the lift together and struck up a conversation. Since we exited on the same floor, we continued talking in the hall just outside the elevators. Among the topics we discussed were family, the business, and his ongoing battle to stay clean and sober. If you haven't seen it, you really don't know how much of struggle it is for someone battling substance abuse. The good thing for Eddie was he was winning his battle. At that time he was more than three years clean and sober. Another thing we talked about was his faith and how rediscovering and reconnecting with that faith saved him and gave him back his family. The conversation wasn't one-sided. He did ask me a ton of questions about my family, my faith, as well as my goals in wrestling. Eddie knew that I wanted more than to just be a referee. I wanted to contribute creatively and in other ways as well.

One of the things I wanted to talk to Eddie about was how he and Rey could part ways with Eddie as the bad guy. After all, in my mind it was a great idea that I thought no one would see coming and be very surprised with. "Here's the plan!" I told him excitedly. I sometimes tend to get just a little too animated when presenting my ideas. I have Greek blood flowing through my veins; I can't help but talk with my hands. I continued to explain my vision to him all the while giving him my hand-assisted recreation. After finishing what I believed was a new and fresh approach to having tag-team partners break up, I waited for any kind of reaction from Eddie. He thought for a moment, turned his head to look me in the eyes, grinned, and said, "I love it! That's great. When did you think of this?" I said that I had thought of it the previous night while on the bus heading back from the arena to the hotel. I explained to him that sometimes, ideas just pop in my mind and that usually it is sparked by something I had recently seen. He laughed and said he was going to suggest my scenario to the boss and was hopeful they would go with it. Eddie then wished me a good night and said we would talk more the next day. I thanked him for listening to my rambling, and we went to our respective rooms.

I guess I should let you in on my master plan. I will endeavour to explain it as best as I can without the use of my hands. The match featured the team of Rey and Eddie, who were already experiencing friction, as they took on MNM, Joey Mercury and Johnny Nitro accompanied by Melina. As did happen during the match that aired on TV, there would be a point in the bout where Rey would accidentally hit Eddie instead of one of MNM. The only change I would have made was during the hot tag. Rey would enter the ring like "a house on fire" as the saying goes. He'd dominate both of his opponents, sending one of them crashing to the outside while isolating the other in the ring. As the match continued, Rey and his rival collide mid-ring and they both end up lying flat on their backs with the member of MNM closer to the babyface corner and Rey lying farther away. As the other MNM member, who was outside the ring, tries to enter to help his partner, the referee prevents him from getting in and interfering. With the referee distracted, Eddie climbs up to the top turnbuckle, about to leap with his signature Frog Splash finishing maneuver. As Eddie leaps from the top, instead of hitting the MNM opponent who was lying closest to him, he would fly over his opponent and come crashing down on his partner, Rey Mysterio. Then Eddie would pull MNM on top of Rey and exit the ring enraged. The referee would then turn to see Rey being pinned, count to three, and MNM are still your world tag-team champions. Eddie would walk away from the ring and his partner, thus beginning a new rivalry with his former friend. That was how I envisioned it going down. I liked it but, then again, I am just a tad biased.

The day of the TV taping arrived and, sure as his word, Eddie went to those in charge and presented them with my layout for his break-up with Rey. When he came to find me to let me know what had been decided, you could see the disappointment in his face. Eddie told me they liked the idea *but* that was not how they wanted the scene to play out. I was really not too upset about it because I understood that it was just business. Just goes to show, there is always more than one way to get the desired results. Would I have liked to see my idea come to fruition? Absolutely! However, what the company went with worked just fine due mainly to the extraordinary talents of Eddie Guerrero. He definitely made that whole thing special.

Anyone who has worked with Eddie can tell you how much he loved what he did. He poured his heart and soul into the wrestling business. I always felt that I was the same way. Maybe that's why we got along so well. When you look at all the guys he was good friends with, they all shared an incredible passion for the business, as did I. As I stated before, you make only a few real friends in this industry and Eddie was one of them.

November 13, 2005, Minneapolis, Minnesota: another day etched in my mind. It began like any other day. It was a Sunday and we were going to tape both *Raw* and *SmackDown* that evening as we were embarking on a European tour immediately following the show. As I made my way to the lobby to check out, I had this odd feeling that something was going on. I checked out of the Marriott Hotel and decided to make the 10- or 15-minute walk to the arena with my friend and frequent travel companion Tony Chimel. The best part about walking over to the Target Center was that you never had to go outside to get there. There is an indoor route one can take to get there and that's what we did. Funny thing is, if we had gone out the front doors of the hotel, we might have noticed all the commotion that was going on. We had no clue that anything was wrong.

At the arena, things seemed normal, nothing out of the ordinary that we could see. Of course, the first order of business was to hit catering. Even before we could get some food on our plates, we noticed something was amiss. Bruce Prichard and Michael Hayes, both influential members of the creative team, abruptly left the catering room. That eerie feeling was now getting stronger. I left without eating anything and made my way down the hall towards the production office to see if I could find out what was up. Before I got there, I ran into Derek Casselman. Derek is one of the main merchandise people working for the WWE and a fellow Canuck. The first thing he said to me was, "Is it true what they're saying about Eddie?"

"What are they saying about Eddie?" I replied.

He continued, "Someone said they found him dead in his hotel room this morning."

I couldn't believe what I was hearing. I told Derek that if this was his idea of a bad joke — Derek stopped me before I could finish my sentence. He assured me it was not a joke and that was what he was hearing. I was in complete shock. Could this be true? He was so darn young, 38 years old, there was no way it could be true. I quickly made my way to the production office and everyone there was sombre. I really don't remember who broke the news to me. It was indeed the truth; Eddie Guerrero had been found in his hotel room by his nephew Chavo early that morning.

To say I was shocked would be a gross understatement. I was devastated. Then I thought, if I was feeling this terrible, I could only imagine how his closest friends and family were taking this tragic news. As I walked out of the production office, a rush of emotions started to overtake me. I quickly ran outside the arena towards where the TV truck was parked, sat on a road case, and began to cry. Eddie's passing touched me very deeply. It is so difficult to express the many emotions that I went through that day. He was more than just a colleague; he was our friend. Just as with the passing of Owen, to this day I find it difficult to put my feelings into words. One thing that did help comfort us during this tragic time was that the WWE mourned Eddie's passing as a family.

Later on that afternoon, Eddie's nephew Chavo, Chris Benoit, and Rey Mysterio arrived at the arena, clearly distraught. I expressed my sincerest condolences, told them that if they needed anything at all not to hesitate to ask, and left them to take care of what they had to do.

The crew was now setting up the arena for a special night of WWE television. Both *Monday Night Raw* and *SmackDown* would be tribute shows to our friend. First up was *Raw*. Every WWE superstar, referee, backstage worker, and crew member gathered on the set as Vince McMahon addressed all of us. Vince spoke about how much Eddie was loved by all those who had the honour of knowing him and how he would be greatly missed. He also said that on this day of mourning, the WWE would celebrate the life of Eddie Guerrero. Then a memorial video package aired on the big screen set to Johnny Cash's cover of "Hurt." The outpouring of emotion was overwhelming.

It was time for us to tape the *SmackDown* tribute show. Veteran referee Nick Patrick handled the ref assignments on this day. I thanked him for giving me the privilege of refereeing the match between Triple H and Chris Benoit. I approached Triple H to ask him what he and Chris were going to do in the match. He put a hand on my shoulder and calmly said, "I really don't know. We are going to call it out there. He's going over rolling me up out of the cross-face somehow. Don't worry about it. Just count three."

It was time for the match and I was having trouble controlling my emotions. Somehow, I managed to get myself together and made my way to the ring. As both Triple H and Chris entered the ring, it became an increasing struggle to maintain my composure. The match itself was a classic encounter featuring two of the best in the world. When it was time for the finish, I counted three and raised Benoit's hand in victory. Triple H stood up and walked over to Chris. I exited, leaving the ring to the two superstars. They embraced and that's when the waterworks began again for me. Triple H raised Chris's hand and left the ring as well. Just then, Dean Malenko entered the ring, and he and Chris hugged and paid tribute to their longtime friend.

When we all finally got backstage, the first person I ran into was Triple H, who gave me a hug and said, "Good job, Jimmy, thanks."

I thanked him and just then, Chris came up to us. He and Triple H hugged and thanked each other. Chris then turned to me, grabbed me, and gave me a big hug. We were both in tears. It was emotionally and physically draining.

As I mentioned earlier, we were all scheduled for an overseas tour to Europe and were taking a chartered flight from Minneapolis after the show. We showered, boarded the buses, and made our way to the airport. As you could imagine, the bus ride as well as the long flight to the UK were sombre and relatively quiet. It was going to be a difficult tour anyway but now the added mental strain of Eddie's passing would make the trip even harder. Not making things any easier was the ten-bell salute before each show on the tour. It is our tradition to remember our fallen friends. Thank goodness we had each other to help us through this difficult time.

The tour finally ended and it was time to head home for almost a week. I couldn't wait to see my wife and family. I was so exhausted that I think I slept for almost 24 straight hours. I really need to thank my wife, Audra. She is the foundation that kept and still keeps me grounded and gets me through trying times in my life. She is truly amazing and I am blessed that we are together.

One last thing I would like to say about my friend Eddie Guerrero: I would like to thank him for being such an influence on me and helping me in so many ways. He was an inspiration to so many of us. I miss you, buddy, and I will never forget you. *Viva la raza!*

CHAPTER 19

Chris Benoit

I had trouble putting my thoughts to paper when the subject turned to my gone but not forgotten friends Owen Hart and Eddie Guerrero. This chapter may be the hardest of all. Searching for the right words given what happened can be a daunting task, but I feel I must address Chris Benoit. How do you find the words when you are talking about someone who was your colleague and friend? Someone who showed you a tremendous amount of respect and you respected equally as much? How does one describe one of the most talented and dedicated in-ring performers under such trying circumstances? A man who has brought so much joy to wrestling fans all over the world and whose actions during his final days overshadowed what definitely would have been a Hall of Fame career?

On Saturday June 23, 2007, Chris Benoit was scheduled for a live event in Beaumont, Texas, for which he no-showed. It was extremely unusual for someone like Chris to miss an event. I'm not sure who contacted whom but Chris spoke with Scott Armstrong and Chavo Guerrero and informed them that his wife and son were ill and that he would be in Houston for the Vengeance PPV the following day. Sunday came and Benoit was nowhere to be found. No one knew what was going on, but everyone commented that something was not right. The show went on without Benoit, who had been scheduled to win the ECW title that night. Still, almost everyone, including myself, were wondering what was going on.

Monday, June 25, 2012, Corpus Christi, Texas. That was the night the WWE was to hold a "memorial service" for Vince McMahon, who had apparently been blown up in a limousine the week before. The talk that day was not about the show but rather where Chris Benoit was. The WWE called a talent and crew meeting that took place in the arena's seating area. Before the meeting began, Vicki Guerrero began crying and left the arena floor. That's when we all knew the news would not be good. A very sombre Vince McMahon began to speak and told us what they knew by that point. Chris Benoit; his wife, Nancy; and his son, Daniel; had been found dead in their home. At that time, that was all the information we had. It was decided that *Raw* that night would now be a tribute show dedicated to the life and career of Chris Benoit, featuring his past matches as well as comments from colleagues. All the praise and kind words about Chris Benoit spoken by his peers that night were genuine and heartfelt. However, things began to unravel once more news about the deaths was revealed.

Late that night and the next day, details regarding the deaths began to emerge. The authorities determined that Benoit had murdered his wife, then his son, before committing suicide. I will not get into the graphic details on how these murders and suicide were done. You can find that information for yourselves elsewhere. All I can tell you is that no one could believe what they were hearing. I myself couldn't believe the conclusions the police came up with. This was not the man I knew. I knew his wife and his son. He adored Daniel. Watching a shy Daniel mimicking his dad as he warmed up before a match, matching his father push-up for push-up, Hindu squat for Hindu squat, made us all smile. How could he do such a thing to that little boy he loved so much?

As more details of the case became public, the press had a field day raking the wrestling business and in particular the WWE over the coals. They tried to place the blame on everything from steroids to unrealistic work schedules to anything else they could make up. All of a sudden, there were dozens of former wrestlers on all the cable news networks adding their "expertise" to the situation. Some were just trying to regain their 15 minutes of fame; others were furthering their own agendas, while some were just trying to explain what they believed this really was. What most of us thought was that this was an isolated incident that no one saw coming. What caused Chris Benoit to brutally kill his wife and son and then commit suicide? We may never know the truth. I can't speak for the rest of the roster. I only know how I felt at that time.

This was a man who called me several times when I had a family emergency and had to fly home. He and Eddie would call almost daily and ask how things were going and tell me if I needed anything to please call. This was a man who a few months before his death had a conversation with me at ringside one day asking about my family. Then out of nowhere, he said that he knew I had regular riding partners but that he would like to travel together because we never had the opportunity to do so and he enjoyed talking to me. He had regular travelling partners in Chavo Guerrero and Scott Armstrong, which is why I found his idea of travelling together interesting. Maybe he meant the four of us together. I don't know. Even now when I think back to that conversation there's a part of me that wonders what it really was that Chris was looking for, if anything. Maybe he just wanted to expand our friendship.

It's just so puzzling to me how this man who was so giving to his peers could commit such a terrible act. If you lined up a thousand guys and asked me to pick the one who would do such a horrible thing, Chris would be one of the last guys I'd pick. That being said, Chris had changed somewhat after his best friend Eddie

Guerrero passed away. I can't put my finger on the change, but he never seemed like the same guy or like he'd recovered fully from the loss. That doesn't mean we saw something like this coming. Never in my wildest nightmares would I have ever expected something so horrible to happen. In my opinion he just seemed sad that his best friend was gone. He was still very helpful to young guys and mentored people such as rising star MVP. He took MVP under his wing because he saw something in him that he identified with. What that was one can only guess, but there was a bond between the two of them. To me, Chris's relationship with MVP was just what Chris needed.

I am honestly having a terrible time finding the right words to describe my feelings. I keep going back and forth with my approach here. Maybe what I need to do is just be honest. The Chris Benoit I knew and worked with and became friends with was not the man who committed those horrible crimes. I will not profess to have known him better than anyone else or to have been closer than others. After all, he never spoke to me about his home life or any problems there may have been there. I believe he kept that all close to his chest. He was a very private man when it came to his family.

I know these were not the actions of a rational person. I will not speculate on the events of that terrible weekend. I believe no one will ever know the absolute truth about what transpired. What I do know is there is nothing that can be done to change what happened. People can choose to remember Chris Benoit any way they see fit. The WWE chooses not to mention him in their history or their DVDs and that's their prerogative. When I think about Chris I want to remember my friend who contributed so much to the wrestling business that I love and helped so many others by passing on his knowledge. Unfortunately, his good work throughout his career and all the positives he brought to the ring will never excuse his actions that night. To this day I find it difficult to come to grips with the events of that day and make sense of it all. I suppose it will never make sense. All I can think of is that another of our brothers is gone. There are too many friends gone too soon. Regardless of the circumstances surrounding their deaths, I still miss them all to this day.

CHAPTER 20

My *WrestleMania* Moments

When I look back at some of my most significant career moments, one word seems to pop up a lot: *WrestleMania*. I have participated in 14 *WrestleMania*s as a referee. There were others in which I did not referee, but performed other duties. I was a team player and did whatever was asked of me, but being in the ring was what I really preferred. When I think back to my first *WrestleMania* and how much of a big deal it was to me I kind of chuckle. Being a witness to how the event has morphed and evolved into what it has become is nothing short of astonishing. Who would have thought that Vince's big gamble back in 1985 would develop into what it is today. The pageantry, the magnitude — it is simply breathtaking. The evolution of the event from my first appearance at *WrestleMania IV* in Atlantic City to my final one at *WrestleMania XXIV* was remarkable.

It may sound to some as if I'm overstating *WrestleMania*'s importance. I beg to differ. As a matter of fact, I think I may be understating its significance and those who have participated in one know what I am talking about. I would love to go through every match at every 'Mania that I have refereed, and believe me I have every one of them on tape or disc somewhere in my collection. Instead, I will cherry-pick just a few of my favourite matches or moments. These are the ones that are dear to me. There were so many, so the selection process is difficult.

Let me begin with *WrestleMania IV* airing from within the shadow of the boardwalk in Atlantic City, New Jersey. In all, there were 16 matches on the card, and I refereed four of them. This was my inaugural 'Mania and what a way to make an impact. Right at the start of the show, Joey Marella and I were shown walking with the Battle Royal trophy to the ring. The winner of the match would be presented with the trophy. What no one knew was that the day before, while Joey and I had a practice run walking the trophy to the ring, we accidentally broke it. Fortunately for us we were at the Trump Plaza Convention Center and there were carpenters on duty. They fixed the trophy for us and all seemed well. That was until the end of the Battle Royal. After Bad News Brown double-crossed Bret Hart to win the match, Bret got some payback by tossing Brown out of the ring and then proceeded to *try* to smash the trophy to bits. I said try because the carpenters who repaired it did a great job. Unfortunately for Bret, they did too good a job. Bret stomped, kicked, and did everything he could to break the damn thing but couldn't. Eventually he gave up and just threw it out of the ring. *WrestleMania* was off to an awesome start.

Next up for me was the first-round elimination tournament match with Don Muraco versus Dino Bravo. Bravo lost the match via disqualification after pulling yours truly directly into the path of a charging Muraco. So in my first *WrestleMania* singles bout, I took my first ref bump of two that night. I'll get to the other bump soon, but this one hurt because Muraco's rather large elbow hit me right on the collarbone. It was painful but there was no selling it once I got to the back. I didn't want to seem like a wimp.

Now it was time for me to ref the final first-round tournament match featuring Jake "The Snake" Roberts taking on "Ravishing"

Rick Rude. The finish here was a 15-minute time limit draw, thus eliminating both men from the tourney. I remembered the finish of the match but I forgot to keep an eye on the timekeeper for the time cues. I was so into the match that I brain-cramped. Eventually they rang the bell, ending the match. I think if you go back and watch this match again and timed it from bell to bell, it might have gone a bit longer than 15 minutes. One day I'll go back and check it out.

The fourth and final match I refereed at *WrestleMania IV* was the Intercontinental title match. The champion the Honky Tonk Man, accompanied by Jimmy "Mouth of the South" Hart and Peggy Sue, defended his title against Brutus "The Barber" Beefcake. The end of this would see me take my second ref bump of the night. The execution of the finish was fine. It was the end result that didn't quite go as planned. For many years there was an urban myth about me being knocked out by Jimmy Hart's megaphone. I can no longer allow Jimmy to be blamed for something he didn't do. He did not knock me out with his megaphone. I knocked myself out when I dropped face first and my chin hit the canvas. I was supposed to slowly come around and explain that Honky was DQ'd but I was dazed. Joey Marella and Danny Davis carried me to the back. I don't recall much once I got there. Let's just say I was done for the night. My first *WrestleMania* experience was in the books and I couldn't wait for the next one.

I was not a part of *WrestleMania V*, which was once again at Trump Plaza in Atlantic City. My next 'Mania was *WrestleMania VI* from the SkyDome in my hometown of Toronto, Ontario. No ref bumps for me in the three matches I refereed this time around. There was of course the Robert Goulet national anthem caper, which I've documented in an earlier chapter. The three matches I refereed were Earthquake versus Hercules, the Barbarian versus Tito Santana, and Rick Rude versus "The Superfly" Jimmy Snuka. I was also part of a run-in to help break up the Bad News Brown/ Rowdy Roddy Piper melee at the end of their match.

For me the entire night was memorable. Being able to perform in front of over 68,000 fans live and millions more on pay-per-view is a natural high that is indescribable. Something I didn't know back then: a young Adam Copeland was in the audience that night about 11 rows back from the ring. Of course you all know the future WWE superstar and Hall of Famer better by his ring name Edge. He would sometimes joke about watching me referee when he and his childhood friend Christian were just kids. I never got upset with him when he said that stuff. What could I have said? He wasn't lying. I smile when I think how cool it is that the kid who watched me at *WrestleMania VI* became one of the most decorated WWE superstars of all time and a deserving member of the Hall of Fame. Even cooler was that he was a major player in my all-time biggest *WrestleMania* moment. More on that in a little bit.

It took me a while before I would get the opportunity to take part in my next *WrestleMania*. For reasons already mentioned in the book, my troubles with a certain superior, it would not be until *WrestleMania 13* in Chicago that I would return to the showcase event for the WWF/E. Although I made several appearances throughout the show, I was not assigned a match on the PPV. Instead, I refereed the pre-show match between Billy Gunn and Flash Funk. I didn't mind reffing that match but I was not on the main show, which is everyone's goal. Billy Silverman, a referee from the east coast whom the WWF used occasionally when running a show in that area, was given a match on the main *WrestleMania* card. I normally do not get upset about these things but in this case, I felt I was more deserving of the spot on the show than him. As usual, I didn't complain and just went with the flow. Still, it was great to be there in any capacity.

WrestleMania XIV in Boston was memorable for many reasons. I got to referee the mixed tag match with Marc Mero and Sable versus Goldust and Luna Vachon. Although I was happy to be on the actual PPV that year, all our thoughts were with Earl Hebner, who had suffered a brain aneurysm a few days before the event. Thankfully he had the presence of mind to call his brother Dave, who called an ambulance. He was rushed in time to a hospital in Boston where they were able to stabilize him. All of us went to visit him the day before the show. He was not looking well at all. His wife, who was flown in to be with him, told us that the doctor said one of three things can happen with an aneurysm: you make a full recovery, you have complications with your health, or you die. It took several months, but Earl made a full recovery and returned to work. He was one of the lucky ones, and we were very happy to have him back with us. Oh yes, we dedicated *WrestleMania XIV* to Earl.

The *WrestleMania* tour continued for me with number XV. It was a busy night for yours truly. I participated in three matches. First was the *Sunday Night Heat* match that featured Miss Jacqueline taking on Ivory. Not much noteworthy in this match but the ladies worked very hard for sure.

My next assignment was match number two on the main card. The WWF tag-team titles were on the line as the champs Owen Hart and Jeff Jarrett accompanied by Debra defended against Test and D'Lo Brown, who were accompanied by Ivory. The champs retained their titles with the aid of Debra, who managed to distract almost everyone in the ring including me.

Later in the evening, I officiated the WWF women's title match. Sable was the ladies' champion and she faced newcomer Tori. The match was moving along just fine until it came time for me to get knocked down and incapacitated for a minute or two. The plan was for Tori to run at Sable in an attempt to hit her with a flying cross body block. Sable would duck out of the way as I positioned myself behind her. Not such a terrible place to be positioned, but I digress. Tori would then hit me with the cross body across the chest. This was supposed to send me crashing to the canvas on my back, where I would sell that the back of my head hit the mat, taking me out of the picture for the proper amount of time. Here's when things went south. Instead of hitting me across the chest, Tori's flying cross body hit me square in the belt buckle. Way too low for me to properly take the bump and sell my head. Trying to think fast, I instinctively and immediately sold my groin area. Tori's elbow did make contact with the family jewels so I figured I might as well go with it.

All would have been just fine if Nicole Bass, who interfered in the match to help Sable, had not entered the ring right where I was selling. I did my best not to see her but to make matters worse, after she did what she was supposed to do, Nicole Bass exited the ring again right where I was selling. Once again I had to do my best to avoid seeing her. I crawled back to the action, counted the pin, and the match was mercifully over. When I got to the back I ran into Kevin Kelly, who was a play-by-play announcer for the wwf at the time, and he commended me for thinking on the fly. He said that under those conditions, I did very well. I very much appreciated his comments. *WrestleMania XV* was in the books, thank goodness.

Anaheim, California, was the site of *WrestleMania 2000*, as it was called. The 16th annual extravaganza aired from the Arrowhead Pond for the second time. I was fortunate to have been assigned the triple threat ladder match for the wwf tag-team championship. The champs the Dudley boys faced the Hardy Boyz and the team of Edge and Christian. This match stole the show. All six men put on a performance that set the standard for any and all future matches of this type. They all gave it everything they had. It did take a toll on their bodies, as all six men were battered and bruised, but they were very happy with their accomplishment. As I said, it was easily the match of the night and put each of them on the wrestling map if they were not on it already. It was one of those moments that had me on edge for the entire match and also made me proud of them all.

Houston, we have a problem! That very well could have been how we remembered *WrestleMania X-Seven* from the Astrodome in Houston, Texas. *WrestleMania X-Seven* is regarded by many as the greatest *WrestleMania* ever from top to bottom of the card. Once again I had the privilege of being assigned what turned out to be the match of the night, the TLC II match. It was a rematch from the

SummerSlam TLC match. The Dudleys, the Hardys, and Edge and Christian tore the house down. Each time these six guys get together in this type of match environment, they always seem to top themselves: a true testament to how good they all are. The highlight spot of the match was when Jeff Hardy was hanging onto the ring several feet above the mat that the title belts were fastened to. Edge climbed a ladder in the corner, took aim, and leaped from the ladder, spearing Jeff in the process as they both crashed to the mat. The entire stadium was on their feet chanting "holy shit" in unison. It was one of the most memorable *WrestleMania* moments of all time.

That match almost didn't take place that evening. There was an incident in one of my prior matches that could have prematurely ended *WrestleMania X-Seven*. It was the Hardcore championship match. The champ Raven defended the title against Kane and the Big Show in a triple threat hardcore match. They started battling in the ring, but it didn't take too long for the fight to make its way to the backstage area. At one point Raven jumped behind the wheel of a golf cart parked in the back. As he pulled away, the Big Show jumped on the back. Raven tried to steer the vehicle clear of the power cables, but his front tires kept lifting off the ground due to Big Show on the back of the cart. The golf cart crashed into a fence where the power cables ran alongside. Fortunately for all involved, the cables were unharmed. Disaster was averted and the PPV was able to continue. *WrestleMania X-Seven* was the best *WrestleMania* that almost didn't happen.

Finally, *WrestleMania* has come back to . . . *Toronto*! That's right; the granddaddy of them all was back in my hometown with *WrestleMania X8*. Besides running around the SkyDome for the Hardcore title's 24/7 rule, I also refereed the European title match, where champion Diamond Dallas Page defeated local hero Christian. With all due respect to Christian and DDP, their match was memorable but the most striking memory I have from the show actually happened well before the doors opened to the public. I was standing out in the stadium leaning on the barricades just taking it all in and remembering back to number 6 and thinking about how things had changed. The set design was elaborate and the production values were marvellous.

As I stood there just enjoying the atmosphere, someone placed a large hand on my shoulder. Much to my pleasant surprise it was the one and only Hulk Hogan. Still with his big paw on my shoulder he said to me, "Now this brings back some awesome memories, doesn't it, brother?"

I know the Hulkster calls everybody brother, but it's still pretty cool nonetheless. I told him it was awesome and that I was having flashbacks from *WrestleMania VI*. He laughed and said, "Yeah, me too, only back then we both had more hair." Again we shared a laugh and chatted about the way the business had changed and the difference between when he started versus then. For me it was just an amazing time shooting the bull with one of the all-time legends in wrestling history.

Later that night when the Rock and Hulk Hogan stood eye to eye in the middle of the ring, I snuck out into the crowd because I wanted to experience it like a fan. I was always a fan and still am to this day, but being out there in the SkyDome listening to the roar of the crowd gave me goosebumps. Toronto was off the hook. I was proud of my hometown.

Seattle, Washington, was the site of *WrestleMania XIX*. What I remember most is not the triple threat tag-team title match I refereed. That match featured the team of Eddie and Chavo, Los Guerreros, versus the team of Rhino and Chris Benoit versus the champs Charlie Haas and Shelton Benjamin. The champs retained in a very good but somewhat rushed match. My most vivid memories are of the main event, where WWE champ Kurt Angle put his title on the line against Brock Lesnar.

These two warriors were having one hell of a match when Brock climbed the corner to the top. Pausing for a second or two, Lesnar attempted a shooting star press, which is basically leaping off the top rope, doing a back flip in mid-air, and landing chest to chest on your prone opponent, who is flat on their back in the ring. As Brock was about to take flight, it appeared that he double-clutched. In other words, he kind of hesitated as he was jumping, which caused him to under-rotate and land on the top of his head. Everyone in the Gorilla Position was frantically trying to communicate with the referee, Mike Chioda, to find out if Brock was injured. All the refs were having trouble with our earpieces that night, so it seemed that Mike was not hearing Gorilla.

Somehow Brock and Kurt got through the match. It was very apparent after the match that Brock did not have all his wits about him. After much coercion from Gerald Briscoe, Lesnar finally agreed to get checked out at a nearby hospital. He had suffered a stinger, which given the circumstances was quite remarkable. Brock dodged a bullet that night.

Kurt Angle was not 100% going into the match and was really feeling the after-effects when he returned backstage. You could see that he was in a lot of pain and his arms were trembling. He too was checked out, but Kurt is a wrestling machine and was there for the next set of television tapings, as was Brock. These two incredible athletes are part of my strongest memories from this *WrestleMania*.

New York, New York, the city so nice they named it twice. *WrestleMania XX* returned to Madison Square Garden, where it all began. I was assigned the opening match, where the United States champ the Big Show took on challenger John Cena. In 2004, John Cena was just two years into his WWE career and you could tell even then that this kid had something. The well-educated and sometimes hard-to-please wrestling fans in MSG cheered this young superstar loudly.

As the match went on, Cena displayed his enormous strength by delivering an F.U. to Big Show. That is a move that required Cena to lift the seven-foot, nearly 500-pound man on his shoulders, then toss him in the air, flipping him on his back. You have to see it to believe it. Usually, that would be enough for Cena to defeat his opponents, but not this time. Big Show surprisingly kicked out of the pin attempt at two, which shocked everyone. Cena thought about it for a second, then went to retrieve the chain he wore to the ring. I, like any good referee would, prevented Cena from using the chain on Show. As I turned my back to get rid of the chain, Cena, without me seeing, pulled brass knuckles from his pocket, punched Big Show with them, and delivered a second F.U. As luck would have it, I turned around just in time to see the F.U. and count one, two, three. John Cena had won his very first WWE title. His career from that point on was pretty good to say the least. It was a special feeling for me knowing that I took part in Cena's very first title in the WWE.

WrestleMania goes Hollywood! The 21st instalment of the yearly classic aired from Tinsel Town, Los Angeles, California, and the Staples Center. For the second year in a row, I refereed the opening contest. As I've said before, the first match on any PPV, especially *WrestleMania*, is the match that sets the tone and the mood for the rest of the show. A good opener gets the crowd into the night early, then it's up to the rest of the card to hold their attention. Rey Mysterio versus Eddie Guerrero did just that. I spoke about this match previously when talking about Eddie. It was one of my favourite *WrestleMania* matches that I have refereed.

The Windy City was once again the site, this time for *WrestleMania 22*: Chicago and the Allstate Arena. I was originally scheduled to take part in two matches this night, the Money in the Bank ladder match and the casket match between the Undertaker and Mark Henry. I offered to give my spot in the casket match to Chris Kay. Chris did not have a match on the show and I thought it would be a huge moment for him to referee a match on *WrestleMania*. It would be an even bigger moment considering it would involve the Undertaker. I spoke with referee Nick Patrick, and we asked John Laurinaitis if he would be okay with the change. John said he was fine with it if the Dead Man was. So we asked Taker if he was cool with the kid being one of the refs for the match. Nick would be the other so there would be a veteran presence manning the casket. The Undertaker gave us his blessing, and Chris Kay had his *WrestleMania* moment.

I was perfectly fine only refereeing the ladder match. Michael "P.S." Hayes explained that I was needed for that particular match because of my experience in those types of matches. It is very comforting to know that your superiors have confidence in your abilities. I was just as happy that I had a hand in making someone else's *WrestleMania* a memorable one. I was just trying to pay it forward.

The Motor City was our next stop for the granddaddy of them all. *WrestleMania* 23 took us back into the stadium setting. Ford Field was the site and on this night, more than 80,000 fans jampacked the arena. Once again, my assignment was the Money in the Bank ladder match. This year, there were be eight participants instead of the usual six. As was the case in every other MITB match, all the guys went above and beyond to entertain. There was one thing that stood out in the match that I believe all who witnessed it still remember. Midway through the match, Jeff Hardy climbed a 15-foot-high ladder inside the ring and on his brother Matt Hardy's urging, he performed a leg drop off that ladder onto Edge, who was lying prone on another ladder outside the ring, set up on the ring apron and the barricade. The impact caused Eddie's ladder to break in half and Edge, along with Jeff, was injured. My first reaction was to check on both men to see if they were okay. Well, not okay but conscious. After we determined that they were responsive, they were eventually carried off on stretchers by the paramedics. Both guys were beat up but they survived. I do think that the toll on their bodies was building up. As we saw a few years later, Edge had to retire from the ring because of all the wear and tear on his body, particularly his neck. That speaks volumes to how much he gave to the business he loved. Thankfully *WrestleMania* 23 was not his last. Edge was back the following year which would turn out to be my final *WrestleMania*.

Whenever I am asked what my favourite *WrestleMania*

memory was or what match was the most significant in my career, the answer to both is the same: *WrestleMania XXIV* in Orlando. The main event was the world heavyweight title match, where the champion Edge faced the Phenom, the Undertaker. This moment might never have happened if it wasn't for Edge.

Originally, I was pencilled in to referee the Money in the Bank ladder match for the third *WrestleMania* in a row. I was told by management that because I had been in so many matches of that type, my experience was needed. I was flattered, but I wanted a bigger challenge. *WrestleMania* is the WWE's biggest event of the year. It is the culmination of many months' worth of storytelling and the resolution to most rivalries. Every wrestler's goal is to appear and one day headline the showcase of the immortals. This is also the goal of all the WWE referees. I would be shocked if it wasn't. I know it was my desire to be in the ring officiating the final match at a *WrestleMania*. Don't get me wrong here, just being on the *WrestleMania* card is a huge honour, but it doesn't get any better than working the main event.

The week before *WrestleMania XXIV* at the final TV tapings before the big event, I was sitting in the locker room preparing to get changed into my ref gear. Seemingly out of nowhere, Edge tapped me on the shoulder. He quietly said that he was going to request me as the referee for his match with the Undertaker at *WrestleMania*. I couldn't believe it. He said it wasn't a slight against any of the other refs. I had been the ref for many of his biggest matches and he felt I should be in there for this one as well. *Wow!* What an honour! I was stunned, shocked, and numb. You name it, that's what I was. At the same time I felt some pressure as well.

I thanked Edge and he left the room. Still a little shocked, I went to get a coffee and ran into the Undertaker in the hall. He asked me if Edge had spoken to me yet. I told him he had and he then asked if I was okay with that. I replied that I certainly was and that I would do my very best not to disappoint either of them. Taker then said, "You won't. That's why we are requesting you."

Did I mention what an honour it was to be requested for the match by the superstars in the match? As elated as I was, it was a subdued elation. This was the main event, the final match of the night. I was putting extra pressure on myself, but this was the biggest match of my career. It doesn't get bigger than being the referee for these two legends.

The night before *WrestleMania*, I had trouble getting to sleep. I was wired and couldn't relax. I decided to go for a walk outside the hotel at about two a.m. It was peaceful as I sat on a bench going over the match in my head. The thing that worried me the most was the Big Boot I was taking from Taker. I wasn't concerned about the kick itself; I was more worried about it looking as good as it possibly could. I didn't want it to look telegraphed or weak. After much thought, I realized that the more I thought about it the more I might mess it up. I said to myself, *Just do what you do best and stop over-thinking.*

It was show day. I was nervous as hell, but it was a good type of nervous. We went over the match one more time; they were ready and so was I. Walking down to the ring and looking out into the crowd gave me goosebumps. When the Undertaker's music hit, a chill went through my body. Not to worry, because the flames shooting up from the stage warmed me up very quickly. I was amazed how much I could feel the heat from so far away. As Taker walked to the ring, the only thing I could think was how breathtaking his entrance is. Then Edge made his grand entrance into the stadium, strutted down the ramp, and called for his signature pyro.

Standing in the middle of the ring between them holding up the world title, I felt this was the crowning achievement in my career and if it were to end the next day, I would be fine with that. The match itself was a clinic in psychology and storytelling. These two greats were having a mat classic as the drama built to the point where the entire stadium was standing. Then my big moment came with the Big Boot to the face. I don't think I gave it away beforehand, but I'll let those who saw it be the judge. I didn't see the boot coming at all. I didn't want to look at it in case I flinched at the last second and make it look weak. I felt the contact but it didn't really hurt. Adrenaline is a wonderful thing. With the boot to the noggin, I was done for the rest of the match. Charles Robinson made the very long run to the ring to finish the match. Me, I was lying outside the ring selling.

After being helped to the backstage area by two of the WWE's athletic trainers, Larry Heck and Jason Crivello, I tried desperately to tone down my excitement. Not quite sure how that worked out because I was pumped. The first person I ran into backstage was Matt Striker. Matt gave me a thumbs up, which made me feel good. I was still a bit worried that Taker or Edge might not have been pleased with my performance. Hopefully they didn't notice me except for those times when I was relaying time cues and setting myself up for that Big Boot.

While waiting for those two to return from the ring, Ricky "The Dragon" Steamboat came up to me, shook my hand, and said, "Great job, Jimmy. The boot looked like it took your head off."

My reply was, "Awesome! How did the rest of the match look?" I wasn't content with having only the boot look good; the rest had to look good as well.

Ricky looked me in the eyes and said, "To tell you the truth, I really didn't notice you during the match. I was so focused on the story Taker and Edge were telling that I didn't notice you. Sorry, Jimmy."

That was music to my ears. "Thanks, Ricky," I shot back. "If you didn't notice me, then I was doing my job properly. I really appreciate the feedback." Now, I just needed to check with the guys in the match to make sure they were happy with everything.

Both men were very tired to say the least after 30 gruelling minutes of excitement and drama. I waited for Edge and Taker to congratulate one another on their masterful exhibition as well as for them to catch their breath. Edge was the first one I approached and thanked for the match. He grabbed me, gave me a big hug, and said, "Thank you, buddy. I'm glad you were a part of it."

I was elated to be a part of the match and Edge knew how much it meant to me. I had been a part of other moments in Edge's career, but this one topped them all, in my opinion. I was starting to get emotional but was able to keep my composure; that is until visiting the Undertaker where he was relaxing before getting changed. I entered the locker room and thanked the Dead Man for the match and allowing me to be a part of this special moment. He shook my hand, thanked me back, and said it was a pleasure working with me. Remember when I said I was feeling a little emotional but was in control? Well, that didn't last too long. After hearing that from the Dead Man, I tried real hard to keep it together, but tears began to flow. No one has ever heard me tell this ever — not even my wife. I had tears of joy from what was the biggest moment of my referee career. I always thought that most of the boys knew how I felt about the wrestling business. I'm sure the Undertaker knew, but if there were ever any doubts, I believe he understood how I felt that night.

WrestleMania XXIV would be my last, but what a way to go out — refereeing the main event with two of the most respected men in the wrestling industry. I could not have asked for a better scenario than that. Thank you, Undertaker and Edge, for making this night the highlight of my refereeing career.

CHAPTER 21

It Was Just Time

Sooner or later, all good things must come to an end. That statement may be true, but it's what you do after the fact that matters. As much as I wanted to believe that I would be a part of the wrestling business forever, I had to be a realist as well. After all, at the end of the day, it is a business and must be treated as such. In the back of my mind, I knew there would come a day when I would have to leave the ring in pursuit of other goals. I hoped that when that time came, it would be the right time.

As I've already mentioned, the most important thing in my life is my family. As passionate as I felt about the WWE, it was always family first for me. It was October 2008 and my family needed me. On a day off from work, I took my father to his doctor's appointment. He had always been able to drive himself before, but for some reason he felt he couldn't go alone and asked me to take him. The doctor examined my dad and then told me that I needed to get my father to the hospital. The doctor said the best course of action was to take my dad home first, make sure he had something to eat, then call an ambulance to take him to Emergency. He explained that if he were to arrive by ambulance, they would look after him more quickly than if we were to walk in. So I did what the doctor ordered and then called my brother and sister to update them. My wife came with me to the hospital and just played the part of glue. She was the calming influence that kept me composed.

Once inside the hospital, they put him right into a bed and began running a battery of tests. Blood work, urine tests, X-rays, the whole nine yards. Looking at his expression, I had an eerie feeling that my dad knew what to expect. I can't explain it, but he wasn't afraid. We waited several hours for the test results to come back and, when they did, we were told that they were referring dad to an oncologist. That was a word we really didn't want to hear. They admitted him that evening so we stayed for a while to make sure he was settled in and that he had everything he needed for the night. As we said goodnight and filed out of the room, no one spoke. I held my wife's hand tightly as my brother comforted my mom. We had an idea this wasn't going to turn out well, but sometimes you just can't bring yourself to accept things.

Two days later we all gathered at the hospital to meet with an oncologist. We were informed by this doctor that my father had been diagnosed with Stage Four Adenocarcinoma. In layman's terms, he had final stage lung cancer. We were floored. We were not expecting good news, but this was the worst case scenario. My sister asked the doctor what the treatment options and prognosis were. The doctor said they could perform radiation and chemotherapy but that they would have little to no effect. As it stood, they gave my father between four and six months to live or with treatment possibly eight months. My mother refused to believe it was anything other than a mistake. She was definitely in denial.

We conferred with Dad. He decided he didn't want the chemo because it would be too hard on his body and that he would just do the radiation. Someone had to be available to take him to his treatments and run errands for my parents. My brother couldn't take the time off work, and he was dealing with a health problem in his family. My sister lived in Napanee, Ontario, and worked in Kingston — almost three hours away — which made it impossible for her to be on call. I figured that the only logical choice would be me. Taking some time off from the road, I spent the next few months looking after my dad, and my mom for that matter. I say I looked after my parents, but *we* would be more accurate. My wife, my brother, and his wife all helped tremendously as well. Even my sister made the commute on weekends to lend a hand. My cousin Julie was also a great support for us. It was truly a team effort, a real family effort.

A few months had passed and my dad was back in the hospital; this time we all kind of knew he was not coming home. He had gone downhill more quickly than anticipated, and it showed. We really didn't know how much time he had. My sister took a leave of absence from her teaching job and was staying with my mom. I don't mean to sound crass, but it had become a waiting game.

Then on January 8, 2009, while driving to the hospital to visit my dad, I got a call from John Laurinaitis. He's the executive vice president of Talent Relations and my direct boss. Now, no one at the wwe really knew how grave my father's situation was. I chose to keep that matter private. All they knew was that I was dealing with a personal family issue. He said that the company was downsizing their workforce by 10%. Without getting into too much detail, after a good conversation with John, we agreed it was time for me to part ways with the wwe. Some things are best left private, and I feel our talk should remain that way. I never had and still do not have any hard feelings toward the wwe. As I mentioned many times, wrestling and in particular the wwe is my passion, and John told me the door was always open. At this juncture in my life there were other priorities that took precedence. Besides, with my father deteriorating rapidly, my heart was not in wrestling at that point. I heard John's words, understood what he said, but it really didn't sink in until much later.

This may sound strange, but I thought I would have been more upset about it. I didn't understand it myself at first, but I was okay with it. Still, no one at WWE really knew how bad the situation was at home. That day I spent with my father. My brother took the evening shift and watched a hockey game with my dad. My dad's favourite team, the Toronto Maple Leafs, played the Montreal Canadiens. My brother was surprised at how much energy he had. He actually got out of bed and watched the game from a chair. Dad hadn't been out of a bed in days so this was remarkable.

Early the next morning, I went to stay with my father for a while. He was in a lot of pain and had nowhere near the energy he had had the night before. Later that afternoon, with the entire family present, Christos Korderas passed away. No matter how much you think you are prepared for this kind of thing, you never really are. It was a difficult time for all of us, but we managed to pull through it as a family.

For the longest time after my father's death, I had no desire to get back to work. We were fine financially, for a while at least, but sooner or later I had to begin working again. That was when it really sunk in. I was no longer working for the WWE. Now the only question was what line of work did I want to pursue? All I had done for almost all of my adult life was wrestling. After much deliberation and discussion with my wife, I decided I wanted to get into some type of broadcasting. It was because of her encouragement and support that I made the choice to give it a shot. I always wanted to try it; all I needed was just a little push. Audra not only gave me that push, she gave me a shove, which was fine by me.

Before I had a chance to do that, my wife's father got sick and was diagnosed with lymphoma. It was another major blow to the family. We had to make a difficult decision. Audra would essentially move to her parents' home in Quebec to care for her parents while I stayed in Toronto to go back to school. Not having Audra around was very tough to deal with but I understood she had to be there for her parents. On a side note, Audra's dad is now healthy and doing fine, fine, fine! I honestly believe that my father-in-law is alive and doing well today because of Audra's TLC. Just ask him, and he'll tell you the same thing.

In the meantime, I went to broadcasting school and set my sights on a career behind the microphone or in front of a camera. Tony Chimel always told me that I had a great face for radio. Little did he know that was exactly where I would end up. While still in school, I was contacted by Arda Ocal, an energetic young man with a mathematics degree from Waterloo University. He was working at the Score, an all-sports television and radio station here in Canada. He and another young man by the name of Corey Erdman had a radio show called *Right After Wrestling* that aired every Monday night right after *Monday Night Raw*. Arda asked me if I would like to do an interview for their show and talk about my time with the WWE. Of course I said yes. The interview went well, and Arda said he wanted to do it again one day. I said sure and didn't think more of it. I thought he was just being nice.

Then I ran into Arda at an independent wrestling show in Vaughan, Ontario. We talked for a while and got along very well. We became fast friends. Then we came up with an idea for his show. Every week we would record a 30- to 45-second bit called Ask the Ref. For the most part it was going to be a tongue-in-cheek segment on the show with the occasional serious answer thrown in. This went on for several weeks. I was having a lot of fun doing the segment and Arda and Corey seemed to like it as well. Then things changed. Corey was reassigned, leaving Arda to do the radio show alone. After recording an Ask the Ref segment, I suggested to Arda that maybe I could come in-studio for a show. Much like the WWE was doing on *Raw* at the time, I could be the guest host for the week. He liked the idea, and I sat in with Arda as a co-host of the show. I guess Arda liked how it went because he asked me if I could come back the next week. "Damn right I can" was what I wanted to say. Instead I said, "Sure, no problem," trying to act cool. That was the break I was looking for and thanks to Mr. Ocal, I had my foot in the door. As the weeks passed, we began to gel as a team. I was learning so much from him and the show was gaining a significant audience. Things were going great and Arda, slowly but surely, was becoming the Canadian version of Tony Chimel.

I was enjoying the radio show immensely, and Arda and I had a good chemistry that was constantly getting better. I continued to learn on the job as I still do to this day, heeding the advice Bobby Heenan gave me many years before. We have fun on the show, and I believe that translates well to our listeners. Things were rolling along as I paid my dues by not getting paid. No complaints; I was new to the industry so that's what you do. Kind of reminds me of the wrestling business. There are many similarities between the two industries, but the biggest difference is you don't have to take bumps on the radio. TV is a different story though.

Again, fortune smiled on me when I was asked to fill in one week for Greg Sansone on the television version of *Right After Wrestling*. Greg was one of the regular analysts on the show and the boss. Now I had been on TV hundreds of times and performed in front of huge crowds, but speaking on TV was a different animal. During all those years I was in the WWE as a ref, fans seldom heard me speak. I only had a few rare speaking roles. Now people could hear what I had to say and that scared me at first. But this was a huge opportunity and I wanted to make the most of it. I was very nervous; however, the duo of Arda and Renee Paquette made me feel comfortable and guided me through the show. I filled in a few more times; then I was asked to be the regular fill-in guy whenever Mauro Ranallo or Greg Sansone was unavailable to do the show. I loved it because I knew I had found my new calling.

As time went on, things began to fall into place. I was contacted by John Pollock of the Fight Network, a combat sports specialty channel here in Canada. Thanks to John, not only was I freelancing for the Score television network, I was now doing previews and reviews for WWE and TNA wrestling PPV on the Fight Network. I was beginning to get a lot of exposure on Canadian TV. Adding to this was the fact that I was now the regular analyst for the Friday night version of *Right After Wrestling*.

Right about this time, the Score was making changes to the *Right After Wrestling* TV and radio shows. The show was rebranded *Aftermath*. Then I was asked to be a WWE analyst for *Aftermath* TV for every show. I was now a regular, and I believe that Renee, Arda, and I have developed a rapport that is fun and entertaining, in my humble opinion. At times I have trouble leaving my wrestling past behind, which was evident when I took a bump on the set of *Aftermath*. Once again I was a part of ground-breaking television. Well, maybe not ground-breaking, but certainly entertaining television. The chairs we sit on when doing the show are reminiscent of chairs you would find at an airport boarding gate. The chairs' legs are more like small skis, if you get my drift. They are placed on a carpeted riser. As we were filming the show one time, I felt like my chair was moving. I wasn't sure if it actually was so I ignored it. That is until the back of the chair slipped off the back of the riser and I was stuck in an awkward position. Fortunately for me I did not fall out of the chair and the chair did not topple over. It was just stuck there on a 45-degree angle. Thanks to cameraman Scott Winters for helping me out of a sticky predicament. We didn't stop filming and just left it in the show. This is a highlight for me to be sure.

Being a freelance analyst for wrestling is mainly what I'm doing now, and I couldn't be happier. I'm not making the money I was making in the WWE, but I am very happy doing what I am doing and I get to be home with my wife and family every night. Also, the people I work with are awesome. They all helped me so much in making the transition to being an on-air analyst as smooth as possible, and I thank them all for their help. Thank you, Greg Sansone, Gordon Fox, Renee Paquette, John Pollock, and especially Arda Ocal. Without your guidance and advice, I would not be in the position I am in today.

I thought with my broadcasting career starting to take flight

I was unlikely to referee a wrestling match for a major company again. Boy, was I wrong. I ended up reffing a few independent events around Toronto for my friends at Squared Circle Wrestling and Max Pro Wrestling. Rob Fuego and Scott D'Amore are the respective promoters and, because we are friends, I worked a few shows for them. I really enjoyed it as I got to see hungry young talent trying to hone their craft and I got to provide them with advice. It was a great feeling having these young men and women asking me for feedback on their matches and other words of advice. I was looked upon as a locker room veteran. Now that's cool!

I had another unexpected highlight in my refereeing career in May 2012. Ring of Honor is considered the number three wrestling promotion in the United States. They were coming to Toronto's Ted Reeve Arena for an Internet pay-per-view entitled Border Wars. One of the matches on the card was a rematch between a very talented young wrestler named Mike Bennett who was scheduled to face the much-revered Canadian wrestler Lance Storm. I knew Lance from his WWE days and we got along quite well. About a week before this event, former WWF/E personality Kevin Kelly, who now works for Ring of Honor, contacted me about refereeing this match on the PPV. I gladly accepted.

This was my first time I would referee a televised match for anyone other than the WWF/E. I wasn't sure how I would be received by the ROH roster. I found out when I arrived at the arena that I had absolutely nothing to worry about. Everyone, and I mean everyone, was so generous and respectful that they made me feel right at home. ROH referees Todd Sinclair and Paul Turner were great. It was also great to see many old friends like Charlie Haas, Shelton Benjamin, Mike Mondo, Kevin Steen, Fit Finlay, and of course Kevin Kelly.

When Lance arrived, we greeted each other and he asked what I was up to. I told him I was reffing his match that night, and he was very happy to hear the news. As match time approached, I started to get a little nervous. I had not refereed a PPV in three years so I was worried I would be a bit rusty. It was now time for me to go to the ring. Steve Corino was working backstage at the show and sent me through the curtain to the ring. As I jogged to the ring, to my surprise, the hometown Toronto crowd started to cheer. The cheers got louder and I received a standing ovation as many fans threw streamers into the ring. The throwing of streamers into the ring is a show of respect by the fans to the wrestlers. I was really shocked when they threw them for me, all I could think to do was clear them out of the ring. I was really touched by this scene, but when the crowd began to chant "Thank you, Jimmy" and clap in unison, I started to get emotional. I had to compose myself. I could never express in words how I felt at that moment.

After the match, in which Lance was victorious, Lance and I hugged in another show of respect for one another. When I returned to the backstage area, I thought that the booker and everyone else would be upset that a referee would get such a response from the crowd. They were all genuinely happy that I received such a warm welcome from the crowd. Once again I have to say I am grateful to ROH, Lance Storm, Kevin Kelly, and especially the fans for one of the most memorable nights I have ever had.

When I think back and analyze my career both in and out of the ring, I am overwhelmed by how truly blessed I have been. Not only did I get to live my dream by working for the WWF/E, the biggest and best sports entertainment company on the planet, I get to live a new dream now. Wrestling has always been a large part of my life and will continue to be. Just like Bruno Sammartino told me early on, once this business gets in your blood, you will never get it out of your system. The only difference today is that I get to examine as well as give my opinions and insight into the world that is the WWE. I never stopped being a fan so this is the best of both worlds. I watch and comment on wrestling and I am home with my family every night. It doesn't get much better than that.

When I am asked if I would return to the WWE, I can honestly say that as of right now, it is not in my plans, but who knows. If the right opportunity were to present itself, I might consider it. There is an old saying in the wrestling business: never say never. After all, it was my home away from home for more than 20 years. Maybe Arda and I will show up on the proposed WWE Network one day. You just never know.

When I reflect and look back on my life, I see a diehard young wrestling fan who became a WWE referee and then transitioned into what he is today, a wrestling analyst. I can honestly say that I have had a blessed career. My life in stripes was fantastic! The shirt I now wear may have changed, but the passion lives on.

Performing in front of thousands of people on a nightly basis was a dream come true for a life long wrestling fan. I have so many people to thank for my good fortune that I'm struggling with where to begin.

First, my parents.

Dad, you are my hero. You were the best teacher any son could ask for. Everything that is most important to me — honesty, loyalty, and hard work — you instilled in me. You were always proud of my accomplishments, but I was more proud of you and honored to be your son. The glue that held our family together was my mom. You always put our family first. You have the biggest heart of anyone I have ever known. Thanks, Mom and Dad.

My brother and sister, despite the age gap, were tremendous role models. My brother, with his quiet strength and good advice that was more than helpful. My sister, for being my protector and confidante. More often than not you took the bullet for my mischievous antics — and then listened when I needed to confess. I couldn't ask for a more loving family.

To my in-laws, thank you for your words of encouragement.

Elio Zarlenga, you were not only the guy who introduced me to the business side of wrestling, you are a good friend who showed me the ropes and had my back — my first real friend in the industry.

Jack Tunney, for taking a chance on a young man with a dream. He was not just my boss; he was someone I respected very much.

Pat Patterson for suggesting to Jack that I try refereeing. Through the years, Pat was a mentor and a friend.

The McMahon family, especially Vincent Kennedy McMahon, for giving me the opportunity to be a part of the greatest wrestling company in the world. I learned so much from the chairman.

Carl DeMarco and all the rest of the WWE Canada office.

Everyone at Titan Tower that helped me with everything from travel arrangements to work permits. Particularly *the* voice of the WWE, Howard Finkel, for being such a good friend and sharing his passion for this business.

To my WWF/E family, I would not have been able to do what I did if it were not for every referee, wrestler, agent/producer, and everyone else on the crew that I have had the honor and privilege to work with. I would love to list you all here but that would fill another book. It truly was like having a second family. All of you have influenced my career and I learned so much from each and every one of you.

Greg Oliver, for your assistance, suggestions, and photos. You have written several excellent books on wrestling, and your guidance and advice with this project is very much appreciated.

Thank you Andrea Kellaway, Charles Robinson, and Steve Argintaru for allowing me to use your photos. I appreciate all the time you guys spent digging out those pictures. They add so much to my book.

The good people at ECW Press for being interested in my story and agreeing have it put into print. I am grateful for all your hard work and patience.

Acknowledgments

The Ontario Art Council for assisting a first time writer in getting his story told.

I didn't want to name any one referee or wrestler because I don't want to slight anybody but there is one superstar and friend I have to single out.

Adam "Edge" Copeland was gracious enough to pen the foreword and I am forever grateful. Your kind words are incredibly touching. I have so much to thank you for but I think you know how I feel my good friend. Thanks, Edgester!

Thank you to The Score TV, the Fight Network, and all the great folks who work for them.

To John Pollock (spelled it correctly this time), for reminding me how to spell your name and for taking the time to read my manuscript and assist with editing. You are a good friend and I enjoy working with you at FN.

There are two people I really can't thank enough for making this book become a reality. First is my very good friend Arda Ocal. You are a true friend who is like a brother to me. You not only took a guy with zero experience in broadcasting and helped give him a voice on radio and television; you constantly pestered me about writing this book to tell my story. I told you stories from my years with the WWE and you took notes on your smartphone, email them to me with the tag, "this story should be in your book." You introduced me to Michael Holmes of ECW Press and the rest is history as they say. Our friendship goes far beyond wrestling. Thank you, bro; I owe you so more than I could ever repay.

There's an old saying that you should always save the best for last. That has never been truer than right now. The person I would like to thank the most is my best friend, the love of my life, my soul mate, and the most positive influence in my life, my wife Audra. Thank you for taking a chance on someone who was "just a referee." You never waivered or complained once about how much time this crazy business took me away from home and our family.

You knew the sacrifices involved and how much I loved wrestling and how much it meant to me. You once told me, "I could never ask you to give up doing something you love and care so much for."

Audra, you were also the one who originally said that I should write a book about my career. I told you I didn't think I could do it and questioned whether anyone would be interested. You always had faith in me and my abilities. I can't imagine doing any of this without you. Audra, you showed me that it doesn't matter how many times you fall, it's more important that you get back up again and again to follow your heart. I have and you are the reason why I always land on my feet. How do I say thank you to someone who has sacrificed so much to allow me to live my dream? I thank God every day for you and look forward to the rest of our lives together. I love you!